# FORMALISM, EXPERIENCE, AND THE MAKING OF AMERICAN LITERATURE IN THE NINETEENTH CENTURY

Theo Davis offers a new account of the emergence of a national literature in the United States. Taking American literature's universalism as an organizing force that must be explained rather than simply exposed, she contends that Emerson, Hawthorne, and Stowe's often noted investigations of experience are actually based in a belief that experience is an abstract category governed by typicality, not the property of the individual subject. Additionally, these authors locate the form of the literary work in the domain of abstract experience, projected out of – not embodied in – the text. After tracing the emergence of these beliefs from Scottish Common Sense philosophy and through early American literary criticism, Davis analyzes how American authors' prose seeks to work an art of abstract experience. In so doing, she reconsiders the place of form in literary studies today.

THEO DAVIS is Assistant Professor of English at Williams College.

*Recent books in this series*

# FORMALISM, EXPERIENCE, AND THE MAKING OF AMERICAN LITERATURE IN THE NINETEENTH CENTURY

THEO DAVIS

CAMBRIDGE
UNIVERSITY PRESS

CAMBRIDGE UNIVERSITY PRESS
Cambridge, New York, Melbourne, Madrid, Cape Town, Singapore, São Paulo, Delhi

Cambridge University Press
The Edinburgh Building, Cambridge CB2 8RU, UK

Published in the United States of America by Cambridge University Press, New York

www.cambridge.org
Information on this title: www.cambridge.org/9780521872966

© Theo Davis 2007

First published 2007
Reprinted 2009

Printed in the United Kingdom at the University Press, Cambridge

*A catalogue record for this publication is available from the British Library*

ISBN 978-0-521-87296-6 hardback

# Contents

# *Acknowledgments*

I thank Sharon Cameron for her challenging and inspiring teaching, which has been absolutely essential to me. I also want to thank Walter Benn Michaels, who was central to the growth of the project. Together they provided an intellectual foundation for which I am deeply grateful. Alison Case, Frances Ferguson, Suzanne Graver, John Limon, and Larzer Ziff read my work and offered important guidance and criticism. Johns Hopkins University and Williams College provided financial support for research and for fellowship and leave years, and New York University provided library support. Ruth Mack's friendship and brilliance are rare indeed, and I've been lucky enough to have her talk me through almost everything since our first year of graduate school. I'd also like to thank Rachel Baum, Tess Chakkalakal, Jennifer French, Jason Gladstone, Christine Heaphy, Katie Kent, Tina Lupton, Imani Perry, Kashia Pieprzak, Chris Pye, Michael Snediker, Abigail Snyder, and Anita Sokolsky. I am grateful to all my family for their abiding love and support, and especially to my father, Eric Davis, who knows a thing or two about close reading.

# Introduction: New Critical formalism and identity in Americanist criticism

How are experience and literary form related in nineteenth-century American literature? I enter into that question, this book's central concern, through literary nationalists' counterintuitive assertion that America was a singularly uninteresting subject. In the words of one such critic, W. H. Gardiner, "You see cultivated farms, and neat villages, and populous towns, full of health, and labor, and happiness . . . Where then are the romantic associations, which are to plunge your reader, in spite of reason and common sense, into the depths of imaginary woe and wonder?"[1] From this barrenly cheerful land American literature magically blossomed – in the literary historical narrative envisioned by nineteenth-century nationalists, and adapted by early twentieth-century critics such as Van Wyck Brooks and F. O. Matthiessen.[2] Celebrating American literature's purported creation of a shared national identity has subsequently been dismantled as a falsely universalist construction obscuring the multiplicities and material negotiations of the lives of individuals and groups within the United States.[3] My intention is neither to revive the early twentieth-century celebration of American literature's role in founding a national culture (as in recent works that would rearticulate American national identity through reference to its literary history), nor to extend the critique of it (a critique which now includes analysis of the wider context of the Americas as constitutive of and obscured by the totalizing notion of "America").[4] For the ongoing commitment to dismantling in order to expand the definition of America, either within the nation's borders or in relation to the Americas at large, actually ingrains still more deeply the belief that some core American experience and identity is the fundamental concern of Americanist literary studies. I challenge that fundamental principle in this book through my accounts of what counts as "American experience," or rather of experience in America. To do so, I begin with the question, What would you have to believe about both literature and experience to think it would be so hard to write about upstate New York, Boston, or Virginia?

To nineteenth-century literary nationalists, the core problem was that recognizably American experiences had not been treated previously in literature: the very fact that American life was an unfamiliar subject meant that it was considered unsuitable for literature. To maintain that position, one must not believe that literature exists as a way to take the specific richness of personal experience, or local experience, with innate value in its very situation in place, time, matter, and self, and transform it into a universally resonant literary artwork. Instead, these writers and critics believed that experience is a repertoire of possible responses to typical objects and events, and that literature uses the written text to call up and then to shape a work of art out of those conceptual, possible experiences. Gardiner specified the conditions of making experience interesting in literature that produced the apparent problem in the first place: "The characters of fiction should be descriptive of classes, and not of individuals, or they will seem to want the touch of nature, and fail in that dramatic interest which results from a familiarity with the feelings and passions pourtrayed [sic] and a consciousness of their truth."[5] Gardiner advances a remarkable notion: the "touch of nature" and the "truth" of "feelings and passions" are to be found in classes of person, not particular individuals, and are evoked by the articulation of generalities. Without such generalities to draw upon, a writer has no hope of soliciting that "dramatic interest" that is consistently seen as central to the work of the writer in this time. (A later critic would approvingly note that *Uncle Tom's Cabin* "seize[d] upon the attention" and held it fast "until the end" – thereby accomplishing "the chief object aimed at by the romancer.")[6] In this frame of belief, it actually would seem all but impossible to write a book using just language and an individual person's set of ideas and impressions of a particular place; the lack of a set of presumptively common ideas about what counted as an idea or a feeling that a person would have about typical events was to lack not the subject of literature, but its very medium.

My central contention in the chapters that follow is that a range of American writers, among them Emerson, Hawthorne, and Stowe, conceived of experience as a domain of hypothetical, typical responses, and that their central literary project was the evocation and shaping of such typical experience. I argue that the present-day theoretical premise that experience is by definition subjective, and that literary form embodies not only subjective experience but also historical context, is at odds with the framing conceptions of major American authors. In the first part of this introduction, I survey this claim about the operation of literature and experience in a significant portion of antebellum American texts. In the second part of the introduction, I contend that current accounts of the relationship of experience to form are not only inaccurate to the texts under consideration, but are themselves untenable. In reconsidering the theoretical problem of form and experience, I suggest that we should no longer cast the study of American literature as the ongoing articulation of American identity.

I

With political independence from Britain solidified by the War of 1812, nationalists increasingly sought to define an independent, recognizably American culture. In literature, this entailed a shift from eighteenth-century articulations of American literature through neoclassical abstraction and the literature of the public sphere, committed to disembodied citizens and universality, to articulations of American literature as a way to address life and experience in the nation in newly particular terms. At the same time, the rise of liberal individualism also drew on and fostered a literature devoted to the privacy and interiority of the subject. These two moves, towards the nationalist literature of American experience, and the liberal literature of personal experience, appear to work in harmony with one another, evoking an interconnection between the liberal subject and national identity. The three major authors I examine in this project have all been seen to exemplify this turn to a literature of experience, both personal and national: in Hawthorne's exploration of sexual, psychological, and national identity; Emerson's declaration of the self-reliance of both the individual and the nation; and Stowe's demand that a commitment to emancipation follow from shared sorrow over the destruction of the family. And the minor figures I discuss, Bronson Alcott and John Neal, seem exemplary in their commitment to rank individualism, which for Alcott opens beyond the nation to the universal, and for Neal is tied to the articulation of American identity. Nevertheless, I argue that these authors articulate experience as an object of disinterested contemplation, a typical experience governed by principles of normality and abstraction rather than the accumulation of an individual's particular life events and responses to them. That common understanding of experience is critical to these authors' conception of literature. Encompassing criticism, fiction, essays, even transcribed conversations, these texts work both to represent and to analyze experience, in so doing composing a writing of analytic invention which would shape and project experience.[7]

The major mode of American prose in the first half of the nineteenth century that I explore seeks to produce in its reader an ideal experience by deploying three main textual practices: first, by representing experiences in terms of the hypothetical or the probable, as when a narrator refers to how a character would be likely to feel, and second, by focusing on types and emblems, such as the scarlet letter or the transparent eyeball. In some cases, authors proceed by generalizing actual experience into types, but they more often explore types and emblems as a medium through which to approach experience. Third, they investigate how emblems and types came to be and how they are likely to affect the reader. The tension between the hermetic image and the unbounded extension of its origins and potential impact characterizes the writing of all the authors I examine. These formal features of the text, however, all point away from themselves and towards the form of the experience of a hypothetical reader. And what is most surprising about literary form, in this body of literature, is the way it is conceived primarily as a property of experience, and only secondarily as a property of the text. Thus, as I suggest in the readings that follow, the formal features of the texts point toward formal features – shapes to be articulated – in the domain of abstracted experience.[8]

My account of experience in this literature contrasts with much of the most important Americanist criticism of past decades in departing from commitment to both the category of identity and subjective experience, and the idea that abstractions must be thought of in some dynamic relation with subjective experience. These commitments grow out of the poststructural critique of the Enlightenment's elevation of reason and the universal at the expense of the body and the contingent. That critique is then applied to the historical narrative of the transition of America from republic to nation, as if the emergence of nationalism evidenced the theoretically necessary resurgence of the material specificities denied by republicanism's rhetoric of abstracted citizenship. For example, in *American Incarnation*, Myra Jehlen argued that modernity freed individuals from their economic, bodily, historical, and social ties but also traumatically cut them off from the world; American ideology and literature would strive for a reunion she describes as incarnation, "incorporat[ion]," or "embodi[ment]."[9] For Jehlen, in America the liberal ideal of the abstracted subject is healed by its transformation into the identity of the American: "Grounded, literally, in American soil, liberalism's hitherto arguable theses metamorphosed into nature's material necessities."[10] Of course, Jehlen was hardly praising this transformation, and an enormous volume of scholarship in nineteenth-century American literature is organized around not only a categorical opposition of experience, framed as entirely personal, embodied, and material, to the abstract universal of reason, but also a dual imperative to unveil the untenability of this opposition, and to subvert it by bringing out the elided grain of experience. Dana Nelson's *National Manhood* explains how the abstract, egalitarian definition of the citizen was replaced with the limited identity of the "white man," as "a nationally shared 'nature.'"[11] Russ Castronovo speaks of how the "abstract personhood" of the US citizen "is rhetorically, if not actually, financed by the experiences, memories, and stories of others; the privileges of (white male) citizenship are tied up with the hyperembodiment of blacks, women, and workers."[12] And Lori Merish writes that "the abjected materiality of the Other's body (and the recognition of unfreedom) continued to haunt the edges of the subject's identity, threatening its fantasies of political liberty."[13] But whereas some critics saw this as revealing the essential corruption of the American individual, and of liberalism in general, it could also seem more like a descriptive assertion about the complex ways in which liberal individualism could be sustained, as in the work of not only Jehlen but also Richard Brodhead, Sacvan Bercovitch, and Lauren Berlant.[14]

Americanist scholarship has, in showing the imbrecations of the abstract and the embodied, increasingly explored the connections between the public and the private, and between the rational and the emotional, in such a way as to revise the frame of a transition from the eighteenth-century's abstract citizen to the nineteenth-century's nationalist liberal. Jay Fliegelman's *Declaring Independence* deems "the age of reason" a "misleading rubric," and persuasively explores how public speaking in republican America worked out "the period's antirationalist preoccupation with ruling passions, desire, and an involuntary moral sense."[15] Criticism on the nineteenth century has also pursued the interconnection of private emotions and the public sphere even in the nineteenth century. A signal work in this direction was Gillian Brown's *Domestic Individualism*, which pointed out that "nineteenth-century American individualism takes on its peculiarly 'individualistic' properties as domesticity inflects it with these values of interiority, privacy, and psychology," and this is through conceiving of the ownership of objects as a form of emotional identification.[16] The implication that the private individual was in a dynamic interaction with the external workings of capitalism has been extended particularly in criticism concerned with sympathy and sentiment. Glenn Hendler's *Public Sentiments* argues that the novel is an institution of the public sphere, and explains how private emotional life is caught up in a drama of being in public.[17] Stacey Margolis's account of *The Public Life of Privacy* attacks the entire tradition of viewing the American novel as concerned with liberal individualism, maintaining that the novel and individualism alike understood the self to be defined only by "public effects."[18] If we once had a historical account of a republican era committed to the Enlightenment citizen and his separation from material interests followed by a subsequent national period in which the citizen was replaced with the identity of the American, we now have an internecine account in which the citizen of the republic was always caught up with body, feeling, interest, and the American was also still engaged in efforts of publicity and universality.

Such reconfigurations of the subject in nineteenth-century America have emerged in tandem with theoretical investigations of feelings and experience as traveling between subjects, notably those by Rei Terada and Martin Jay. Terada argues that emotion and experience are by definition incompatible with the notion of a subject. The "ideology of emotion," writes Terada, "diagrams emotion as something lifted from a depth to surface." In this specious logic, "expression tropes" serve "to extrapolate a human subject circularly from the phenomenon of emotion."[19] Terada also attacks a content theory in which "emotions entail beliefs and apply to objects," as emotion is used to posit a link of inner to outer world. In contrast to the expression and content theories, Terada argues that emotion is the product of the interpretation of representations: "We are not ourselves without representations that mediate us, and it is through those representations that emotions get felt."[20] Terada's overarching claim is that the interpretation of mental representations splits the subject, and produces emotion and experience. In Terada's words, "experience is experience of self-differentiality. The idea of emotion is as compelling as it is because in the honest moments of philosophy it has served as the name of that experience."[21]

The idea that experience might not be tied to the individual subject is also central to Martin Jay's recent history of the concept of experience in Western philosophy. Jay aims to undo the basic sense that the Enlightenment wrested the contingent materiality of the subject from the abstract, universal function of reason; in so doing, he works against the identitarian, possessive account of experience. Jay points out that in broad terms the Enlightenment produced a "split" between "the psychological subject with all its personal history and idiosyncratic appetites" and the objectivity of experience in both empiricism and Kantian transcendentalism, in which experience constitutes "the imposition of categories and forms by the transcendental mind on the multiplicity of sensations."[22] Not only does experience, then, *include* subjectivity, objectivity, and transcendence as possible formations, the category of experience itself can be conceived of as the venue in which the split of universal and particular, and more locally of subject and object, might be integrated.[23] Later accounts of pragmatism and poststructuralism that Jay explores also investigate how experience can appear to be the way in which the subjective and the universal are reconciled.

Jay takes a capacious survey of the term's incarnations in which, notwithstanding its myriad aspects, it always means a progressive openness to otherness. Opposing the "exclusivist fortresses" of possessive and identitarian experience, Jay concludes that experience "involve[s] a willingness to open the most seemingly integrated and self-contained subject to the outside, thus allowing the perilous, but potentially rewarding journey to begin."[24] For Terada, every account of emotion turns out to be an experience of self-differentiality, and this serves as a cumulative empirical demonstration of what experience is. Jay and Terada both offer theories of experience that they support through empirical analysis of a series of texts in temporal progression, as if proof of what experience is must be accrued through exemplification of what experience has been. But it's also critical that for Jay, the commitment to experience is a commitment to how experience structures belief; he is expressing a pragmatist account of experience as the ever-expanding ground of ever-changing beliefs, which is ultimately to posit what we are instead of what we believe, but only to do so on that grand scale – hence his commitment to a highly inclusive method, and to a subject who seems to open himself up to swallow the world whole and still have room for more. In his commitment to melding experience with belief, Jay shares much with Terada – for she too, envisioning a world where there are no subjects, only the self-representation of emotions, posits a fusion of meaning with being that represents the triumph of identitarianism, insofar as being committed to the connection of representation and belief to experience and affect is to be committed only to experience and affect. Hence historical accounts of how experience has always worked serve, for Jay and Terada, in place of arguments for what experience is or what we should believe about it. This is perhaps why, although Jay and Terada are both interested in experience without a subject, the subject remains central to each of their accounts, to be rather ecstatically annihilated, or cowered from, in Terada and to be gently exposed and transformed by an encounter with the world in Jay. Thus, these theoretical approaches are close to the historicism of the Americanists: for all, the historical location of cases in which the subject has been pried out of its isolation serve implicitly as arguments that the subject is always thus compromised and that the notion of possessive experience that has been so central not only to accounts of nineteenth-century America but to modern identity theory is theoretically, because historically, untenable. In so doing, of course, such works maintain the logic of possessive experience (you are what you've been through).

In the articulations of American literary experience that I analyze, there is a single, coherent understanding of a typical experience, not a negotiation of two differing registers, private and public, feeling and reason. In the account of experience, and of literary experience in particular, in American literature that I offer, the notion of the individual and his possessive relation to experience is marginal; the notion of "my experience" as somehow inherently relevant and interesting, because it is either different from or analogous to yours, is basically absent. The subject can appear to evaporate, to stand as a shadow, or to be a pedestal for the full formation of experience; it is used and abandoned with little fanfare. The subject is not so much critiqued, expanded, or revealed as imbricated in the market, the social, or the public sphere, as shown to be incidental to concerns about experience as literature can evoke and shape it. This means that the major recent accounts of American literature (as a falsely universal project rejecting the contingency of experience, or as a pragmatist and cosmopolitan negotiation of the contingent and the universal) share a commitment to the primacy of subjective experience in opposition to abstract universals that does not fit the texts they consider. In other words, I contend that the entire concept of the contingent as it relates to the universal is based on a mistaken conception about the framing terms for speaking of experience and literature in America in the first half of the nineteenth century.

The concept of literary tradition as an expression of national identity to which some critics have begun to return depends on a misreading of the operation of experience, nation, and literature in the very works most often marshaled for evidence of such accounts of American literature. My point is not that we can happily see that in fact American authors got it right, and thus pursue a corrected account of experience that is still an American tradition. Nor am I arguing that experience should be wiped aside; without a better account of it, we will not move beyond the current dynamic between universal reason and contingent experience. We can't move beyond that dynamic by picking one side over the other, or by collapsing them together – because neither approach really gets at the form of literary experience.

II

To discuss experience as part of literature has been, in Americanist criticism and theory, to do one of two things: to talk about the experience of reading as a fact about the subject, or to talk about the experience of reading as a way in which the meaning of the text is brought into being.[25] Experience is, in either case, seen as fundamentally subjective – defined by the person reading (the difference is whether the interest is just in the subject, or in the way the subject makes meaning). My concern with experience is, in the readings that comprise this book, neither with the subject, nor with the way the subject shapes meaning. It is, instead, with the proposition that experience is a projection out of – caused by, not shaping – certain texts. Such experience is crucially distinguished from the actual experience of any subjects.

My readings depend, in other words, on an account of experience different from that present in the criticism of two major Americanists, Walter Benn Michaels and Myra Jehlen. Both Michaels and Jehlen perceive the urgent question of this time to be the divide between the commitment to identity, as a commitment to experience, and a commitment to beliefs and meanings independent from identity. If commitment to identity embraces tolerance for the way each of us is differently shaped and has different access to cultural discourse, it is also inarguable and thus leads to either a peacefully fractured society or a global condition of violence between identities. Commitment to beliefs as knowledge that we have reasons for, and that we can argue our way into or out of (rather than just inhabit, as if we were all allegorical images of our pasts) offers the universalism of a world where all parties can speak with one another on the same terms. But it also depends, as has been frequently objected, on a belief in the irrelevance of experience to our beliefs (it is not all right for me to be Catholic and you Protestant just because we were brought up that way – one of us is going to hell), and a belief in the universality of reason, which can be heedless of the power of experience and identity, and even coercive in its commitment to the possibility or prospect of agreement. In the face of this broad problem, Michaels argues against identity per se, while Jehlen argues for the adjudication of the relations between identity and belief, and between the contingent and the universal. These concerns turn, in each case, on a commitment to a certain account of how experience is relevant to meaning: Michaels argues that we must not consider experience, only meaning; Jehlen argues that experience is necessarily part of and constitutive of meaning. However, their very opposition to one another about the relevance of experience to belief and to meaning is founded upon a shared commitment to experience as subjective in its entirety. Subjective experience is, in both their accounts of literature and of culture more broadly, a blanket term in which no distinctions can be made, in which everything must count, and count equally. For each, moreover, this account of experience as by definition subjective is bound up in an interpretation of New Critical formalism as itself an appeal to the way that meaning can be fused into such experience, so that New Critical formalism's commitment to how a thing is expressed becomes a commitment to how a thing is experienced. Each critic frames identitarian commitment to the dependence of meaning and belief upon experience as a version of New Critical formalism's commitment to literature as a fusion of the concrete experience with the universal.

Yet to be committed to form does not necessarily involve either an elision of experience altogether or a surrender to subjective experience, even if these are the options presented in the work of Michaels, Jehlen, and new formalist criticism. Here I rely particularly on Steven Knapp's *Literary Interest*, a brilliant investigation of why literature might seem to matter. Knapp co-authored with Michaels the essay "Against Theory," which argued that the text's meaning was identical to the author's intention; thus, appeals to intention to explain meaning were empty.[26] Knapp and Michaels argued the impossibility of believing that different beliefs were equally true – the impossibility of really believing, in other words, that belief is relative. They explained that we really do believe what we believe (that's what makes a belief different from a surmise, a preference, or even an opinion), and that we believe it for reasons. Hence, we are always capable of being persuaded to change our beliefs by appeals to better reasons, and are not bound to them by our experience or identity. Notwithstanding the shared authorship of "Against Theory," Knapp's position in *Literary Interest* upon experience differs importantly from Michaels's in *The Shape of the Signifier*. And as I will discuss below, the difference between their accounts of experience turns on a difference in their accounts of the New Critical formalism of W. K. Wimsatt and Monroe Beardsley.

In *The Shape of the Signifier*, Michaels maintains there are two mutually exclusive ways of looking at a text: interpreting its meaning or exploring one's experience of it. If we take the (mistaken) route of choosing to think our experience of a text matters, "we have no principled reason not to count everything that's part of our experience as part of the work."[27] This commitment to all of experience is, in Michaels's account, the ambition of Minimalist art: it wants everything around it to be part of it, as if a sculpture were no different in kind from a table. In Minimalist art practice, we see that to choose experience is to choose everything in it: "there are no boundaries *within* your experience, no boundaries other than the physical limits. Everything that is contributing to the experience (the wall on which the painting is hung as well as the painting) is as much a part of it as everything else" (90). In contrast, Michaels argues that Robert Smithson's work depends on making a distinction between art and the rest of our experience. In regard to Smithson's framing of piles of rocks, Michaels observes: "it's the act of containment that produces the concept of art. It is the 'container' (the frame) that makes the art because it is the frame that renders much of the experience of the beholder (his experience of everything outside the frame) and thus his experience as such irrelevant" (93). In this quotation, Michaels allows a possibility of a partitioning of experience in the phrasing of a boundary that "renders much of the experience of the beholder (his experience of everything outside the frame)" "irrelevant," for if this is so, some part of his experience remains relevant. To say part of the experience matters and part of it doesn't is to have departed from the original definition of experience as something that axiomatically matters in every aspect of its appearance to the individual subject. But Michaels asserts instead that "experience as such" is "irrelevant." For Michaels, to propose that part of an experience matters and part of it doesn't is to have represented a meaning and to have declared experience per se out of the question. As he puts it, this is so even just in *looking*: "[Smithson's] glance leaves the shape of the ground – its topography – untouched but utterly alters its ontology; it is the difference between the infinite and a map of the infinite, between a thing and a thing that represents" (95). The claim that making a distinction within experience is to move out of experience and into representation also occurs in Michaels's discussion of James Welling's photographs. What concerns him is the way they bracket or crop the things they are photographs of, so that the photograph no longer reads as a view of that object per se. Once the photograph isn't a view of an object, it is a "representation" (105). In Michaels's account, abstraction (not representing something) is indistinguishable from Minimalism's version of art as just objects; for form is just an object of experience. Once a distinction is made within experience, it has to be a shift into representation of meaning; it can't be a marking of shape, of pure form.

In Michaels's discussions of deconstruction's commitment to the shape of the mark and New Criticism's commitment to the rules of language, each of these is a commitment to the experience of the text rather than to its meaning. In regard to deconstruction: "as long as the relevant criterion [to deciding if marks are signs] is formal (is shape), the question of whether the formations really are letters is a question that is crucially about your perspective. Hence, the commitments to the primacy of the materiality of the signifier (to shape) is also a commitment to the primacy of experience (to the subject position)" (87). In this respect, deconstruction shares its commitment to the experience of the thing that the text is, instead of what it means, with the New Critics. New Critical formalism was committed to the idea that the author's intention is irrelevant to the meaning, which has to be located in the text as a piece of language. Thus hermeneutic disputes would rely on the rules of the language, not on the appeal to the author, and, writes Michaels, this commitment to the rules of language is a commitment to the text as a thing that we experience – and, therefore, "the appeal to the rules of language is actually a way of committing rather than avoiding the affective fallacy"(115).

Describing form as an object of subjective experience and of the essential critical choice as one between meaning and experience is also to categorize the aesthetic as still more subjective experience. Kant's claim was that although it was an experience, the aesthetic judgment was nonetheless not private or personal – it was subjective and yet universal, something we would hold as true for all persons and not simply about our opinions or preferences. For Michaels, the idea that the experience of an artwork could be something different from our own private feelings and reactions, and yet not be identified as the work's meaning, must be a mistake. This much is evident in his discussion of a moment in "The Affective Fallacy" concerning Coleridge's disgust at some tourists' response to a waterfall. Wimsatt and Beardsley wrote:

The tourist who said a waterfall was pretty provoked the silent disgust of Coleridge, while the other who said it was sublime won his approval. This, as C. S. Lewis so well observes, was not the same as if the tourist had said, "I feel sick," and Coleridge had thought, "No, I feel quite well."[28]

Michaels comments in *Shape of the Signifier*:

The difference between sublime and pretty is a difference in the object, not in the response to it, and the point of the commitment to objectivity is not to find some method for determining whether the waterfall really is sublime or pretty, it's just to note that the question of whether something is sublime or pretty is a different kind of question from the question of how it makes you feel. If you say it's sublime and I say it's pretty, we disagree; if you say it makes you sick and I say it doesn't make me sick, we aren't disagreeing, we are just recording the difference between us. (72)

It's clear that Wimsatt and Beardsley are asserting that there are responses that are just about us, and these are precisely not things about we can be said to disagree. And the judgment of the waterfall as sublime or pretty is clearly something we can disagree about, and thus is different from a fact about us. But is the disagreement exactly "a difference in the object"? For the fact that Coleridge feels disgust at the judgment of "pretty" suggests something more than a mistake – we don't tend to be disgusted if someone is wrong about the plot in a novel, nor even if someone misreads a street sign. Another odd thing about the passage is that Coleridge is silent, rather than pointing out that the person is wrong or explaining why he thinks it's sublime. Even if we were disgusted with someone for getting us lost or being unable to get *Moby-Dick*'s plot right, we would be able to explain to the person why he was wrong. With the aesthetic judgment, at least according to Kant, we can't give such reasons – hence its dependence on the cultivation of taste through norms, and hence the fact that Coleridge is consumed with "silent disgust": he knows the tourist is wrong, but there's no way for him to argue the point.

Of course, aesthetics debates whether qualities of beauty and sublimity are experiences of the subject or qualities of the object. But even if we were to take the position that there are beautiful and sublime objects, and that we are able to explain to other people why something is or is not sublime, we still wouldn't go so far as to say calling an object "sublime" is to say that the object means sublimity. But Michaels does imply that once we are making an objective judgment about the waterfall, as sublime not pretty, we are talking about an interpretation of its meaning: "the main idea of 'The Affective Fallacy' was that the question of a text's meaning (like the question of the waterfall's sublimity) is a question about it, whereas the question of its effect is a question about us – how are we feeling?"(72). However, when Wimsatt and Beardsley conflate the judgment of the object as sublime with an account of the object's meaning (as they do later in the essay, but not in the waterfall passage) they contradict their own insight in this passage that the aesthetic is not a subjective experience, and yet is not a meaning. After all, the waterfall is a natural object: it is meaningless. There is a difficulty with questions about the waterfall's sublimity, and the difficulty is that they seem to be accounts more of meaning than of our feeling, and yet (as Michaels's parenthetical "[like the question of the waterfall's sublimity]" recognizes) not precisely the same thing.

Quoting Anatole France with their characteristic aplomb – "To be quite frank . . . the critic ought to say: 'Gentlemen, I am going to speak of myself apropos of Shakespeare'" – Wimsatt and Beardsley assert that in speaking of one's experience of a text, one barely speaks of that text at all.[29] Wimsatt and Beardsley defend their polemic that the reader's experience is irrelevant – evident in their approving citation of France – in part by noting that the experience is a "result" of the poem. This seems like another deployment of the genetic fallacy, but increasingly it seems that for them this causal relationship is instructive. The experience is caused by the poem instead of by the person, for they write, "the more specific the account of the emotion induced by a poem, the more nearly it will be an account of the reasons for the emotion, the poem itself"(34). For Wimsatt and Beardsley, our experience of a poem, far from being a fact about us, is actually a fact about the poem. This is to say that they think we *can* make distinctions within our experience (between the parts of our experience of reading Shakespeare that are about ourselves, and the parts of it that are really about Shakespeare).

To make those distinctions, Wimsatt and Beardsley separate affects into two classes: those which are about the subject, and those which are about their object. The conclusion Wimsatt and Beardsley draw from the waterfall passage is: "A food or a poison causes pain or death, but for an emotion we have a reason or an object." In other words, they suggest that there are *two* kinds of experiences: bodily experiences ("pain or death," caused by physical objects and events) and emotions, which are judgments regarding objects outside oneself. The account of the tourist's objective judgment of the waterfall is, according to Wimsatt and Beardsley, that it is an emotion, not a physical condition. On Wimsatt and Beardsley's account, all that is really subjective is one's body; other than that, one's entire emotional life is an interpretation of one's external conditions, an interpretation that can (moreover) be entirely mistaken. They hold what Terada calls the content theory of emotions – in which emotions are about objects, not about the subject. Wimsatt and Beardsley go even beyond the content theory, however, to maintain that our experience of a poem turns out to have nothing to do with us: there is no "evidence that what a word *does* to a person is to be ascribed to anything except what it *means*" (25–26). To talk about how Shakespeare makes you feel is actually to talk about Shakespeare, because (a) that's what your emotion is about and (b) that's what caused the emotion. The critic who speaks of himself "apropos of Shakespeare" has failed to really read Shakespeare – he's not talking about the experience of reading Shakespeare at all, but about himself. "Apropos" is exactly the point: he doesn't speak of his experience of Shakespeare, but of his experience in relation to, on the occasion of, Shakespeare.

When Wimsatt and Beardsley write, "the more specific the account of the emotion induced by a poem, the more nearly it will be an account of the reasons for the emotion, the poem itself" (34), they make a critical locutionary shift. As long as they are insisting that the experience of a poem is caused by the poem, and that the experience of a poem is about the poem (related but not identical claims), they are still maintaining a separation between that experience and the poem, a point that would suggest experience is not relevant to criticism. But they suggest here that giving a good account of "the emotion induced by a poem" is actually to give "an account of . . . the poem itself." The only way that this can make sense is if the poem is the same thing as the experience – otherwise, why should giving a good account of something mean giving an account of the thing that caused it? The emotion, that is, seems to be the same thing as the poem; but something cannot cause itself, nor is that the force of the statement. We are left with the idea that experience of a poem is exactly  like the poem which causes it. If the meaning were indistinguishable from the affect – either the same thing or a perfect replica – there would be no need to discuss them as separate entities (purely subjective experiences such as nausea would be obviously irrelevant). That is exactly the implication of their statement that a good description of a response is a description of its cause, the meaning. Even though, then, the essay commits the affective fallacy that it means to denounce (as Michaels points out), it is critical that this depends upon the *distinction* within experiences they proposed in the waterfall example. They can understand their commission of the affective fallacy to be logically consistent with their refutation of it: the affective fallacy is talking about yourself and your physical being, and good criticism is talking about an experience of a poem which is identical to the meaning of that poem.

Wimsatt and Beardsley's claim that experiences fall cleanly into two distinct categories, subjective physical experience and objective emotional experience (which is caused by and about an object to which it then turns out to be identical) is, however, implausible. They themselves cannot maintain this clear distinction between physical experiences and those experiences that are about, caused by, and ultimately the same as their objects, for in their own epigraph they liken poetry to wine: "We might as well study the properties of wine by getting drunk" (21). Not only is this to equate poetry's objective effect on the emotions with wine's physical effect on the body (the kind of thing that makes one feel sick), but getting drunk is not just a physical but an emotional experience. Wimsatt and Beardsley's division of affects into subjective responses and accounts of objects is a strategy to deny the inevitably complex quality of experience and to deny the normativity that emerges from such a combination of subjective and objective elements. Wimsatt and Beardsley's commitment to splitting apart objective experience (emotion) from subjective experience (physical sensations) is dedicated also to the preservation of objective judgments rather than inarguable personal experiences. But, as their elitism indicates, Wimsatt and

Beardsley's practice depended on making judgments about experiences, not just objective judgments about objects. Coleridge's silence and disgust alike suggest this aspect of the issue: on the one hand, aesthetic experience is a judgment, the kind of thing that makes us consider other persons' views to be either right or wrong. Yet those judgments are not arguable, as Coleridge's silence, even his recourse to disgust rather than argument, also suggests. One could say, then, that art should be treated like food, just an object of subjective experience and preference. But the problem is that it is in the moments when we feel capable of and justified in judging others' experience, but unable to justify or to argue that judgment, that we resort to disgust.

 For Michaels, the commitment to experience is by its very nature a commitment to identity and against both meaning and belief. There is argument about meaning, and there is either passive retreat to opinion or aggressive recourse to violence (pushing the tourist over the waterfall, perhaps). I want to contend that the experience of literature is relevant as a formal property, but that this entails neither an attack on meaning (by either substituting experience for meaning or insisting on the imbrecation of experience with meaning) nor an endorsement of identity and subjective experience. I have begun to do so by raising questions about whether dividing experience must mean entering from experience into meaning and representation, and by questioning the way in which Wimsatt and Beardsley think of experience as either objective and identical to meaning or entirely about the subject. I will extend these questions below in regard to the work of both Jehlen and Knapp, but first I want to point out that the alignment that Michaels makes of identity with New Criticism is borne out at least as a description of a clutch of recent criticism that has focused more on close reading than on archival and historical research.

 When critics talk about returning to close reading and about reading for form, more often than not they are rediscovering their own deep commitment to thinking of language as a material in which ideas can be incarnated. Frank Lentricchia and Andrew DuBois assert that both "formalist critics" and "the nonformalists who have dominated literary criticism and theory over the last decades of the twentieth century" share "a commitment to close attention to literary texture and what is embodied there."[30] The "texture" is a figure for the difficulty and complexity of the way words are put there, and "embodie[s]" is a figure for the notion that some reality, some *thing* other than ideas and sound-images, is physically located in a text. This commitment to formalism as a commitment to thinking of language as the object of experience is evident even in work that uses close analysis of the text to approach the experiences outside it. As Bercovitch notes, a certain new Marxism "compels an even closer reading of the text – a more rigorous attention to paradox, irony, and ambiguity – than that dreamed of by the New Critics. The text, it would seem, has been invested with all the subtleties of historical process so that history may be understood through the subtleties of literary criticism."[31] Whereas Wimsatt and Beardsley suggested that an account of the emotion caused by the poem would increasingly be an account of the poem itself, Bercovitch suggests that an account of *Uncle Tom's Cabin* would increasingly turn out to be an account of the cause of the novel, its historical context.[32]

The idea that close reading will tell us all we need to know about the *cause* of the text, both the author and the historical context, can be seen in a number of fairly recent texts. For Peter Coviello, in *Intimacy in America*, "the very grammar and syntax, the peculiarities of form that characterized a particular author tell us immensely consequential things about the individuals' relation to the notions, objects, and ideals that we will later come to think of history."[33] In Hendler's *Public Sentiments*, close reading is of interest for what it reveals about the beliefs about the structure of the psyche that caused the text, as in the following passage describing the character Christie's debut as a public speaker in Louisa May Alcott's novel *Work*:

> The women see her not only as "a genuine woman [who] stood down there among them like a sister" but also as "one of them; for the same lines were on their face that they saw on their own." Sympathy here reaches its public apotheosis: it is mutual and reciprocal, simultaneously producing identities and breaking down the distinctions between them. Again, Theodore Parker's phrase for the sympathetic orator – "Feeling, [s]he must make others feel" – describes Christie's role here perfectly.[34]

This version of close reading is paradigmatically anti-New Critical in its embrace of intentionalism, either of the author-psychology stamp or of the broader historical-causality kind. The premise is that the text is a symptomatic result that can be peeled back to reveal a preexisting event or condition that is, because it is the cause of the expression, its most salient feature. But notwithstanding such intentionalism, these critics maintain a New Critical focus on the text as self-sufficient object of special interest because they frame the analysis of both author psychology and historical background as necessarily approached through the language of the text. They claim, that is, to be able to uncover this information in the text instead of in the external evidence that the intentional fallacy should draw a critic into. (As is pointed out in Wimsatt and Beardsley's withering analysis of "the whole glittering and pointless parade of Professor Lowes'

*Road to Xanadu*," an account of the sources of "Kubla Khan," which traced
out the "gross body of life, of sensory and mental experience, which lies
behind and in some sense causes every poem" that "can never be and need
not be known in the verbal and hence intellectual composition which is
the poem.")[35] In these readings of the experience informing the text, we
are supposed to be able to see the road to Xanadu – the context and the
psyche that caused the text – in the text itself. That's the force of Hendler's
repeated quotations of "Theodore Parker's phrase for the sympathetic
orator – 'Feeling, [s]he must make others feel'": in that particular phrasing,
the logic of sympathy is lodged as it is nowhere else. And in the belief
that the experience that causes the text is best exemplified in the richness
of the text, these critics remain focused on the verbal icon even as they assert
otherwise.

   The belief that talking about language is really a way of talking about
the reality outside it evidently structures Jay Grossman's *Reconstituting the
American Renaissance*, which explicitly links close reading to attention to
material, contingent experience. For Grossman, the fact that Emerson wrote
drafts of his ideas "within the covers of his father's notebooks" means that
his ideas are part of not only the materiality of those books, but even of those
ideas of his father's that were recorded on the pages that Emerson ripped
out of them.[36] Emerson cannot really mean anything other than where
he came from, as, Grossman argues, American literature of the nineteenth
century cannot stop meaning the same thing as American literature of the
eighteenth century. If, on the one hand, the claim is one of a thoroughgoing
intentionalism, on the other hand it is an equally rigorous commitment to
affective criticism. Grossman's account of "reading closely" Emerson's letter
to Walt Whitman includes his account of what it would be like to encounter
"the actual material characteristics of Emerson's words as they appear on the
spine of the 1856 edition."[37] It might be, worries Grossman, "difficult to
reconstruct" what "I greet you at the beginning of a great career" meant in
1856, but that is not to say we should not try: "For the few browsers who
actually glanced at the spine of the 1856 edition in the shop of Fowlers and
Wells at 308 Broadway in Manhattan, the 'you' greeted by 'R W Emerson'
may have seemed initially to refer to themselves *as readers*."[38] The reason
it is hard to reconstruct the experience of encountering this book spine in
1856 is not that the past experience is gone, but that there is a lot more
experience under the bridge since then: "We, for example, already know
who Emerson is, and . . . already understand the significance of Whitman's
gesture in light of what we perceive to be the overall movement of his
career."[39] And the reason it is not as hard as it looked to be to reconstruct

the experience is that, insofar as it's central to Grossman's whole project that the past experience is always with us, it doesn't even need reconstructing: it's all there in the "imprinted words."

Thus, although the return to close reading seems like a move hostile to most new historicist criticism, it is really an extension of it. This is something that Myra Jehlen seems to have known all along: America as an identity is also America as a great work of art of the very kind that New Critics valued. She noted, "When the liberal idea fused with the material landscape, it produced an 'America' that was . . . symbol, its meaning inherent in its matter."[40] Linking the New Critical ideal poem to American identity still more directly, Jehlen wrote that John "Donne is a useful reference . . . for the ideal–material fusion in America also rises to the metaphysical through paradox."[41] This alignment of identitarian thinking with New Critical formalism is part of the point of the way that recent returns to the text emphasize the importance of form because of its relevance to content or to meaning. Thus, the return to form that has  striven mightily to insist that it is not about the isolated literary work, but always about the work as the embodiment of an endless train of what Grossman calls "concrete inheritances," entails actually keeping on with the same account of what makes a literary text valuable – the way that it encapsulates, includes, bespeaks, something else. If it is true, as Michaels and Jehlen both contend, that the commitment to form is a commitment to experience (instead of, confused with, knowledge), the return to form must be what it has been to date: a continuation of new historicism, and identitarianism, and New Criticism alike.

But that is not how the return to form has to develop. The issue depends upon the question, raised already in regard to Michaels, of what making a distinction or frame within experience entails. I now return to this question by way of Jehlen's essay on the Guggenheim Museum in Bilbao, Spain. Jehlen begins the piece describing herself "stepping into the lobby," "pass[ing] through Richard Serra's *Serpent*," and passing another piece "on the way to the stairs."[42] But, finding herself in "an uncooperative mood," she leaves the museum to "[get] a cup of coffee."[43] The problem is the building's refusal to be an object of subjective experience, a place to just walk through, and this is also evident in the description of the museum as "a dream and a nightmare to photograph, for any angle offers a striking picture and none really captures it . . . Virtually all the photos are dazzling and unlikely . . . The pictures do not lie: no one has been able to visualize this building clearly, not even its builders."[44] Photographs of the Guggenheim, Bilbao, are like James Welling's photographs (as Michaels reads them) because they are not *of* objects, nor are they seen from the perspective of the human eye or subject: "one cannot picture it, cannot view it."[45] Jehlen evidently wants the museum to be like Minimalist art (objects to be experienced by subjects, just like tables or chairs), and she seems irritated by its refusal to be an object she can walk into, see with the naked eye, or photograph in a way that makes it look like a building instead of a "dazzling and unlikely" image.

Observing that the Guggenheim, Bilbao, "can swallow any art, let alone any viewer," and provokes "a strained disorientation," Hal Foster finds it a repudiation of Minimalism's commitment to subject and site.[46] Foster understands architect Frank Gehry's rejection of site and subject to be part of a larger severing of the museum from the cultural context, noting that the museum (and other recent Gehry works) "could be dropped, indifferently, almost anywhere" (40). Gehry's rupture of the museum's ground in the subject's experience and in the local context amounts, in Foster's analysis, to an assertion of personal liberty and formal abstraction that is politically oppressive and aesthetically empty. Foster objects that Gehry's work is an expression of one individual artist's liberation, against which all others are "unfree": audiences are disoriented and all but throttled by the spaces of the Guggenheim, Bilbao, as the economically disadvantaged are disoriented and throttled by the flights of multinational corporations, a twinning evident in the use of the museum's form as a brand logo (40).

Jehlen shares Foster's concern with Gehry's privileged whimsy as a threat to the subjective experience of the viewer (the anti-Minimalism) and to the culturally located subject. But unlike Foster, Jehlen sees this as a problem regarding intentionality. For Foster basically disagrees with Gehry, writing that it seems "as if Gehry . . . designed in keeping with 'the cultural logic of late capitalism'" consciously, and objects to the oppressiveness of this aim (37). In contrast, for Jehlen the problem is not with Gehry's intentions but with his understanding of intentionality. The case is complicated by the fact that Gehry maintains that his work is not the expression of his individual vision, subject and culture be damned, but that it is sensitive to both. For Foster, "the claim that Gehry is sensitive to context does not hold up" (39). Jehlen takes this claim of Gehry's more seriously, however, and objects to the fact that Gehry thinks he, as "a singular artist," can speak for an entire culture. It's not that Gehry claims to express the culture but really just expresses himself (that's Foster's view of the problem), it's the very way that Gehry's individual "express[ion]" is propounded as a form of cultural expression with which Jehlen takes issue.[47]

As she writes: "the community . . . has been internalized: it has become an aspect of selfhood, of individual identity. Actual roofs, windows, and toilets are then without personal significance to the architect and extraneous to his art."[48] The idea that "roofs, windows, and toilets" can be ignored is, for Jehlen, important evidence of how Gehry thinks he can take the experience of the community into account, without taking everything about it into account. For example, he claims to be sensitive to context in using a fish motif for the seaside Guggenheim, Bilbao, but the building bears no visual relation to the immediate surroundings. It is Jehlen's belief that the subject's experience of the building, and the cultural identity at stake, has to include everything – the windows, the toilets, the bad moods. In this way, we can say that Jehlen's commitment to Minimalism is even stronger than Foster's, for the very notion of Gehry expressing himself as apart from the cultural context and subject's experience, as well as of expressing part of the cultural context (the fishing heritage but not the buildings next to the museum) is what she objects to. In other words, we should just have the community's expression, without any one person's intention at all, which is another way of saying we should just have everything in the subject's and culture's experience.

Jehlen does not assault expression or intention per se. Rather, she specifically assaults the claim that intention could be thought of as distinct from all the rest of experience – that, in other words, the fish motif can be thought of as distinct from the toilet. In this way, what she leans toward is a hybrid of Minimalist commitment to the relevance of everything in the experience and a New Critical commitment to experience conceived of as intertwined with meaning. This combination is evident in one passage in which she compares meaning to a roof: "Even writing *Finnegans Wake*, James Joyce had to convey a cognitive message; the building Gehry made for the Fishdance restaurant had to keep out the rain."[49] If meaning something is just like providing a roof so people don't get wet, meaning is just another object of experience. And if it's wrong for Gehry to separate one object from another, that's because for Jehlen, to be committed to meaning/experience is to be committed to the entirety of experience. Where Foster disagrees with what Gehry means, Jehlen disagrees with Gehry's premise that he could mean something apart from the whole experience of the building, but yet connected to some part of the experience of being in and from Bilbao, Spain.

As a consequence of this difference, while Foster's piece is a polemical attack on Gehry – he should stop making this kind of building – Jehlen's essay turns out to be hostile praise for it. Because she objects to the theoretical principle of meaning separated from experience that Gehry's whole building would rest upon, she must think it impossible for him to succeed in that very ignorance to culture for which Foster denounces him. Jehlen must, and does, concede that the cordoning off of toilet and street from the Guggenheim, Bilbao as art is actually part of the art:

In the hypermodern American building standing proud and incongruous on its historic Basque site, two major disjunctions of recent years seem to have materialized: the first, at once aesthetic and epistemological, is the disjunction of form and function that has rendered form freely expressive but also vertiginously arbitrary. The second disjunction is the political opposition between multiculturalism and cultural nationalism, or between the transnationalism of the rich and the localism of the poor . . . Frank Gehry's church of art, brilliantly prophesying the gospel that closed the second millennium, celebrates schism: to each era its message.[50]

The upshot of her account, in which Gehry can't just mean what he wants to, but his building materializes its era perfectly, is that meaning (the authorial intention, say) is impossible. Thus, rather surprisingly, Gehry's presumption that his own view will be communal turns out to be something that Jehlen shares: "to each era its message," insofar as all messages will be identical to the era.

Jehlen and Michaels share a commitment to the idea that there are two choices: seeing meaning as separate from experience, and seeing meaning as part of experience, and they both think that formalism belongs on the side of meaning as part of experience. Where they differ is on which side is the right answer – to Michaels, the latter is to have denied the existence of meaning at all, while to Jehlen the former is a mistaken account of meaning. What Michaels and Jehlen also share is an account of experience as the subject's total experience – of it including the wall, the floor, the toilet. However, Michaels's convincing account of meaning's constitutive break from experience won't be enough to do away with the appeal to experience in criticism, and that's precisely because experience is actually in a more curious relationship to form than in either the collapse of form into subjective experience or the definition of form as part of meaning. Experience doesn't matter in regard to any account of meaning (or rather, needn't and shouldn't); but this is not the sole ground on which it might claim relevance to criticism. When Jehlen tells us in the middle of her account of the Guggenheim, Bilbao, that she went out to get a cup of coffee, it's a move like saying "I feel sick" at the waterfall – it's just a fact about her experience. But this comment is also different from other comments Jehlen makes, such as her notation that the museum "feels bigger than it is" or that it "appears serenely self-contained."[51] The reason the coffee break is such a strange moment is not that she thinks experience might be important to the building, it is that she thinks her experience of drinking coffee is as relevant as (is of the same order as) her experience of how the spaces of the building shift. That is why she thinks there is something wrong with Gehry for thinking of the museum as art, without taking into account the windows and toilets: he thinks we can all tell they aren't relevant to the experience of the museum, whereas she (like Michaels) thinks once it is experience that is at issue, everything in it matters.

But why should we think that whatever it is in art objects that is distinct from their objecthood, it must be their meaning? Why should we call a glance of an eye that distinguishes one thing as mattering versus another as a representation, as Michaels does? And why should we think that we are incapable of distinguishing between aspects of our experience? Once you've used a frame to demarcate that part of an experience matters and part of it doesn't, you've clearly indicated some discernment into the question – but this is really only to point up that experience is often about precisely the way that the mind distinguishes among the sensations that it perceives. Were we unable to make distinctions between what did and what didn't count in our experience, we would find it extremely difficult – not to say impossible – to conduct our lives, in part because we would never be able to say that we had enjoyed the conversation at dinner but didn't like the food, that the weather was pleasant even though the car broke down, and so on. There's a reason why Jehlen needs to travel to Bilbao and see the museum: that some part of the experience of being there is necessary to grasp it (as when Foster describes its spaces as "mystifying"); so too, we wouldn't be inclined to trust a critic who wrote about paintings only by looking at their reproductions, or about books without reading them. We also wouldn't think their stomachaches and caffeine fixes mattered, which is to say that these are kinds of objects to which parts of our experience matter, and parts of it don't. Our accounts of such objects cannot just be interpretations of their meaning, but neither can they be recitations of all of our experience. And it is missing the distinctions within experience, and the distinction of form from both meaning and experience (and from their fusion), that makes us think we have to choose between meaning or experience/form/meaning – when, in fact, what we need to do is not choose between meaning and experience but choose among our experiences, to be willing to distinguish between what is relevant and what is not.

Steven Knapp's *Literary Interest* is largely about why literary form and the experience of reading might matter to anyone (or, really, why it should not). In Knapp's argument, every attempt to explain the ethical imperative of literature and criticism turns out to be an argument that it performs a special union of the particular and the universal, and that is a union that just doesn't need literature. Knapp argues that there is nothing inherently ethical about that suspended interest and contemplation that literature produces, and that there is nothing particularly valuable about any of the ways that literature seems to bind together universals and contingencies. Moreover, he points out that even the recent labor of new historicist critics to connect literature to historical "actuality" is only another attempt at binding the contingent and the universal, which simply reproduces the quintessential literary interest in the interrelationship of two things without providing a substantive intervention, such as the amelioration of suffering or the rectification of injustice.[52]

As Knapp sees it, interest in or thoughtfulness about the literary ("any linguistically embodied representation that tends to attract a certain kind of interest to itself")[53] is different from the meaning of the text. One example of this is that "there is an interest in metaphor that goes beyond any interest in figuring out what thoughts the writer intends to communicate."[54] Throughout, this interest in the representation itself, in the words and the form of the representation in addition to in its meaning, is an interest in the experience of the representation rather than in its meaning. Knapp points out that Wimsatt's essay, "The Concrete Universal," focuses on "a texture of concreteness which does not contribute anything to the argument but is somehow enjoyable or valuable for its own sake."[55] But lest this look like "an irrational turn from meaning to experience," from interest in that which is represented to the experience of the manner in which it is represented, Wimsatt maintains that the image is itself necessary to the meaning.[56] Wimsatt suggests that not only does the manner of representation refer to what it represents, but what it represents refers back to the manner of its representation. Knapp writes that Wimsatt "*reverse[s] the referential relation by treating the experience itself as in some sense pointing back to the literary symbol* that both occasions it and refers to it"[57] (original emphasis). For example, the apple that falls from a tree is a way to illustrate gravity, but it isn't crucial to it; yet, to Wimsatt, in the case of metaphor and the concrete universal, the manner of illustration develops a substantive imbrication with the idea, as if gravity could not be understood without returning to the apple as an illustration of it. This circular referentiality produces, according to Wimsatt, "a new conception," the concrete universal.[58] This is the central idea of New Criticism, a fusion of form and content that is equivalent to a fusion of subjective experience and universal meaning.

This union of the subjective experience to the universal meaning (universal because its meaning is not dependent on the form in which it is expressed and the subjective way any one person comes to see it) is in Knapp's account the argument for the importance of literature. Knapp maintains that the concrete universal is, however, no new thing that goes above and beyond the opposition of experience to meaning, but is just more commitment to experience. He writes, "the 'new conception' for which there is no other expression is not in fact a conception at all but an experience," which experience is nothing but "the thrill produced by encountering this particular configuration of metaphors." Thus, New Critical formalism is just a commitment to "an experience – whose contours are uniquely defined by the particular cognitive and emotive effects of these metaphors and the temporal order in which they succeed each other."[59] That meaning which cannot be extracted from its context is just another experience, not a meaning at all.

But Knapp's argument about New Criticism as commitment to experience, unlike its appearance in Jehlen and Michaels, doesn't mean that it must be a commitment to all of experience. Instead, it is a commitment to "an experience" (as opposed to "experience") that can have "contours" "defined" by particular aspects of it. In other words, to an experience defined as having limits, a frame around it, if you will. Knapp argues that in a poem,

the "objects" by which the emotions are suggested must be *types* of objects or occasions, not particular remembered ones. Otherwise it would make no sense to expect the objects constituting the critic's "reasons for emotion" to constitute similar reasons for the reader informed by the critic's account, unless one supposed that they shared the same particular memories. But if the emotion can be communicated only insofar as it is associated with a more or less general *type* of object, then the experience of such an emotion necessarily involves a reference to a *range* of possible occasions for experiencing it.

Thus affective experience, if it is communicable at all . . . must have a built-in generality that already complicates any stark opposition between private emotion and public knowledge. The objects with which emotions are associated are general *types* of objects, and the emotional responses must have a similar typicality, since otherwise a reader who understood the type of object referred to would not even be *likely* (except by chance) to share the appropriate response. Emotions, consequently, don't need to be inserted into a semantic structure in order to be rescued from irrational particularity; they already *have* a semantic structure.[60]

Knapp's point is that because experience isn't radically subjective, there's no need for literature to come along and give it structure. But Knapp's theory, I want to underscore, offers a semantics of the experience of a text that is distinct from the meaning. And unlike the theory of New Critical formalism, which binds experience to meaning, thereby collapsing them incoherently into just more experience, Knapp's point suggests that the experience of an object can be regulated by the meaning of that object, even though the two things are separate.

In this case, the perception that Michaels and Jehlen share of a stark choice between a commitment to meaning and a commitment to form and experience is inaccurate. To say we should choose meaning instead of experience would be to continue the misapprehension of experience as limitless subjective experience. Experience and its formal properties are more complex, more typified, and more distinguishable from subjective experience than they seem when, in both Michaels's and Jehlen's work, New Critical formalism is read as definitive of formalism per se. And it's only from the point of view of critical commitments to meaning as only founded in and through experience in its all-embracing, subjective sense, and from the point of view of concern with how such subjective experience has to be thought through in relation to the universal, that the New Critical commitment to experience as transformed in and through form appears so perfectly to complement these concerns. Formalism in general is not entirely identified, after all, with Wimsatt and Beardsley; but, as I have suggested above and as Knapp differently suggests here, even Wimsatt and Beardsley's account of experience is markedly less subjective, less irrational and indistinguishable than the account of it in recent Americanist critical thought. Thinking about form is not the same thing as thinking about subjective experience, or as thinking about how subjective experience might be united with meaning. The tendency to read New Critical theory as inflected with the concerns with identity and experience of the last twenty years is itself another example of the appeal to historical continuity to defend critical claims about our beliefs today. This is part of an ongoing identitarianism, in which experience and literary form are what they always have been. This is both to misread Wimsatt and Beardsley – to misinterpret the past – and to mistakenly assume that formalism is what it has been. Formalism today need not be construed as constitutively "new," as a revival and renovation of the inheritance of New Critical formalism.

Moreover, American literature never fully delivered that fusion of experience and language in the metaphoric image that New Critics sought. Even Matthiessen wrote that Hawthorne suffers from "the frequent disproportion between the weight of what [he] wanted to say and the flimsiness of the vehicle he could devise to carry it," and regretted that Emerson rushed through images as if they were undeserving of extended reflection.[61] The reason for this is that American writers in the first half of the nineteenth century – the very time when literature was emerging as a profession, and increasingly understood as distinct (both in its high and low form) from other forms of writing and scholarship – did not think of experience, particularly of the experience relevant to texts, as that undistinguishable subjective category that it so prominently seems to us to be today and that fueled New Critical formalism. Knapp's account of experience as possessing a "semantic structure" defined through types is much closer to that in American writing centrally concerned with articulating an "American experience" than are the various forms of experience that are preeminently particular. However, Knapp's account is still not entirely sufficient to describe the form of experience in this nineteenth-century American literature (not that this is a flaw in his theory, only that it cannot entirely describe the way the belief works in these texts), for experience here will turn out to demand a curiosity and be attributed a discrete integrity apart from the particularity of individual subjects who would enter into that structure of experience.

In Knapp's conception, the literary reader is

> caught up in an irreducible oscillation between typicality and particularity: between (on one side) the forms of action that an agent must understand in order to make sense of herself as the possible performer of certain actions, and (on the other side) the concrete history without which the agent could not distinguish herself from those who might, otherwise, just as well replace her.[62]

Yet in reading Hawthorne, Emerson, and Stowe, one is asked not just to hover at that threshold between being a real person and a typical one. One is asked to suspend one's particularity and to move into a form of being governed entirely by the typical. In this sense, American literature asks its reader to go somewhere other than that tension between the individual and the typical that Knapp pinpoints. It asks us to abandon our subjectivity altogether and to consider the experience of a text as a composition made from the analytic narration of emblematic images. In the texts I shall turn  to, paradigmatic moments of focusing on the external grain of the world, or on the peculiarity and value of the individual, turn out to be articulations of a set of ideas about experience, an abstraction to which authors are referring and also asking their readers to abet them in shaping. This conjuring and articulation of abstract experience – (not held in the text, not given over to the individual reader, but managed as one directs a kite) – is the literary work. For Knapp the idea that experience must have a form means that literature is somehow irrelevant – experience doesn't need literature to give it shape. But the writers I will be exploring here understand the idea that experience has form not as a condition that renders literature largely moot, but as the necessary condition upon which it can come into being. As such, the form of experience that Knapp points to constitutes not something for literature to feed off parasitically, abrogating to itself an interest beyond all merit, but the medium in which it can be made.

In this section I have maintained that experience has form, and that it is not an indistinguishable morass of subjectivity standing in opposition to meaning and belief. In what follows, however, I shall primarily be providing an account of how form and experience are understood in nineteenth-century America. Of course, many texts that seem committed to subjective experience make recourse to the typical and the general (according to Knapp, they have to). Stendhal's posthumous autobiography, *The Life of Henri Brulard*, is consumed with how circumstances have shaped his innate character into still more individual form. He tells us that "My skin is too delicate, a woman's skin (later on I always got blisters after having held my sabre for an hour); the least thing takes the skin off my fingers . . . Hence maybe an insurmountable revulsion for whatever looks *dirty*, or *damp*, or *blackish* in colour." But even here, Stendhal "borrow[s] for a moment the language of Cabanis" and remarks that his idiosyncrasy is also "to be seen at the Jacobins at St-André."[63] Yet not only is Stendhal's concern with how his own skin has affected his response to the world a kind of particularity that is utterly different from that in, say, Emerson, but even the way of connecting that particularity to the general in another's phrasing and comparable examples has a quite different aspect. There is a specificity to the way these American texts use abstraction as a form of experience – a general observation that spurred many critical observations about the distracted airiness and intellectuality of an author such as Hawthorne in comparison to Dickens or even Austen. The widespread belief that America had no history to turn to, and the fact that because of its provinciality American literary culture used the Scottish theorists much longer than did those abroad, helped to bring about these beliefs about form and experience and the writing practices that emerged from them. But these together do not constitute a set of determinative conditions, and so I don't think it is a lock-step form that can encase every author in the period. I do think the specifics of this writing practice, in which abstract emblems and types project trains of possible and typical experiences, distinguish this American writing from contemporary British and European writing, but I don't think it is a uniquely and transhistorically

American practice) Although such discussions lie outside the scope of this project, the differences between this antebellum abstraction and that of both Puritan and republican-era writing are more substantive than their occasional surface similarities. And the problem of making American literature in the nineteenth century is markedly alien to contemporary discourse, in which memoirs derived from the authentic grain of an individual's life are presumed to be of gripping interest to others.

# CHAPTER I

# Types of interest: Scottish theory, literary nationalism, and John Neal

"The emotions produced by a fine landscape and the singing of birds, being similar in a considerable degree, readily unite, though their causes are little connected."[1] This sentence, from Kames's *Elements of Criticism*, passes no judgment on the accuracy or truth value of responses to landscapes and birdsongs, and considers only the similarity and relation of those responses. As in that one example, core epistemological questions are consistently sidestepped throughout Common Sense philosophy and aesthetics, in favor of concern with the properties of experiences rather than with the information they might provide. Faced with the spectacle of Lockean empiricism's trajectory into Humean skepticism – with the way that basing knowledge only on one's senses could never lead to certainty about the truth value of one's knowledge – Scottish Common Sense philosophy, as its name implies, worked to regain a basic faith in the senses. And faith is the operative word, because the Common Sense philosophers do not really disprove skepticism, but rather adopt a strategic blindness to the fact that we have no way of knowing if our experience is at all trustworthy. In practice this led to, among other things, a body of writing on psychology and aesthetics which is largely descriptive, outlining how thoughts and emotions follow from one another and from objects in the external world. The result is an assertive and analytic account of the mind, but not an argument for the accuracy and validity of the mind's impressions.[2] Associationism inverts the empirical method (the use of experience to gain knowledge about objects outside the self), recasting experience as *what* we know, not *how* we know. As Adela Pinch observes, in this tradition emotions are conceived as "somewhat autonomous substances," rather than as interior, personal property.[3] What is central is that experience is disentangled from the subject or the person; concomitantly, it is entertained as an object of aesthetic contemplation.

In so approaching experience, the Scottish critics laid out a way of thinking about experience as the observable, typical experience that crucially inflected the way that "American experience" was thought of in the formative phase of literary nationalism in the early decades of the nineteenth century. I take this to indicate that the fundamental distinction between subjective imagination (producing the romance) and grounded observations of objects (producing factual writing) is a mistaken paradigm for American literature as it developed under the rubric of nationalism. In this chapter, I first explore the cases of Lord Kames and Archibald Alison, to show the way they conceive literature as the projection of abstract experiences through the use of types, pointing at a work made only in that projected experience, not in the text itself. Then, in the second section, I argue that this idea is not just a check, in nationalist literary criticism of the 1820s and 1830s, on the idea of a native experience's expression, but that it leads into a conception of experience in American literature as something forecast out of types and general ideas. Thus literary nationalism's conception of an American experience is disembodied, a point I extend in the third section through analysis of one particular writer in this period, John Neal, whose most fervent nationalist sentiments and personal revelations occur within the bounds of a commitment to the literary experience as a projected, typical experience rather than as an outpouring of embodied emotion.

I

Scottish philosophy was a pervasive presence in nineteenth-century American literary criticism and teaching.[4] Criticism which has examined the effects of the Common Sense philosophers on American literature tends to possess two complementary emphases: the Scots define the real as the literal or the actual, and the Scots define mental conceptions, particularly imaginary ideas but also abstractions and possibles, as degraded forms of the actual, importantly in danger of becoming subjective and, in short order, false. In Terence Martin's understanding, for example, "The whole movement of Scottish Common Sense metaphysics was out of the mind; indeed, its total structure rests on the foundation of objectively, actually existing reality."[5] The alternative to such strident insistence on the category of the materially present real was the category of internal mental activity. It is in favor of avowedly untrue internal experience that authors would turn to the romance, which was, again in Martin's words, a genre which "dealt with private, internal experience – or with experience formed in a private, personal manner."[6] Michael Davitt Bell made a similar claim, and further maintained that American romancers sought to combine the objective with the subjective through "connecting or 'mingling' imaginary ideas with 'real' materials" and thereby join literature back to the real.[7] This implies that there is an effort to objectify the imaginative and the subjective realm of internal experience, an implication which I follow out in this chapter. Yet for Bell, the situation remains one of a firm opposition between objective external objects and subjective internal experience, even if authors try to combine the two, and it is precisely that division which will not hold as an account of the Common Sense tradition and its relevance for American literature.[8]

While Martin and Bell focused on the objective stress of Common Sense philosophy, other critics worried the reverse, that it was too subjective. Walter Jackson Bate pointed, for example, to the significant title of James Beattie's *Essays on Poetry and Music, as They Affect the Mind*.[9] Both Bate and René Wellek had serious reservations about associationism, because they found that it nullifies questions about the quality of a work of art and replaces them with questions about the reader's or viewer's experience. In this respect, Scottish-influenced criticism is a subjective critical method in which the art object disappears. That disappearance is crucial, but not for the reason Bate and Wellek would cite, that it signals the turn to subjective appraisals of art. When the art object disappears, associationism presents in its stead an appraisal of the reader's experience. The process of responding to a work of art becomes an object in the criticism of associationist Scots and their American adherents. Moreover, it is exactly in that process that the distinction between objective, external reality and subjective, internal reactions which Martin and Bell employed loses its applicability to this body of thought.

Kames's and Alison's thought, most particularly, contained a foundational belief that experience might be an aesthetically coherent object of spectatorship. That is, they held that we may regard our own thoughts and emotions as we view a painting or read a novel. Their interest in the structure and quality of experience preempts any discussion on their part of the validity of basing beliefs upon or gaining knowledge from experience. They neither deny nor aver that experience tells us the truth, and this peculiar unwillingness to contend with the question, is experience a ground for knowledge? – an oblique relationship to what would seem to us among the most pressing and obvious questions about experience – will recur in the writers I examine in subsequent chapters. This resistance to considering the category of experience as it tells the truth is a refusal to define experience as an individual person's subjective reactions to objects. It offers instead a definition of experience as the typical person's hypothetical, pro-jected responses to typical images, situations and possibilities.

The analysis of experience requires one axiom: experience is not just how we know things, but something we can know in itself. In the first sentence of  the first chapter of the *Elements*, Kames makes this key distinction between consciousness and experience, which consists of perceptions and ideas: "A man, while awake, is conscious of a continued train of perceptions and ideas passing in his mind" (*E*, 31).[10] One would think that consciousness consisted of perceptions and ideas, for how could one's consciousness of perceptions and ideas be anything other than still more perceptions and ideas? Nonetheless, in that sentence Kames makes just such a separation of consciousness from perception and ideas, and implicitly relies upon the existence of a consciousness that sees our seeing and knows our knowing. In Kames's understanding, one is a spectator to that process of thoughts and feelings called experience: persons have what he terms the "consciousness" of "an internal object" which is "within the mind," and such consciousness is distinct from that passion or thought.

Kames's entire analysis of experience is of the principles upon which the trains of thought and feeling proceed – as one might, say, observe the principles of gravity, or the course of a bird in flight. What causes these trains of thoughts and feelings? How are they organized? These are the kinds of questions he is interested in asking of experience. If one cannot control one's experience, and it is not determined "by chance," Kames wants first and foremost to know, "by what law is it governed?" (*E*, 31). That law is connection, and it regulates the train of thought, a disparate segment of experience, similar to a stretch of beads on a cord. Thoughts and impressions succeed in linear order, and continually cross-reference one another. Two principles bind experience from one moment to the next: the connections among phenomena, and our attraction to, and in some cases choice among, those connections. Kames notes "the various relations that connect" "external objects" to one another, such as "cause and effect, contiguity in time or in place, high and low" (*E*, 31). In this case, mental links occur at the prompting of connections which, to Kames, exist outside the mind. The idea that the connections between objects are independent of the mind is evident in his comment that "the train of our thoughts is in a great measure regulated by [those] relations," while the mind seems passively to receive the connections between objects: "an external object is no sooner presented to us in idea, than it suggests to the mind other objects to which it relates" (*E*, 31). Yet, the train is not entirely directed by the outside world. Because "there are few things but what are connected with many others," we must choose which to follow and "insist upon one, rejecting others" (*E*, 32). In this sense, the mind does not just receive connections, it must also direct them. If my account of Kames sounds mechanistic, that is part of the point: for Kames the mind responds to objects and discriminates among those responses in a manner that is largely predictable.

Even though discriminations among responses follow set rules, those rules vary for different types of character. The "law of succession" may be undiscriminating contiguity, as in the case of the garrulous woman in whose mind "thoughts and circumstances crowd upon each other by the slightest connections," or that law may be governed by some principle, as in the case of the wise man choosing on the basis of the most "substantial and permanent" connection, or even the wit who chooses connections which are intentionally "distant and fanciful" (*E*, 33). Such variations in the law of connection are nonetheless standardized, for variant connections are divided into classes rather than ascribed to abnormal, stray individuals. And Kames is comfortable outlining a standard of pleasurable connection, a standard which he ascribes to all persons despite the variations mentioned in the passage above. We gravitate toward particular connections in order to prolong our mood, and to stabilize and lengthen whatever state we may be in. One may choose a connection to match one's "present tone of mind: for a subject that accords with that tone is always welcome" (*E*, 32). If continuity is inherently pleasurable, it may even seem desirable to sustain *any* experience, even an unpleasant experience of misfortune (who wants cheerful images when in the throes of despair?). Steady, smooth extension and elaboration of a mood are not only comfortable but beautiful for Kames. He goes on to assert that the ceaseless variety of connections may be bound together into the stable entity that is the train of thought, possessing a beginning, an end, and a principle of connection between its elements.[11] That is partly what the wise man does in sticking to a steady ground of connection between one idea and the next rather than veering perversely (like the wit) from one thought to an opposite one. When Kames deems those connections to be most pleasing which are orderly and smooth, the pleasure is in the continuity and sameness that result: "When an object is introduced by a proper connection, we are conscious of a certain pleasure arising from that circumstance" (*E*, 35). It is the organization and the consistency of our responses that is enjoyable, and it is desirable for our state of mind – even fear or grief – to endure and cohere.

I noted above that experience must be independent of consciousness if it is to be analyzed at all. In addition to that separation of experience from consciousness, in the *Elements* experience is strikingly separated from phenomena. One sign of that is that Kames allows for only a negligible difference between direct apprehension and imagination. He does distinguish between what he designates the *perception* of "external" objects of awareness (such as "every object of hearing, of smell"), and *conception*, the capacity to entertain images and ideas presented at second hand, as when one reads of "an ebony ship with sails and ropes of silk" (*E*, 10). But the difference between the "perception" of a living flower and the "conception" of that flower received through a painting has nothing to do with the inherent difference between a plant and a painting, nor does it have anything to do with the difference between the nature of the image each prompts in us. The difference between seeing and picturing a flower is only in our belief about the flower: perception "includes a conviction of the reality of its object," while conception "does not" (*E*, 10) – in which case, we could "conceive" of a real flower so long as, in gazing upon it, we believed it to be unreal.

The distance between objects like a living flower and our images of them (which allows perception and conception to be so close) also informs Kames's counter-intuitive account of memory, in which experience and memory are virtually indistinguishable:

> Objects once perceived may be recalled to the mind by the power of memory. When I recall an object of sight in that manner, it appears to me precisely the same as in the original survey, only less distinct. For example, having seen yesterday a spreading oak growing on the brink of a river, I endeavor to recall these objects to my mind. How is this operation performed? Do I endeavor to form in my mind a picture of them, or a representative image? Not so. I transport myself ideally to the place where I saw the tree and river yesterday: upon which I have a perception of these objects similar in all respects to the perceptions I had when I viewed them with my eyes, only less distinct. And in the recollection, I am not conscious of a picture or representative image, more than in the original survey; the perception is of the tree and river themselves, as at first. (*E*, 11–12)

What is crucial here is that experience is so much like memory that they are all but indistinguishable.[12] The point is not that memory is especially immediate, but that original experience is especially abstract, as it is cleanly separated from its object. For only if the object is incidental to the experience can the memory be so much like the original experience once the object is gone. Kames is, it is true, approaching a claim about the life-like nature of memory, about memory as a true reliving in which a person "transport[s]

[him]self ideally to the place where [he] saw the tree and the river yesterday." In that respect, experience and its memory would be alike because they share a connection to the original object — memory would be life-like in so far as it revives the object, "the tree and river." But even to think that one can mentally return to "the place" and the object, or to think that memory can be a reliving rather than a representation, one must already understand that present experience to exist at a remove from the tree and the river. Only if the presence of the object is distinguishable from the original experience can memory be said to even approach the relationship of the original experience to that object, once the object is no longer present. To call memory just a representation is to stress the important reality and presence of the tree and river in our original experience of it, while to call memory a reliving (as Kames does) is to rely upon the nonessential or subsidiary role of tree and river in the original experience.

Kames extends this distinction between objects and our experience of them even within the moment, as a distinction between body and mind. He separates "qualities of the objects we *perceive*" from "qualities of the emotions we *feel*," and distinguishes the perception of warmth by the senses from the "sensation" of "the pleasure arising from warmth" (*E*, 10). For instance, first there is a reactive "impression" made "upon the palate by an apricot," and then there is a response of the mind to the sensation itself, which we must be careful not to "assign a wrong place to"; we must see that pleasure in taste belongs not to the apricot but to "the mind" (*E*, 24). Kames maintains that qualities inhere in objects (that an apricot has a certain taste) but portrays those inherent qualities as merely circumstantially and causally related to our experience of them. The important thing is our perception and feelings about the apprehension of an apricot's taste, not about the apricot in and of itself.

In such passages, experience is understood as a separate, extra-personal and extra-phenomenal register. Kames grants something to inhere in objects, and something to inhere in the mind; yet the principle of connection is a third category, the "relation," which seems to exist between or beyond those two options. As I have already noted, Kames distinguishes between objects' "inherent properties" and "the various relations that connect them together." In declaring that relations are "remarkable," Kames is saying that they are "distinguishable" or "identifiable" but still not "inherent" to the object. Relations somehow follow from objects yet are not in them or a part of what they are. At the same time, the relation isn't in our mind; it must depend on something outside the person, because "we cannot add to the train an unconnected idea" (*E*, 32). The relation, the principle of correct connection between ideas and between forms, is of this third category: (neither world nor self.) What Kames avers here of the relations between objects that our minds observe holds throughout the *Elements*, as Kames characterizes all of experience as a category of non-self and non-world. This is to categorize experience as a set of abstract rules rather than as a matter either of subjects or of objects.

At this point, we may reconsider the terms of Bate's and Wellek's concerns over the affective element of associationism. For those critics, an aesthetics must be concerned with one of two things: the work itself or the viewer's response. Yet response in Kames isn't truly the viewer's; he describes a spectatorship of one's responses which is explicitly not a log of subjective reactions. Kames writes:

> Viewing a fine garden, I perceive it to be beautiful or agreeable; and I consider the beauty or agreeableness as belonging to the object, or as one of its qualities. When I turn my attention from the garden to what passes in my mind, I am conscious of a pleasant emotion, of which the garden is the cause: the pleasure here is felt, as a quality, not of the garden, but of the emotion produced by it. (*E*, 72)

There is no disproportionate rapture in this passage, for in it the foundational assumption is that the "I" can speak that which is true for any observer. Kames is looking at his own experience as something alien to himself, looking at his observations from a cool distance. He may well lose sight of the garden in this passage, but he apprehends the pleasure taken in it with that fineness of attention which Bate or Wellek would direct to the garden itself. So although this passage describes a shift of attention from object (garden) to experience, that experience is in turn made an object, one which is seen by the "I" or observer. It is not an experience of the self, but a moment when one steps back and analyzes one's perception as from a distance, "felt, as a quality . . . of the emotion" (rather than simply felt).

The separation of experience both from phenomena and from consciousness (or from objects and subjects) also underlies what Kames calls "ideal presence," a state of fully sensed and yet imaginary experience one may have while reading. Reading, for example, "a lively and beautiful description" of Hannibal and Scipio "at the famous battle of Zama," we no longer "consider it as long past." Rather, writes Kames, "I perceive them brandishing their swords, and cheering their troops; and in that manner I attend them through the battle, every incident of which appears to be passing in my sight" (*E*, 65). At that moment, the reader forgets his place, his own life:

The power of language to raise emotions, depends entirely on the raising of such lively and distinct images as are here described: the reader's passions are never sensibly moved, till he be thrown into a kind of reverie; in which state, forgetting that he is reading, he conceives every incident as passing in his presence as if he were an eyewitness. (*E*, 65)

The reader is disembodied, removed from his own time and memories in order to apprehend ideal presence. There is here a moment of presentness that is not quite real; Kames refers to some extra-epistemological awareness; an entity or perhaps an event which is cognitive without belonging to a mind, and which has attributes resembling those of objects without consisting of them.

In the passage above, experience is abstracted from the person as much as it is from the world, and even abstracted from time. A scene feels real when the past, "2000 years ago," becomes the present moment; the reader is gripped in an instant of excitement exactly when this moment seems replaced by a past event. The reader's sense that ancient history is happening in this instant requires temporal extension: the gripping instant's description is "spread out" over time, notes Kames, unlike the "slight or superficial narrative" which stays put in the past. Temporal duration of the writing, in which the ideas and pictures are drawn out and developed over time, causes the impression of an atemporal, frozen moment. Hence language evokes passion better than pictures: "a picture is confined to a single instant of time, and cannot take in a succession of incidents," when "our passions, those especially of the sympathetic kind, require a succession of impressions; and for that reason, reading and acting have greatly the advantage, by reiterating impressions without end" (*E*, 67). He imagines painting lasting only one instant, because it only depicts a single moment, and the viewer does not look at a painting over an extended period of time.

In ideal presence, the instantaneous and the extended are arrested into one sense of reality: experience is both temporal and atemporal. So too, forgetting that one reads, a person is removed from his own experience only to be thrust into an ideal experience, where Scipio and Hannibal battle before his eyes. The text disappears, the reader forgets himself, and Hannibal has been dead 2000 years, but without all those factors there is still a vivid experience, one suspended in a vacuum: in this passage, ideal presence is a heightened experience which exists in the absence of both a subject and an object. At such points in Kames's *Elements*, the belief that one can apprehend experience becomes a formulation of abstracted experience with its own coherence, independent of persons and the world. In that transcendent quality – its ideal independence of person and object – experience becomes, like a poem or a work of art, an aesthetic  object and duly outshines the text which caused it.

In 1790, thirty years after Kames's *Elements*, the Scottish scholar Archibald Alison published *Essays on the Nature and Principles of Taste*. Alison shares with Kames an interest in how emotional and mental states are sustained and bound together, but in Alison's account the train of thought is even more distinct from the phenomenal world, and more nearly subjective.[13] If we see "the savage majesty of a wintry storm," nonetheless "we are conscious of a variety of images in our minds, very different from those which the objects themselves can present to the eye."[14] Such "trains of pleasing or solemn thought" (*T*, 5) occur in the mind, and are only partially determined by the original object, "the simple perception of" which "is insufficient to excite these emotions" (*T*, 4). While people's sensory impressions of the world (such as the impression made by an apricot upon the tongue mentioned by Kames) do not differ (*T*, 8), the trains of thought which those impressions occasion do in that they come from the individual, and are determined by his "different habits and occupations of life" (*T*, 85). Thus, there is no error in the reaction of a "Mathematician . . . who read the Paradise Lost, without being able to discover in it anything that was sublime," but whose "blood [ran] cold" over Newton (*T*, 88). Nevertheless, to understand Alison as committed to the subjective, or possibly to the relative (as when he suggests that people brought up in the city do not enjoy the countryside), is to miss his embrace of Kames's intimation that experience may achieve an aesthetically pleasurable wholeness and interconnection of parts, which can be assessed objectively and recommended unilaterally. Even if Alison allows that reactions vary depending on one's context and personality, he still believes that all reactions can be observed from a detached and objective position, and moreover that from such a detached position it is possible to judge the clarity and coherence, even the pleasurable continuity, of those reactions.

Alison conducts an exact analysis of how trains of thought and emotion must be organized (perhaps by an artist's work, perhaps by a beautiful natural scene) in order to be tastefully pleasing to the person in whom the experience occurs. Ideas of the sublime and the beautiful must first cause emotions, and then combine those emotions with thoughts to form a "complex idea" (*T*, 77). What results is a train of thought that must be a coherent whole; each idea or emotion is similar to that which precedes it and to that which follows it. Furthermore, each idea or emotion in the train has some relationship to every other one, even if they are not placed side-by-side in the train. Yet another requirement for aesthetically coherent experience is that each idea must relate back to the first one, such as the concept of the wintry storm which prompts a reverie. In fine, there is "not only a connection between the individual thoughts of the train, but also a general relation among the whole, and a conformity to that peculiar emotion which at first excited them" (*T*, 78). The ideas do not progress in a vector, but move away from their starting point only to turn and head back towards it. The exhaustive cross-referencing among different points gives the train of thought a duration and a boundary, as well as a clarity and a wholeness beyond what we usually witness in our reactions and thoughts. These criteria of complex cross-reference and the resulting wholeness allow Alison to distinguish between the rush of ordinary experiences and the discrete train of thought which occupies his critical judgment in *On Taste*.

His isolation of trains of response implies that Alison treats those same responses as discrete, aesthetic works. The tendency in *On Taste* to consider the aesthetic quality of experience (rather than of painting or writing) is brought home when Alison argues that the best art is art which disappears, leaving one to reflect upon trains of responses to the art rather than the art itself.  Alison values unity in art because it doesn't interfere with the mind's own processes of imagination: "simplicity" is "welcome to us, as permitting us to indulge, without interruption, those interesting trains of thought which the character of the scene is fitting to inspire" (*T*, 30). This transfer of interest from the work to its effects suggests that the response – the train of thought and emotion – is, in fact, the real art object. Alison's only real criterion for a good painting or poem is that it be consistent; his objections all center on violations of such consistency, as when an "unhappy image" "is singularly ill-suited to that tone" of feeling "which the poet has everywhere else so successfully maintained" (*T*, 137). The motivation for Alison's ideal of consistency is that changes of tone interrupt and frustrate the train of one's response to a work: in Virgil's *Georgics* an image of unexpected "tameness and vulgarity . . . dissipates at once the emotion we had shared with the Poet" (*T*, 136). That discord reveals a difference between the reader and author, because it shows that a single image makes the reader and the author think of two different things. And, when an author diverges from his reader's expectations he interrupts the reader's reverie and forces him to attend more closely to the text. That attention to the author's work rather than to the reader's reverie disrupts and ruins the harmony of that reverie. For Alison, criticism deadens literature when it pays excessive attention to the text itself, making us "attend minutely to the language or composition" of a poem (*T*, 11). The implication of Alison's ideal of consistency is that one does not want to pay very much attention to artworks: any actual piece of art is a necessary evil. He writes,

The landscapes of Claude Lorraine, the music of Handel, the poetry of Milton, excite feeble emotions in our minds when our attention is confined to the qualities they present to our senses . . . It is then, only, we feel the sublimity or beauty of their productions, when our imaginations are kindled by their power, when we lose ourselves amid the number of images that pass before our minds. (*T*, 6)

What Alison means when he says that an artwork is good is that it allows us to forget about it entirely and to delight in the smooth trains of associations it has caused.

Alison's preference for imaginary elaborations, which are only loosely connected to specific texts, also leads him to advocate art which need not rely too much on the visible world. The drawback of depending upon the visible, in Alison's account, is that an artist can't trust an audience to respond to realistic depictions of the external world exactly as he wishes it to.

The Painter can give to the objects of his scenery, only the visible and material qualities which are discernible by the eye, and must leave the interpretation of their expression to the imagination of the spectator. (*T*, 132)

Suppose a painting portrays a scene in the country; it is then prey to whatever thoughts the viewer may or may not have about country scenes in general. If the man is city-bred, the work fails because he has no pleasant associations with the country: "The charms of the country are altogether lost upon a citizen, who has passed his life in town" (*T*, 37). But a poet may do more than represent a landscape, he can convey the associations it is supposed to have "by bestowing on the inanimate objects of his scenery the characters and affections of Mind," that is, by describing an experience of the scene in addition to its brute appearance. By describing the experience, not its object, "the Poet can give direct expression to whatever he describes" and "produce at once an expression which every capacity may understand, and every heart may feel" (*T*, 132). In this respect, the ideal work might not depict anything at all, and might instead recount trains of responses to a vanished object.

Like Kames, then, Alison aspires to erase the object altogether – to make experience regular and fixed without the touchstone of the poem or the world beyond the subject. Even further, that is exactly what literature does for the two critics: it removes the object of experience, rather than serving as one. For in such reading as Kames and Alison imagine, the problems of empiricism – the troubling unreliability of our responses to objects and our inability to know if they are absolutely true – is unrecognized. The question of knowing anything is dispensed with; there is only an analysis of experience, not an attempt to compare it to the objective world, nor even to one's own sense of self or individual psychology. To Kames in particular, language is a transparent medium, which transmits what are still termed – perplexingly – perceptions: Kames writes that "by language every man's perceptions may be communicated by all" (*E*, 15), with no trace of any change or degeneration of the perception. Writing can make a reader into a spectator by making itself disappear. The reader, in a passage discussed above, is "thrown into a kind of reverie; in which state, forgetting that he is reading, he conceives every incident as passing in his presence as if he were an eyewitness" (*E*, 65). Successful writing makes us forget that we are reading, and puts us in a position to witness an abstract reality, such as Kames's ideal presence. Hence, the stress on aesthetic experience entails a certain oblivion to the object in question, such that the first-hand experience of an "eyewitness" requires only a vivid mental image, not physical perception – either of the book in one's hands, or of the event (in Kames's example, the battle of Hannibal and Scipio) that book describes. The inconsequence, finally, of literature to aesthetic experience results in the inconsistent and puzzling superficiality of Kames's and Alison's analyses of specific texts, for the work itself only seems to merit attention if it is awkward enough to get in the way.[15]

The attempt to form a judgment about objects outside the self also vanishes. Alison writes,

The leaves begin then to drop from the trees; the flowers and shrubs, with which the fields were adorned in the summer months, decay; the woods and groves are silent; the sun himself seems gradually to withdraw his light, or to become enfeebled in his power. Who is there, who, at this season, does not feel his mind impressed with a sentiment of melancholy? or who is able to resist that current of thought, which, from such appearances of decay, so naturally leads him to the solemn imagination of that inevitable fate, which is to bring on alike the decay of life, of empire, and of nature itself? (*T*, 16–17)

The passage begins by describing autumn, the falling of leaves and the shortened days. But from these objects, Alison then describes what everyone feels and thinks upon seeing such sights, thereby assuming that the relation between falling leaves and melancholy is universal. However, he is not completely willing to embrace that assumption, for he still does not describe the thoughts of melancholy with the flat, empirical quality with which the trees changing are described – the image of fall in itself isn't quite enough to bring about the reaction of melancholy. Tellingly, Alison's prose shifts into the rhetorical question, which appeals to a common response without entirely counting on its being there; it presupposes that everyone feels melancholy in the fall, but also allows that perhaps someone has *not* felt so.

What is the reader responding to at this point? Not to the falling leaves, but to the unwinding of associations that Alison performs and asserts at once, like the poet who can describe the "expression" of a scene, not just the scene itself. The education of the sense of taste which animates all of associationist criticism comes to the surface here, for writing sets down associations in words and in so doing contributes to the diffusion of conventional responses. So, ultimately Alison appeals to an "acquaintance with poetry" in order to "giv[e] *character* to the different appearances of nature" and "connect[ ] them with various emotions of our hearts" (*T*, 66). Literature, he contends, builds on a conventional repertoire of associations between objects and responses, which it then contributes to disseminating and perpetuating. Responses may vary from person to person, and yet overlap in the main and, importantly, be judged typical from atypical, normal from abnormal, because they are determined by convention.

The question persists, though, of what the force of such conventionality is. For if Alison felt that melancholy in the fall were purely conventional (i.e., that melancholy bears no necessary relation to the turning of leaves) it's hard to see what the imperative to institutionalizing that connection would be, aside from the desirability of agreement among persons. It is this point on which Alison is most elusive, and his lack of clarity about the difference between the conventional and the true indicates the basic philosophical insufficiency of associationism and Common Sense philosophy. As critics including Dabney Townsend have elaborated, the ultimate philosophical test of associationism is an appeal to majority: either to what most people think currently, or to what people have consistently thought over time. This appeal to majority has two different premises: first, the natural character of responses – that which inheres, like melancholy in the fall – is visible when we take a large statistical sample. In this spirit, Alison hopes that through "varied and patient EXPERIMENT" he could "ascertain the peculiar qualities which, by the CONSTITUTION of our NATURE, are permanently connected with the Emotions we feel" as distinguishable from "accidental[ ]" distractions, including "the state of our own minds," which distort any one act of observation (*T*, xiii–xiv). In this conception, the universal, unchanging quality of human responses to the world will be made clear in a wide enough sample pool. The second, contrasting premise is that experience becomes regular only through education, practice, and social interaction. In this respect, instances of response are not meant to discover a universal and innate characteristic of experience, but to reinforce and disseminate an arbitrary convention or norm until it becomes as good as universal. Kames and Alison perform a combination of establishing and discovering universals: they tell us how to respond and describe how we already respond, and they do so without acknowledging the difference between the two.[16] The "incipient circularity" that Townsend notes is a philosophically unsatisfying compromise between the conventional and the innate, and the reciprocal animation of outer and inner world emerging in Common Sense philosophy has obvious shortcomings as an epistemology.[17] But it weighs experience as an aesthetic object, with definite rules of connection, unity, and extension.

But what, then, would an associationist artwork look like? As we have seen, associationism suggests the near-irrelevance of any particular work, indeed of any object outside the self. On the other hand, it suggests that in our experience those objects outside us are caught up in a standard grammar of responses, and it is clear that associations need an object to begin with, some spur outside the mind and heart. This problem of what an associationist work would look like is a crucial element of early nineteenth-century literary nationalism's conception of American literature as an almost impossible notion. The theoretical principle of the associationists that experience was detached from persons and objects, as a combination of perceptions, ideas, and emotions standing as a general, hypothetical repertoire through which any individual might pass, and which any individual can conjure up for observation and analysis, can explain the otherwise quite strange approach to experience, and to literature, of the American authors who were formed through reference to the Scottish tradition. The terms of Kames's and Alison's writing help to locate the ways that apparently inauthentic and differently unsatisfying language – fanciful extravagance, extreme assertiveness, overdetermined conventionality – is placed in a privileged relationship to experience. Experience is, in the American works to which I devote the following chapters, best represented and best produced through writing that does not itself bear the mark of or channel the essence of sensory and emotive presence. And as the Scots background also helps us to see, experience is figured as a collection of responses, ideas, and emotions that may require the presence of persons and objects to come into being but yet stand ungrounded in them.

II

Reviewing Washington Irving's *A Tour on the Prairies*, an attempt to satisfy the public's demand for books on American subjects, the critic Edward Everett suggested that writing about such subjects was particularly difficult. Such writers,

> No matter how cold, and barren, and desolate the scene; – they fill it with life and motion; with interest and passion. They strike the desert rock and it flows with the full tide of fancy . . . If the subject is low, it is raised into importance, by a magic infusion of mind; and though it belong to the dull routine of business, one touch of the creative wand invests it with significance and curiosity.[18]

No matter how "low" or "dull" this nation's materials were – with the "magic" "fancy" of literary art, its bland aspect could be made resonant with interest and meaning. As if with a "creative wand," such interest was invented out of thin air. Yet in contrast to that line of thought, when Everett writes that "they strike the desert rock and it flows with the full tide of fancy," it would appear that American writing needed to do more than just invent interest and "infuse" a "dull" world with it. For the figure suggests that American writing must unearth an interest and meaning already contained within its borders; the hand of genius does not just paint interest over the rock, it makes even that which a writer explicitly "creat[es] . . . out of nothing" seem instead to be the outpouring of the object's very essence.[19] After all, Everett had already praised Irving earlier in the review because "he catches his tints from nature, and dips his pencil in truth, which is always fresh and racy," figuring the subject as an inkwell from which the author draws his materials.[20] So in Everett's view, American literature needs both to reveal latent interest and significance, and to create fancies out of nothing. This contradiction in Everett's analysis is one which he shares with the critics W. H. Gardiner and Edward Tyrell Channing, who also published criticism in the *North-American Review* in the 1820s, and it is a contradiction that also can be detected in the writings of Irving, James Fenimore Cooper, and Charles Brockden Brown. This contradiction is a foundational principle in the literary nationalism of the 1820s in New England, one that reveals that its commitment to local experience as a source of American literature is a commitment to experience conceived as an abstracted, conventional category.

We can begin to approach the subject by noting how recycled Everett's image of a fertile desert was, even in 1835. The image had been used by Irving himself in his tribute to the English writer William Roscoe in the *Sketch-Book*:

[Nature] scatters the seeds of genius to the winds, and though some may perish among the stony places of the world, and some be choked by the thorns and brambles of early adversity, yet others will now and then strike root even in the clefts of the rock, struggle bravely up into sunshine, and spread over their sterile birth place all the beauties of vegetation.[21]

Henry Wadsworth Longfellow sounded a similar note in his 1825 "Graduation Address" at Bowdoin, promising that "Every rock shall become a chronicle of storied allusions."[22] In 1828 John Neal claimed that America was a "dry soil" full of "hidden sources of fertility."[23] William Ellery Channing's 1830 "Remarks on National Literature" objected that "mind is not the creature of climate or soil," and that anyway "rocks and sands" were really a superior climate.[24] American literary nationalism focuses, it might be said, on the image of America as a barren rock, one which authors must subject to a dual gesture: pasting interest onto it and uncovering a latent, innate interest within it.

The conventional and nonmimetic quality of literary nationalism, exemplified in the reference to a generic rock rather than to a specific piece of land, must qualify its otherwise powerful impression of natural expression. For national literature is commonly cast as natural efflorescence: in the passages I have just mentioned, American literature is imagined as a kind of plant, drawing nutrients from dry soil to produce verdant, natural writing. But such "natural" expression is manifestly conventional, and even that convention is about the difficulty rather than the inevitability of natural growth. Further complicating the notion is the heterogeneity of the image of natural expression: is it a plant or a fountain that is produced, and does it spring from a rock, a desert, or a glacier? Such specifics are irrelevant; what counts is that each one is an example, a token, of the general type of referring to the topic of the nation as a barren place from which life can be forced. And at the very least, the notion of the natural is quite distinct, now, from the naturalness of plants: it is an abstract premise of a barren place rendered fruitful, with conventional currency and a variety of potential ways of being particularized.

To believe that America, or any one place rather than another, presented a problem for literary representation, one must believe that specific material objects bear little relation to the elicitation of interest. Arguing that point, in his review of *Tour on the Prairies*, Everett noted that "the Journal of the expedition under Colonel Dodge" made in 1834 to "the same region" held none of the interest that Irving's treatment of it did.[25] In the 1820 preface to *The Spy*, his first novel set in America, Cooper bluntly worried that "the very familiarity will breed contempt";[26] Gardiner duly criticized Cooper for being too literally documentary in *The Spy*, indulging in "that excessive minuteness, which leaves nothing for the imagination to supply."[27] Edward Tyrell Channing comparably disdains "disgusting familiarity," a dwelling in ordinary detail that was not only uninteresting but actively repellant – in Cooper's words, "breed[ing] contempt."[28] The United States might well be compelling as a place to live, even as a place about which to read descriptions, as De Tocqueville's *Democracy in America* and Cooper's *Notions of the Americans* unequivocally demonstrated.[29] Yet in the view of Gardiner, Everett, Channing, and Cooper, interest in actuality cannot be counted upon to correlate with the presumptive interest evoked by literature, insofar as the latter demands something other than the specification of fact, and may even actively destroy such interest.

Kames had argued that description of the visible world was insufficient to set off a reader's imagination, and these authors agreed that literature needed not description but the elaboration of associations. People had no compelling or romantic ideas associated with the familiar, commonplace scenes that were part of their everyday life – the streets they walked down, the plants and animals they saw within their fields. In other words, recognizably American subjects did not trigger trains of images, as did Europe's enviably affecting "moss-clad ruins."[30] The point was not that there is a qualitative difference between American and European subjects – in fact, Gardiner contended that America did possess topics of inherent interest.[31] But the existence of such subjects mattered little so long as readers had no associations with them: "Where then are the romantic associations . . .?" For subjects cannot become interesting until they can function as types, such as the Gothic ruin. One needs, too, not just one's own actual reactions to a subject (an idiosyncratic fascination with New England farmhouses), but a knowledge of what would be the typical, possible response to it. So it was the lack of enchanting associations with known American scenes that prompted Cooper to lament that his readers "required" that novels allude to "moated castles, draw-bridges" and other objects of interest familiar in literature.[32] Everett could insist that geniuses might turn even a world as devoid of features as Greenland's "eternal glaciers" into one "as gorgeous, as various, as full of action, as ever moved in courts or castles," but *still*: an American reader might travel over a covered bridge every day and think of it as just a bridge, one which suggested nothing to him, not even picturesque rural calm.[33] Where for Bell and Martin the problem was that subjective, author-specific imagination could not really be joined up to external objects, here the problem is that there is no shared vocabulary of response to objects – authors need a medium, so to speak, of common associations in which to work.

What produced associations, in the eyes of Cooper and the *North-American Review* critics, was classification and typification of objects and scenes. Apologizing in the 1832 introduction to *The Pioneers* for having included too much specific information drawn from personal experience in that novel, Cooper argued that fiction demanded the depiction of "characters in their classes."[34] As Gardiner had put it, "the power of creating interest in a work of fiction, so far as it arises from development of character, lies in this generalizing principle which substitutes classes for individuals."[35] Biblical and classical figures, or ones from English literature, formed a vocabulary of standard scenes, figures, and events that were embedded in a culture of allusion and association. Yet those types would not serve nationalist literature; that demanded an American repertoire of types, in which Philadelphia or Ohio was to become a new Athens. (Comparing American subjects to biblical and classical types could begin to make associations and interest around American figures: for example, when Longfellow compares "our native hills" to "those of Greece and Italy," he begins to attach such hallowed associations to local places.)[36] Furthermore, as Cooper was keenly aware, using contemporary materials lent an increased urgency to the expectation that literary types be accurate: as "others are as familiar with their homes as we are ourselves . . . if we make any mistakes every body will know it."[37] As a consequence of nationalism's contact with Scottish aesthetics, then, writers articulated the need for images that were general types also possessing recognizable detail, and connected to a range of associations.

Literature of the early national period begins to examine ordinary experience with a new attention to ordinary lives and material details, yet it still aims to fashion widely available types out of such local currency. So Gardiner, in arguing that there were subjects of interest in America, contrasts "the highminded, vainglorious Virginian, living on his plantation in baronial estate, an autocrat among his slaves, a nobleman among his peers" to "the active, enterprizing, moneygetting merchant of the East, who spends his days in bustling activity among men and ships, and his night in sober calculations over his ledger and day-book."[38] He implies that neither type is interesting in itself, as he weaves their contrasts against each other. And he names with clarity and precision – but not particularity – a number of characteristic elements: "active, enterprizing, moneygetting" are ways to specify the type of the Eastern merchant without describing a Massachusetts textile dealer with his own name, history, and quirks. Cooper and his peers wrote with a realism which operates in terms of generality, not particularity, and connected such general reality into a range of reader's expectations. Yet rather than join the particular to the typical and general through either induction or deduction – gathering instances and generalizing from them, or proposing a priori types and then producing specified tokens of them – one finds instead that authors propose types which implicitly refer to a literal world but seem neither to be drawn from actual observations nor to form a starting frame from which to make such investigations into the American world.

The above principles are explored with particular subtlety by Edward Tyrell Channing, Harvard Professor of Rhetoric and Oratory and editor of the *North-American Review*, and a major figure in the perpetuation of Scottish associationist aesthetics in the United States.[39] Channing's survey of the career of Charles Brockden Brown in the *North-American Review* forms the occasion for a critical investigation into associationism's implications for a literature that would focus on American subjects. In it, the critic articulates a bicameral approach to American fiction, in which a gesture is made to the empirical description and, simultaneously, a gesture is made to the invented idea. Channing wrote that the supposed barrenness of American life was due "not to the entire absence of romantic incident, situation, and characters, but, which is just as unfortunate for the writer, to the want in his readers of romantic associations with the scenes and persons he must set before us, if he makes a strictly domestic story." As we have seen, the problem with America is not that it is intrinsically uninteresting, but that Americans are not interested in reading about it; they find it "too stubbornly familiar and unpoetical" because they have no ideas connected with it. In claiming that America has "romantic incident[s]" even if no one has any "romantic associations" with it, Channing suggests that a place could be inherently romantic without anyone finding it so – as though interest, that is, could exist in the absence of any person actually being interested. On the other hand, in lamenting the want of "romantic associations" and arguing that America is fit material for such associations, he still holds to the principle that literature depends upon typical associations to make it interesting, not upon any inherent interest of its subject.[40]

Because of his equivocation on the question of how much interest inhered in objects, and how much interest depends on acquired, external associations, Channing has been seen as a transitional figure, loosening the grip of neoclassicism to let in Romanticism's more restrained innovations. Channing will not, for example, really distinguish between seeing things as they are and adding one's fancy to them. Consider a comment such as "a powerful

imagination can imprison us with any thing that is not spiritless, or incapable of suggesting something like reality to the mind" (64). Is his meaning
that the author's imagination, or the thing it latches onto is suggestive? Is
our impression one of an imaginary, unreal scene, or of something literal?
Channing's phrase "something like reality" does not acknowledge that it
might be important to distinguish between the real and "something like"
it, which we might term fiction. Yet Channing's alternate, but not entirely
differentiated commitments to the realistic and to the typified (to depict-
ing objects which are themselves interesting, and to constructing interesting
associations with objects that are nothing but triggers for such associations)
are not simply the signs of a literature in transition from one paradigm to
another. Channing's is a distinct aesthetic based on the complementarity of
realistic description and imaginary associations, derived from Kames's and
Alison's theory that responses are both natural (making realistic descriptions of objects sufficient to produce them) and conventional (requiring
literature to invent and perform responses as a way of inculcating them in
readers).

The entire essay on Brown shows Channing feeling his way towards a
definition of literature's need to combine realistic descriptions with the
recounting of trains of imaginative reactions to them, as he tacks back
and forth among a variety of positions. At one point, the critic admires the
novelist for his realism, for showing us our home country as it really is, apart
from both conventional and invented responses to it. Channing stresses
Brown's clear vision of the subject, his "great closeness and minuteness of
observation," and writes that the novelist "discovers every where a strong
sense of the presence of objects"(73). Impressed with Brown's ability to
show us the world as it is, Channing claims that Brown's "simple," almost
"bald" style (73) presents things themselves, not his elaborated images of
them: "He appears to be above the common temptation . . . to decorate
scenes with borrowed beauties till they have lost every thing which could
distinguish them, or even persuade us that we were in our own world" (77).
Here it is important to Channing that Brown brings us into contact with
things as they are, as if Brown's business were only to show his readers an
America which is interesting or "romantic" in itself, without the need of
"associations" or added-on ideas.

Yet the "simple" style of description which Channing praises is not
engaged in anything like a restrained realism referencing a concrete outer
world. Channing notes that "no one will charge [Brown] with a disgusting
familiarity," (68) for in his work "there is little which is too humble and
familiar for interest" (70). It is a fault in the literature if "the reality seems

too near" (70) or "a ludicrous importance is given to trifles" (71). Detailed description is not, then, what Channing means by revealing "the presence of objects." To the contrary, he seems to mean that the presence of objects is revealed when Brown barely describes them at all. For instance, to realistically describe "a deserted house, silent and dark in the day-time" is to capitalize on a response we all already have to deserted houses.

*description*
*vs.*
*response.*

> Brown . . . is peculiarly successful in describing a deserted house, silent and dark in the day-time, while a faint ray streams through the crevices of the closed doors and shutters, discovering in a peculiar twilight that it had been once occupied, and that every thing remained undisturbed since its sudden desertion. The sentiment of fear and melancholy is perhaps never more lively, nor the disturbed fancy more active than in such a place, even when we are strangers to it; but how much more, if we have passed there through happiness and suffering, if the robber has alarmed our security, or if a friend has died there and been carried over its threshold to the grave. (74)

Channing invokes a type of location, designated "such a place," and "a deserted house," where the "a" works precisely to specify – a single house – and to generalize – any house that is "deserted." He then moves on to name the emotions of "fear and melancholy" associated with it, entirely in his own words. Brown's writing is not even quoted, because Channing is not assessing how the novelist's description of a deserted house evokes a feeling of dread, but how the *idea* of such a house does so. There is no sense that Brown adds anything to our thoughts and feelings about deserted houses; he plays into those expectations, almost without appeal to the way such a house looks in fact, or even to how the writer might make us see it. Channing argues that Brown's plain, unvarnished style serves to show ideas of things, and to let the reader's ideas about the house expand without the irritation of artistic affectation, much as Alison understood the beauty of Milton to reside elsewhere than in the actual wording of the poetry.

In praise of Brown's description – simple, uncomplicated transmission of the concept of the deserted house – Channing performs the train of details, emotions and associations it provokes. Brown's writing isn't quoted, nor is the text it appears in named. Channing presents the associations prompted by the description, almost in place of the description itself, or as if the associations were a way of showing us the passage. It is the critic who makes the connections to "peculiar twilight" and "faint ray[s]," and makes the analysis of the relative strength of "fear and melancholy" as well as "disturbed fancy." These are descriptions of how any person would be expected to feel in reaction to the idea of the sight: an analysis of general human nature. All the details he imagines – "closed doors and shutters," "peculiar twilight," a viewer who has actually lived there and suffered some trauma – are elaborations of general, possible qualities of the scene. It is very much like Alison's comments about the perception of fall and its production of melancholy: the general concept of the scene prompts the reader to spin out a number of associations, which reference specific, material details and specific personal experiences (life transitions, robbery, death), yet none of them are his own, individual property. They are hypothetically so – "if we have passed there" – but not actually so. His transition into the first-person plural is crucial here: it is the imaginary response to the passage which enables this reference to a fund of potential traumas that "we" all have at hand as triggers of melancholy, if not – perhaps because not – actual experiences we have undergone. And this enunciation of an experience without a concrete subject or object (the idea of responding to the idea of a description of a deserted house) is also at work in the critical method of suggesting the experience of responding to the passage, without actually quoting the passage and even without describing it. Just as the house becomes a type, not a specific place, so too Brown's text becomes a type of description, not a specific one.

Thus far, for Channing what Brown's writing does is unobtrusively proffer objects with which "we" already possess associations, so that when the critic details the responses to the deserted house he may assume that his readers follow his train of thought. But another facet emerges: he also praises Brown for invention, admiring him for so transforming his subject that it appears totally unknown. We know it only through Brown's imagination and vision: "We are not thinking of accustomed modes of living or our ordinary experience, but are held captive by the force of character, the intensity of intellectual suffering" (69). Brown seems to control and even co-opt the reader's thought, as Channing notes that "a spell is thrown over our imaginations" (69). Channing thereby touches on what has become the standard view of Brown as a psychological novelist, caught up in his own mind and emotions. What is really happening, however, is that Brown is presenting a train of ideas and images that is completely transferable to his reader. Brown's psychologism does not penetrate the individual mind's depths, but instead presents streams of reactions and ideas to the world, which the reader is expected to try on and even inhabit. What emerges is not a picture of the world, nor a picture of particular characters (or passages), but a sequence of impersonal experiences, thoughts and sensations, which themselves become the center of attention. So when Channing details his thoughts about the deserted house, he is not just performing our ready-made responses to the idea; he is performing responses which are, somehow, controlled and mandated by Brown's very invention. Channing's idea that conceiving of objects is an occasion for spurring trains of invention, not for drawing out their essence, is the very heart of the literary ideal of this period. And the point is ultimately that this experience is set into motion by the author's language and then becomes anyone's experience, so much so that even a critic's train of responses can describe the experience as well as, perhaps even better than, the author's words do.

Channing's criticism elucidates the reading experience in itself as an occasion to depart from personal boundaries and spin together sense and imagination. He writes,

We have alluded to the distinctness and particularity with which he describes the city visited with pestilence; the dwelling-house, the hospital, the dying, the healed, all appear before our eyes; the imagination has nothing to do but perceive, though it never fails to multiply and enlarge circumstances of horror, and to fasten us to the picture more strongly by increasing terror and sympathy till mere disgust ceases. (73)

For Channing, Brown does not create false pictures, but he is no realist either: rather, he makes only minimal use of the phenomenal world as a reference-point, and allows the imagination to run its course, without being forced to come back to the phenomenal world *and* without being forced to pay undue attention to the phenomena of the text. The account of the yellow fever epidemic to which Channing refers is usually singled out as Brown's greatest piece of realism.[41] But what may once have been a freshly observed experience becomes a leitmotif, not only because the yellow fever figures in both *Arthur Mervyn* and in *Ormond*, but because that same description is lifted almost verbatim from a passage in the earlier "A Man at Home." The description, once made, can be repeated ad infinitum and almost out of context; it becomes a type of foreboding desolation in addition to a localized realist description. What the imagination does come back to is "the picture" or idea of experience that the passage cues, and the responses the reader has to that mental picture. The odd claim that "the imagination has nothing to do but perceive" indicates both that, in Channing's estimation, Brown's description transcends realism to become a new type for literature, and that at the same time the type seems so descriptive, or real, that the imagination is explicitly described as "perceiv[ing]" rather than dreaming.

This is the experience central to this phase of literary nationalism: one prompted by reference to types and classes of objects, unhampered by close attention to or foundation in an author's style, unconnected to one's actual life experience, but instead tapping into a vocabulary or repertoire of generalized images with standard, conventionalized associations. This is an experience without much reference to the notion of the authentic: it has to seem plausible, yet in no sense does experience per se become the ground of any authoritative claims. Instead it is a strata of imaginary and conceptual moves into which one may enter, and in which one's own identity, and the actual objects around one, have little role or reference.

> We read with delight of those who are separated from us by their institutions and manners as well as climate . . . because they resemble us in every thing except that distinguishing character and those prevailing tastes which are ascribable to the peculiar circumstances in which they are placed. We love to see the common world moulding the mind a thousand ways, and multiplying our studies and pleasures without lessening our sympathy and attachments.[42]

Here, Channing suggests that the experience of reading fosters a sense of universality, and an awareness of the commonality of mankind. Perhaps this is precisely because sympathetically entering into a text is to undergo an ideal experience, a general experience without reference to one's own individual boundaries. Reading about a specific culture's "institutions and manners as well as climate" brings to us a sense not only of the differences between cultures, but also and more fundamentally of the essential qualities of a shared humanity. Channing's viewpoint here is symptomatic of a widespread preoccupation in American literary nationalism with the notion of a reader who was generalizable, not just as an American but as a universal reader. Nationalist literature gestures toward location, experience, even the domestic as a touchstone which all people can rally around, not as a private or personal reference nor even as an element of American self-reflection. William Cullen Bryant wrote in 1825 that the romance reader "beholds the scenery of a distant land, hears its inhabitants conversing about their own concerns in their own dialect, finds himself in the bosom of its families, made the depository of their secrets, and the observer of their fortunes, and becomes an inmate of their firesides without stirring from his own."[43] Anyone would be interested in literature about America – not just Americans who had experienced the world it depicted.

The account of American literary nationalism as embodied and particularized has been overstressed; we see this in the belief that experience as it is related to American literature is not about an experience of one's literal being, but about producing and disappearing into the ideal of experience which consists of normal ideas and feelings about types of objects, represented in emblems. To express the native essence is conceived of as an abandoning of the literal place and the literal self for a participation in conventions and their associations: the rock/glacier/desert springing forth a fountain/plant; the Virginian; the Eastern merchant. These types are stapled, we might say, back onto what is visible to the eye in certain moments, but the repeatability of emblems such as Brown's picture of the diseased city or Channing's notion of a deserted house testifies to their generality. That suppression of objective reality is what allows the performance of conventional responses to conceptions of classes or types of objects and scenes to become an "experience," as "the imagination has nothing to do but perceive": perceiving, knowing, sensing and reacting begin to take place without concrete connections to literal and locatable subjects and objects. The objection to such generalities is that they exclude the local, the material, and the contingent. Indeed, such exclusion is precisely the point, although it is actually the condition of inclusion rather than of exclusion, in as much as anything too particular is seen as lacking interest for others. In the period's literature, experience is conceived in terms of the universal, entertained as a field of reactions and responses to general concepts which can be adopted without regard for one's personal character or actual events in one's life.

III

While Channing and the *North-American Review* stand as voices of authority in the literary culture of their time, John Neal's writing was compared to that of "a madman or an id[i]ot."[44] He quickly fell into a durable obscurity, and figures in American literary history as little more than an early example of the artist as social outsider and renegade.[45] His very atypicality, his commitment to his personal eccentricities, have been linked to his faith that narrating local events in American lingo and experimental dialogue would form the essence of a American literature.[46] Neal maintained that *Rachel Dyer*, a novel containing heavily accented local voices using colloquial expressions such as "Rattlesnake an' toddy," was a book "written not only in a universal, but in what may be considered as an everlasting language" (*R*, 162, ix). Yet Neal was an ardent literary nationalist, *American Writers* being the first history of American literature, and I shall argue that despite his notable eccentricity and engagement in ostensibly private material he maintains a commitment to the typicality of experience that bespeaks an underlying agreement between himself and critics such as Channing.

In this section I begin by examining Neal's specific attempts to create American types, of the order of those entertained in the *North-American Review*. Although he quite explicitly means to produce new American types, his efforts at so doing turn into assertions about the lack of fundamental relation between abstract qualities and external appearances, and into elaborations of figures which seem simply to lose sight of the real world altogether. Such efforts, I contend, show that what Neal imagines is a literature in which pure fancies are understood as being true even without any specific connection to visible objects. I then examine the importance of dialogue to the novel, which is most profoundly a cacophonous aggregate of voices, none of them in agreement, continuously staging disorienting scenes of confusion. Such dialogues of confusion obscure the plot and the characters, as well as the setting, to become the only object to which the reader has access. The possibility of declaring the object world unavailable, and thus of problematizing empirical proof, is the enabling condition on which Neal's *Rachel Dyer* joyously spins page after page of shouts and recriminations, questions and musings, rather than expressing fundamental anxiety about epistemological incoherence. Recourse to dialogue about nothing, really, outside itself, becomes an answer to the demand for American types, by focusing less on types per se and more on arranging projected responses. As in the Scots' case, Neal is not concerned with one man's experience; rather, he is concerned with the experience of an entire community, rendered externally in dialogue. Finally, I consider the problem of experience in Neal in terms of his authorial voice. Here too, even when he seems to speak of himself, he is trying to turn his personal voice into one owned by the public, to render the "I" into an "anyone."

In *Rachel Dyer* Neal is explicit about his attempt to indicate that the Puritans were useful literary subjects: he says in the preface that he means to "call the attention . . . to what is undoubtedly native and peculiar, in the early history of our Fathers" (*R*, iv). He is also committed to making interesting types out of ordinary people, as he contends that despite what literary conventions tell us, "a man may have a club-foot, or a hump-back, or even red hair and yet be a good man" (*R*, iv). The nominal "heroine of our story" (*R*, 148), Rachel Dyer, is precisely the opposite of the typical heroine: "a heroine without youth or beauty, with no shape to please, with no color to charm the eye, with no voice to delight the ear" (*R*, 148). She is proffered as an answer to the injunction to make ordinary Americans serve the talismanic function that, say, a beautiful gentlewoman would serve. But it's interesting to see that Neal isn't tossing aside the category of beautiful heroine. He is still, in fact, defining Rachel in terms of the type she is not: to say she has "no shape to please . . . no color to charm the eye" is to continue using pleasing shape and charming eyes as the categories in which to define one's heroine. One can say she is or is not those things, but it seems she cannot simply be something else.

Neal's idea that Rachel Dyer can be his heroine is particularly complicated around the relation of her impeccably moral, pious, and kind heart to her exterior. The premise "that moral beauty *may* exist where it appears not to have been suspected by the chief critics of our age, and of past ages – namely, in a deformed body" (*R*, iv) is a version of the nationalist's ambition to show the innate worth of a rock. Neal must find interior value undetected by the naked eye, and produce value where there seems to be none. The point of the exterior, though, is that it has no fundamental relationship to what's inside (it "*may*" contain goodness, but doesn't necessarily do so). That is to say, no one in the novel begins to associate red-haired humpbacks with goodness; instead, they begin to see that Dyer's goodness can't be seen at all. In her finest moment, her physical appearance is described as manifestly irrelevant:

Every eye was upon her . . . It was Rachel Dyer – the red-haired witch – the freckled witch – the hump-backed witch they saw now – but they saw not her ugliness, they saw not that she was either unshapely or unfair. They saw only that she was brave. (*R*, 226)

What this heroine does is present a physical appearance which is insistently detailed in its ungainliness, and a moral beauty that can be intuited in qualities other than the visible. This is to say that her appearance is both stressed and set aside in almost the same breath – "they saw . . . they saw not . . . they saw not . . . They saw." Creating an American heroine is to declare that the visual image of a hump-backed redheaded dwarf is associated with goodness, but also to stress that there is no essential connection between that appearance and those qualities. In this vein, it seems logical rather than sloppy or strange that *Rachel Dyer* has very little to say about Rachel Dyer: she may be deemed the novel's "heroine," but she plays a small part and doesn't even appear until halfway through the story – she is glimpsed but not taken in. One may have a heroine, but one can look at her only rarely and momentarily to see her talismanic ugliness, and then conceive of her in terms of invisible character traits.

Neal's encomiums to the American landscape similarly declare the value of the ugly without quite looking at it. Again in the novel's preface, Neal claimed that he wrote

to show to my countrymen that there are . . . barren places to all outward appearance, in the northern, as well as the southern Americas – yet teeming below with bright sail – where the plough-share that is driven through them with a strong arm, will come out laden with rich mineral and followed by running water. (*R*, xvi)

At first glance, it seems as if Neal is writing to reveal an inherent, essential interest: I promise you, he says, that America *is* interesting, fertile, filled with "rich mineral" and "running water," though to your eyes it looks "barren." One must merely look more closely: "if you but lay your ear to the scented ground, you may hear the perpetual gush of innumerable fountains pouring their subterranean melody night and day among the minerals and rocks, the iron and the gold" (*R*, xvi). Neal says he is showing us America up close, as it really is – exactly as if he is claiming that if we only know how to look at it, we will see that America is intrinsically interesting.

And yet the passage essentially shows us nothing. As the scrambled image of the ear confronting a scent testifies, Neal appeals only to the concept of perception, the idea of looking at the land, without truly doing so. Instead, fanciful language far outstrips any literal description of America:

the pilgrim or the wanderer through what he may deem the very deserts of literature, the barren-places of knowledge, will find the very roots of the withered and blasted shrubbery, which like the traveler in Peru, he may have accidentally uptorn in his weary and discouraging ascent, and the very bowels of the earth into which he has torn his way, heavy with a brightness that may be coined, like the soil about the favorite hiding places of the sunny-haired Apollo. (*R*, xvi)

This is no description rendering the familiar subtle and shadowed, but a careening run through Neal's imagination with exhausting clusters of detail and allusions. The "earth" so full of interest is not American soil but a symbol of that land – though one so bloated with detail that it is barely recognizable as such. In trying to convince us that America is richer and subtler than we have noticed, he invokes a land with gold beneath the dry topsoil available to the eyes of a mythic "pilgrim or wanderer," utterly abandoning the idea of a clear-eyed delineation of America's compelling landscape.

So, Neal claims he writes to show us how interesting America is, in itself, but he pays virtually no attention to America per se and instead spews out trains of images and ideas connected with some very minimal notion of the nation. That contrast reveals the essential disconnect in the literary theory of the time between the attempt to see American objects, and the attempt to construct associations with them. Neal is willing to leave bare (or, unable to conceal) the fundamental break between the reality of American scenes and the network of associations connected to them. That quality is his greatest strength as a writer – although from another perspective, it is his Achilles heel – for in Neal we can see precisely the way that American literary nationalism does not graft the associations, the constructed interest in the nation, back onto the objective reality of the place itself. The reason for this is that what I'm here calling literal reality – the material object world – isn't what counts as the relevant reality for Neal. Yet, this isn't to say that Neal's shifting to romance, because he still means this, somehow, to be an account of that objective reality. It's just that to access that objective world, to tap into the experience of such reality, is in this formulation to elaborate associations upon an image which indirectly refers to that world, not to present an actual description of it. The experience of American objects is, we might say, seen as quite distinct from the literal observation of them.

Channing saw the problem with Neal perfectly. He wrote that the "description" in Neal's poems "rather [told] what things are like than what they are," that Neal neglected "the prominent object" and distracted his reader with "a string of similitudes." Neal's images, rather than describing "the matter at hand," were "sparkling" and entertaining, and in effect obscured what they should have revealed.[47] Describing something and making something interesting by attaching associations to it required a particular kind of judiciousness, satisfying both the need to appear true and the need to appear compelling. Perhaps Neal continually erred on the latter side; nevertheless, he maintains as an overt principle the same balance of description and association that Channing did. In *American Writers*, Neal himself criticized Leigh Hunt's images because they "frequently take off your attention from the principle object: outshine, overtop, that, of which they should be only the auxiliaries" (*A*, 135) – despite their differences, Neal and Channing take it for granted that extended figurative imagery is what produces a sense of experiencing the object world.

The notion is to dream and also be right: it was for just that achievement that Neal applauded Benjamin Franklin in *American Writers*. Neal says he finds "gratifying" Franklin's "faculty of explanation, which, half a century ago, when most of the subjects, upon which he wrote, were little understood, made whatever he thought as intelligible to other men, as if they themselves had also thought it" (*A*, 106). Franklin is especially creditable because he has not just had an original idea; he has been able to make it into common belief. The idea of electricity first occurred, Neal writes, to

Abbe Nolet, but for the Frenchman "It was only one of those accidental vague thoughts, continually to be met with in the works of brilliant, flighty men" without real force. Franklin, in contrast, can make such dreams real, can establish them with science and can make his own experience "intelligible to other men." He thereby establishes an equivalence, a commonality between his own vision and that of everyone else.

On those grounds, Neal had high praise for Washington Irving as well as Franklin. Neal wrote that Irving reveals what "nobody knew where to look for" (what no one has seen), and that this is also what "everybody could see": the invented image that is taken as common knowledge.

Who has not felt, as he stood in the solemn, strange light of a great wilderness; of some old, awful ruin – a world of shafts and arches about him, like a druidical wood – illuminated by the sunset – a visible bright atmosphere, coming through coloured glass – who has not felt, as if he would give his right hand for a few simple words – the fewer the better – to describe the appearance of the air about him? – Would he call it *splendour*? – It isn't splendour: *dusty*? – it would be rediculous. [sic] – But what if he say, like Irving, "*dusty splendour*?" – Will he not have said *all* that can be said? – Who ever saw those two words associated before? who could ever wish to see them separated again? (*A*, 136)

Neal sees Irving using style to articulate knowledge that we already have; to evoke a feeling of both familiarity and newness. Despite the passage's focus on the specific phrasing of "dusty splendour," of putting two words together in a new way, the crux of the matter is really that although one has always felt Irving's statement to be true ("Who has not felt" this to be the case?), now we savor this familiar knowledge.

The appeal to experience in Neal's account of Franklin, as in Channing's description of Brown, is not an appeal to anything which may specifically have happened to us. It is to a general fund of experience which it is rhetorically asserted that we all draw on (although there is also Neal's indulgence in images of "coloured glass" and "druidical wood"). In arguing, "Who has not felt," Neal cannot really be suggesting that we all have been in the space of ruins or wilderness and thought over the matter for ourselves. Instead, the rhetorical question works perfectly (as in Alison's passage about melancholy in the fall) to ask us if we can imagine feeling anything different in such a situation – and to assert that all that we can imagine is as he says it must be. Irving's passage accomplishes just what the poet as mathematician would: it presents a fanciful image of the author's, yet manages to link it to a register of common knowledge, expected and standard responses to a typical object. Such a conception of how Irving works, to Neal, also helps explain that contradiction in the *North-American Review* over interest as both invented and revealed: invented interest is used as a way of generalizing about objects, and in that sense truthfully revealing them.

And yet, the question persists: "Who has not felt . . . ? Who could ever wish . . . ?" *Rachel Dyer* swirls around its author's desires for a standard nationalist melding of individual views into general ones, and around his apparently skeptical sense that such agreements are never reached – there are always those who do *not* feel – and that even if reached, such agreements would tell no truth at all about the world. Contemporary novels about the witch trials focused on the injustice of the events, as a precursor to the Revolution's struggle between liberty and tyranny.[48] But that approach not only presumed a coherent community in the present, it presumed that the witch trials could be established as unjust executions of the innocent. In contrast, the focus of Neal's novel is doubt about the connection of ideas to reality – of interest to inherent qualities, of the nation to the people and the land – and even doubt about the injustice of the trials. Yet those doubts are disingenuous: Neal's doubt is so closely connected to his volu-bility that it may be seen to function as a condition of possibility for his work, as a cause of his prolificness. (And in the ease with which Neal wears this doubt he may seem most similar to Hawthorne.) To doubt the real-ity of the objective world, apprehended by individual subjects, is to insist on the power of imaginative experience, on the capacity of literature to spawn more literature, and of interest in literature to be bred only with the slightest, dubious link to the object realm. Significantly, this isn't played as a competition between the false imagination and the true reality; the image and the object are kept in some relation to one another. It's urgent for Neal that getting at the object world per se is not so much impossible (though it may be that too), but unprofitable, irrelevant – uninteresting. His doubt about access to the object world through empirical observa-tion is an extension of that lack of interest in lowly familiarity which *North-American Review* critics enunciated. It does not, however, qualify the pervasive sense that the reality of experiencing objects may be conveyed most effectively through reference to communal norms and practices of articulation.

The ostensible plot of *Rachel Dyer* is the return of George Burroughs to Salem, where he finds the town in the midst of the witch trials; he protests mightily against them and is finally condemned as a witch along with Rachel and her sister Mary. However, the heart of this novel is neither its plot nor its characters – each of which is as difficult to discern as is the actual place in Neal's effusion about the "teeming . . . bowels of the earth" – but in the sweep of dialogue. Neal writes, in one exemplary passage:

Who is it! .... who is it! cried the people as they rushed forward and gathered about him and tried to get a sight of his face. Who *can* it be!

Burroughs – Bur – Bur – Burroughs, I *do* believe! whispered a man who stood at his elbow, but he spoke as if he did not feel very sure of what he said.

Not George Burroughs, hey?

I'd take my oath of it neighbour Joe, my Bible-oath of it, leaning forward as far as he could reach with safety, and shading his eyes with his large bony hand –

Well, I *do* say! whispered another.

I see the scar! – as I live, I do! cried another, peering over the heads of the multitude, as they rocked to the heavy pressure of the intruder.

But how altered he is! .... and how old he looks! .... – and shorter than ever! muttered several more. (*R*, 69)

In passages such as this Neal presents streams of dialogue, uses no quotation marks and shifts silently between anonymous speakers. Someone stands at Burroughs's elbow, another is called Joe; but Neal picks people out only to drop them quickly back into the chorus indicated by phrases such as, "muttered several more." The writing conveys so little sense of individual character that one often cannot tell who is speaking. It seems not to matter, for instance, whether "But how altered he is! .... and how old he looks! .... – and shorter than ever!" is a single sentence, which is repeated or spoken in chorus by "several more," or whether a separate individual is supposed to speak each of those clauses. Individuals are glimpsed, but they are linked into loose constellations, connected by dashes and ellipses, and not rendered with any fullness. Depth and life emerge instead in the body of the dialogue as a whole, which sweeps along with its own impetus, forming a lattice of outbursts without foundation in specific speakers.

Neal's manner of narrating primarily through dialogue shifts the focus away from the events and objects in the novel, and onto people's perceptions of them. Those are perceptions which, as we have seen, are presented as a cacophonous aggregate, and although the crowd in the novel serves as a window through which Neal shows us the witch trial, the scene it shows us is hazy. When Burroughs appears, the "oath" of a man straining to see him and the unsure stammering "Bur – Bur – Burroughs" of "a man who stood at his elbow" hardly add up to a confidence-inspiring identification of the novel's hero. And, although the crowd's voice may be somehow general, as I have suggested, it is not internally consistent, nor does it depict harmonious agreement. The persons who make up that group can talk right past one another, as if in the dark, about an object they cannot clearly discern. Such confusion is one of the most prominent features of the novel, as the following examples show:

Why, Matthew – look at me. . . . Do you not – know me?
No – no – who are you? (*R*, 231)

O father – father – O *my!* – there, there! – there he goes!
Where – where – what is it, my poor child?
Why – Burroughs – Burroughs – there, there! there now, there he goes again! –
that's he – there, there – don't you see him now, father?
See whom, dear? – see what? (*R*, 190)

Hark. . . . hark! said Elizabeth, interrupting her sister.
Well, what now?
I heard a voice. . . .
A voice. . . . where. . . . when. . . . what was it like? (*R*, 206)

In a serious manner, nothing is at stake in these exchanges. As with many other moments of misrecognition and confusion, they are generated without any important relationship to the plot: the confusion is cleared up as a simple mistake, and the novel proceeds as though nothing has happened, only to restage the process shortly thereafter. In more than one instance, a chapter ends with the cliffhanging expression of panicked confusion, only to have the next chapter open with an anticlimactic realization such as that a nonthreatening, familiar character has been knocking at the door. In regard to the plot, then, the confusion is entirely gratuitous. However, because it is so frequent, and so much more prominent than the obscure and shaky plot and the undeveloped characters, the confusion is central, and the plot and characters gratuitous.

The confusion is almost always about empirical evidence: what is seen and heard. Burroughs tries, for instance, to provide visible evidence controverting the witch prosecutions. When Bridget Pope testifies that Sarah Good has conjured a half of a knife, Burroughs sends for Bridget's friend Robert Eveleth, to whom Bridget had earlier given the other half of the knife. This proves the knife was not conjured, but always belonged to Bridget: and yet, the apparently compelling physical evidence has no weight with the jury whatsoever and Sarah Good hangs. The majority of the novel is comprised of similar courtroom scenes, in which ostensible forums for the establishment of common truths are shown to founder in incoherence. Burroughs, seeing the futility of concrete evidence, abandons himself to filibusters and does not even offer "witnesses" at his own trial for witchcraft – "Of what use could they be?" he asks (*R*, 224). Cotton Mather delivers a long speech about the importance of belief without testimony at all, for "Able men believe much, *because* they are able men" (*R*, 139). The final effect, though, is not to make it clear that Mather is deluded and Burroughs is right, for Burroughs himself comes to wonder "how could he say, after all, that they were *not* bewitched?" (*R*, 196). It is rather to make present a world of pervasive doubt, and injunctions to credulity, in which there is no clear foundation – neither empirical nor procedural – to decide.

In fact, in one scene, as villagers look out for an Indian attack, which no one but Burroughs believes is an actual possibility, disagreement about what has been seen is so extreme that it extends to whether anything has been seen at all:

> Look. . . . look. . . . there's a glitter and a confused motion there. . . . can't you see it?. . . . just where the sun strikes on the verge of the hill among the high grass, where a – my God. . . . I thought so!
>
> I can't see nothin'. . . . the sun hurts my eyes; but as for you, you can look right into the sun. . . . Hullow. . . . where now? (*R*, 162)

Burroughs, the first speaker, strives to make the others see the attack, crying out warnings "in a voice that might have been heard a mile." Yet no matter how loud his cries are, they do not worry the others in the slightest; to his call "To arms!" they lazily respond, "Rattlesnake an' toddy. . . . what for?" (*R*, 162). The more Burroughs points to the visible threat ("there – did you see that?"), the more the villagers dismiss him ("See what?. . . . you *air* cracked") (*R*, 162–63). But that increase is exactly the point: as subjects and objects increasingly appear to disintegrate, the patter of noisy voices ascends to a presence of its own. This presence is based not on character, not on objects, but on the rhythm and forward push of exchanging words.

The scenes of empirical and epistemological confusion and failure become occasions for displays of verbosity. Consider the manner in which the topic of "proof" is raised repeatedly. Burroughs proposes that "goodness itself may be a thing of opinion or hearsay, incapable of proof" (*R*, 101) (much as Rachel Dyer's goodness cannot be seen in her appearance). His assistant suggests that Burroughs, in Sarah Good's trial, "slip in a remark or two about the nature of the proof required in witchcraft," not so much to answer the problem but to "tire [the opposition] out if we can't do anything better" (*R*, 118–19). Then, at the trial's summary:

Proof, cried Burroughs – proof! taking away his hands from his pale face – and speaking through his shut teeth. Call you that proof which proves nothing? (*R*, 128)

To which the chief judge responds, "I would have you observe that proof is proof" (*R*, 134), as if tautological repetition were an argument. Indeed, the emptiness and the force of the word seems to burst out in the following exchange:

Well . . . what does that prove?
Prove!
Yes – prove – prove – you know the meaning of the word, I hope? (*R*, 188)

The novel's answer to the question, what is proof? is its repetition, "prove – prove," or "proof is proof." The idea that empirical proof could be a conundrum (the cause of Common Sense philosophy's retreat into knowing experience rather than knowing external objects) is the condition of the novel's extension. The entire text is a pattern or collage of statements about the challenges to proof, the difficulty of reaching proof, with no answer but the rephrasing, the restating of the word and the problem. We might say that here the notion of asking about proof – the problem of empirical testimony, even – has been converted into an emblematic occasion for generating reactions and making the literature come into being. When George Burroughs mulls, "I have said little that I meant to say, and much that I did not mean to say; hardly a word however even of that which I have said or meant to say, as I would say it, or as I could say it" (*R*, 118), he reveals that the failure to express a coherent view of oneself or the world around one is a way of allowing ever more language to be produced.

The epistemological challenge propelling the novel's dialogue is addressed explicitly in the first chapter's discussion of belief in witchcraft. Here, Neal imagines a test-case in which "a body of witnesses of equal worth were equally divided" into halves, one claiming some event to have occurred "at such a time or place," the other claiming it did not (*R*, 29). If two people look at the same scene and see two different things, whose eyes should be trusted? Neal argues that we must trust those who claim they saw the event, not those who did not, because it is "much more easy to overlook that which is, than to see that which is not; much more easy to *not* see a shadow that falls upon our pathway, than to see a shadow where indeed there is no shadow" (*R*, 29). By denying that the senses are reliably equivalent in all people, Neal has essentially rejected empiricism – he does not even trust the senses to see what is there before them, and turns instead to some other mode of judgment. In this passage the rhetorical question, "Are we to believe only so far as we may touch and see for ourselves?" has implicitly been answered in the negative (*R*, 30–31).

This is a perplexing moment, because most of the novel seems to assume that the witch trials were unjust, and that those who say they see witches are wrong. Why then does this novelist say that one should believe the superstitious colonists? The rationale appears to lie in the meditations on literary nationalism which introduce the novel. The discussion of witchcraft with its critique of eyewitness testimony comes immediately after the preface, in which Neal surveyed his arduous and ardent battle for literary nationalism in terms of showing the interest in American soil, history, and persons who appear unprepossessing. In that context, the accuser who sees a witch whom no one else sees occupies the same role as the novelist who sees an interest in topics which his reader does not. In fact, this was the position Neal makes Cotton Mather deliver in Sarah Good's trial: just as "The wild Irish have what they call their banshees, and the Scotch their second-sight, and the French their loup-garoux, or men turned into wolves," so we in New England have our witches (*R*, 137). This novel believes that witches are wrongfully prosecuted but that we should believe in them all the same. One has to believe, without any justification, any common evidence, any common experience, because it is just such unverifiable conviction which is necessary to make American literature interesting.

Neal's depiction of a nation as a compelling, cacophonous patter of voices in a futile discussion of belief and proof, and of how the visible relates to the invisible, the empirical to the associated or the ordinary to the imaginary, is accompanied by an undercurrent that explores the role of race in national founding. For example, it is in the scene where an Indian attack is impending that the sun hurts a man's eyes and no one can agree on what, if anything, they see in the woods before them. George Burroughs is the child of an Indian and an Englishwoman, brought up for his early years with his father's tribe, and later trained by the English as a missionary. At one crucial moment in the novel he tries to represent a group of colonists in a clash with Indians by dressing up as a Mohawk: when he disappears with the Indians, the colonists do not know if he has treasonably switched sides or if he has bought their pardon with his own life. At one point, he explicitly states his divided loyalty: "I will not war with white men . . . I will not be the foe of a red man" (*R*, 171). The foundationlessness of the nation that Neal depicts fosters an intuition that there's no real reason why natives are excluded and whites are included. In the dialogue of "who" and "what," such a clear referent seems impossible to locate – as Burroughs's own divided identity suggests that racial difference cannot draw firm boundaries between groups. As in the notion of seeing the hump-backed body of Rachel Dyer, identifying the characters clearly or even developing a plot are quite beside the point – just nubs of a subject to balloon into a volley of noisy reactions. This novel of confused, intertwined voices has no final coherent position – no individual subject position, no community coherence, and no grounds of racial identity – from which to argue.

*Rachel Dyer* is, in the end, a novel that finds its force in knitting together voices, however contradictory and incoherent they may be. What counts in an ongoing dialogue between an unruly man and the official enforcer of speech decorum is not the reconciliation of the two, nor the embrace of one of their views. It is, instead, the way that their speech mixes them together:

Here's the devil to pay and no pitch hot – whispered a sailor-looking fellow, in a red baize shirt.

An' there's thirteen pence for you to pay, Mr. Outlandishman, said a little neighbor, whose duty it was to watch for offenders in a small way, and fine them for swearing, drinking, or kissing wives on the sabbath day.

What for?

Why, for that air oath o'yourn.

What oath?

Why, you said here's the devil to pay!

Ha – ha – ha – and there's thirteen-pence for *you* to pay.

You be darned!

An' there's thirteen-pence more for you, my lad – ha – ha – ha – (*R*, 70)

A scuffle ensues, in which Burroughs shouts that the "sailor-looking fellow" ought to be tossed out of the court, even if he does turn out to be "a soldier of tried bravery" (*R*, 71) and, as such, intimidates the court officers. But what seems to count most is the way that the attempt to enforce norms turns into a verbal tug-of-war, where one person is made to echo another and where the offender begins to fine the officer of the court whom he has made to repeat his own swears. The novel turns on such explosions of word-games, which upend the sense of distinct personages and instead render a tightly interlaced – if also highly contentious – combination of speeches.

Its bravura performance finally exhausted, the novel folds. Neal follows it with what he heads, "Historical Facts," reprinted documents, so "that the reader may not be led to suppose the book he has just gone through with, a sheer fabrication" (*R*, 265). The effect is to render the history a locus out of which Neal has spun his novel, and in so doing shows how limited the role of such factual reality actually is in the book: just a brief afterthought. That qualifier "sheer" intimates that the book is to a great degree a fabrication – just not one without any connection, any location in actuality. The presence of such "Historical Facts" at the end of the novel shows, too, its own sense that it has not incorporated a literal reality into the world of the fiction, but kept them separate.

The works of Kames and Alison implicitly raise the question, "what does an associationist artwork look like?" In the criticism of the *North-American Review*, the answer is one filled with descriptions of emblematic characters, scenes, and events, which are plain but not too literal, fanciful but not too much so. But although *Rachel Dyer* begins with that clarion announcement that it exists to render American material into types of interest, something rather different occurs: a powerfully present rendering of dialogue. Beginning with its blindness to the character and appearance of its "heroine," continuing through its incoherent fancy of American topsoil, and proceeding into a patter of voices reacting to an object world it can't agree about and to which readers are given no access, the novel does not actually invent any such types (except in the extent to which it contributes to making the witch trials a privileged site for historical fiction). The immersion in dialogue begins to suggest that an associationist work must represent trains of association, rather than present objects to cause those trains. In so doing, Neal performs a version of what Channing's criticism does: it presents a series of reactions or associations to an object which all but disappears. It is as if his novel is itself a reading of the historical documents, a production of associations, which it weaves together into a coherent, convincing presence, and then shows to have a causal origin in some literal text. So the novel suggests that the experience that is of interest to the nation is no one person's – it is not concerned with one man's experience of witch trials, but those of an entire community. The associationist novel, here, is concerned with how individual ideas combine into general ones to form an impersonal if heterogeneous edifice which counts as an experience of the real. This is so even though the novel never actually tries to connect the observation of the literal real with the experience of a specific subject and, in fact, strives loudly to discredit such forms of understanding experience.

In the foregoing discussion, I placed some stress on the fact that the voices in *Rachel Dyer* were able to be knit together into a single, cacophonous wall, in part because the persons to whom such voices belonged were rendered almost invisible. It is important to register how much Neal's specific authorial voice also reaches into anonymity, particularly because his reputation is that of an eccentric whose individual personality forms the core of his writing identity. To begin with, one can see that the critical piece *American Writers*, Neal's best known work, collides abstract and personal perspectives even at the level of its basic structure. His accounts are, undeniably, highly subjective and almost slanderous: John E. Hall, editor of *The Port-Folio*, "has foregone the privileges of a fool . . . by his appetite for vulgar notoriety" (*A*, 116); James Madison is a "bad man" with the devil's "cloven foot" (*A*, 146); puffery of Brockden Brown is so extreme that critics have "slobbered him, as the anaconda would a buffaloe" (*A*, 61). But such pert diatribe is organized into an alphabetical, encyclopedic form, which suggests the capacious rationality of eighteenth-century intellectual history, and *American Writers* was the first comprehensive critical survey of the nation's literature.

Because he published *American Writers* anonymously, in it Neal easily might have critiqued himself in the third person; instead, he chose to quote John Neal's "own account" of himself, *"precisely in his own words"* (*A*, 155). That is to say, Neal presents himself as someone else reading his own work, only to then sidestep that pretense and present Neal's critique of his work, written in the first person. Yet the first-person account is presented as a quotation, so that the critic disingenuously presents an honest first-person account as the words of someone other than the author of *American Writers*. And when the quoted "John Neal" does discuss his works, he chooses works that were published anonymously – so that even within the quotation, the author does not admit a transparent moment of self-analysis. All in all, even though the critical voice in *American Writers* is not the anonymous voice of the citizen, we do not want to say that this is the voice of John Neal, for Neal's own voice is markedly difficult to locate among his odd diction, jokes, and censures. Even the author's moods alternate between asserting himself as an individual and as a member of a community: the book is a weird mixture of the the dictatorial and the flirtatious, as when he says of one author "Nevertheless – in mercy – that we may not break his heart, altogether – drive him stark, staring mad – we must allow him a word or two of comfort, after this – a spoonful of syrup – a lump of sugar – to quiet him" (*A*, 100). He is at once committed to correcting errant writers, and to laughing at his own pretension that his criticism might drive an author "stark, staring mad" (a commitment to both establish and flout standards which marked the dialogue over fines for cursing in *Rachel Dyer*).

The novels also playfully turn the author's self-analysis into a public discourse. For example, Monmouth, a character in *Randolph*, critiques Neal's previous work *Keep Cool*: Monmouth finds that novel "a foolish, fiery thing" and notes that Neal's poetry contains "some barbarisms and vulgarities, that will constantly provoke you."[49] (Less a moment of self-critique than of instruction to the reader: be provoked.) In that discussion, Neal intentionally misspells his own name "Neale" and adds a footnote explaining the error – on the part of the speaker? of the novelist himself? This transformation of himself into a subject of discussion within his own fiction, and the transformation of his own name into a sign easily misspelled and then corrected by the "– Ed." blurs the individual, actual Neal, who might otherwise seem offensively "familiar" to his critics, into a more general type of "Neal," which might contain "Neale" and any number of other instances.

In that spirit Neal denied writing many of his novels – even the autobiographical ones. The consistency of these gestures indicate that Neal was not so much toying with the truth, but that he wished, or even believed, that someone else *could* write his autobiography. "These incidents are *known* – there can be no doubt of it; and they must be remarkable, or nobody would remember them: – consequently, they are the legitimate property of the publick, and subject to the appropriation of any novel-writer, whatever."[50] So Neal had denied penning one of his obviously autobiographical novels by claiming that his private life was so infamous that it had already become a part of the public domain. The insistence is that his experiences had achieved a public currency which placed them in the quiver of any novelist – as much the property of another as it was of the man to whom it had actually happened.

Neal wants to upend that republican citizen position by speaking of himself, but to still let that writing "I" become a version of an anonymous or pseudonymous voice. This point is crucial precisely because it counters the standard assessment of Neal as a dyed-in-the-wool individualist, committed to his eccentricity and also to a groundedness in the personal, local experience. As Teresa A. Goddu has claimed, Neal "call[ed] for a literature of the blood and heart, to be connected to emotion and natural expression and for which the Indian's 'savageness' was to provide the passion," and she herself suggests the profit of "resurrect[ing]" and "rematerializ[ing]" Neal, making his bodily presence central to his literary-historical profile.[51] In this view, Neal opposes the intellectual gentility of the *North-American Review* with an explicitly physical understanding of American literature as the spontaneous outpouring of blood, race, and feeling. Dana D. Nelson has also focused on Neal's interest in an American embodiment, describing his "muscular style" of writing.[52] Both Nelson and Goddu, then, stress that Neal envisions American literature as importantly embodied, connected to a gendered and to a racial identity.

Each critic also notes, however, that Neal betrays contradictory impulses toward formality. Goddu stresses Neal's divided directions in *Logan*: he "exposes the bloody ground of the nation" in violence, but he also suggests United States history is a "narrative of civilization and progress."[53] Nelson, in contrast, suggests that Neal's effort is to blend the claims of racial authenticity into claims of legal authenticity, in a gesture of mystification and misrecognition whereby embodied realities linked to the enactment of repression are turned into abstracted, civic realities that anxiously strive to eradicate such traces of material origins. Despite the significant differences in argument, at a basic level both Goddu and Nelson see

Neal struggling over his essential commitment to American literature as the expression of a rugged, full-blooded and "muscular" identity, and his superficial commitment to the narratives of American openness, nondiscrimination, and universal abstraction. The opposition central to both Goddu and to Nelson – namely, the opposition of, and consequent attempt to negotiate between, embodied particularity versus abstract universality – does not hold for Neal. For example: in his novel *Randolph*, Neal violated the standard of the public sphere that Michael Warner persuasively outlined in *Letters of the Republic* by referring by name to Baltimore lawyer and politician William Pinkney, savaging Pinkney for a panoply of sins, among them having a "red, fat English face" and a bearing which combined "natural superciliousness and affected courtesy."[54] This would be Neal at his most personal, his most un-republican (so to speak). But when Pinkney's son took offense and challenged him to a duel, Neal refused to acknowledge that he had offered the kind of personal affront that would be appropriately resolved through a duel – he insisted that his comments were within the sphere of acceptable public critique. This is not, I think, a case of confusion and opposition of ideals; it is evidence of Neal's conviction that personal matters *were* public (not just negotiated with the public, but of the public). For instead of hearing an embodied and complex subject, speaking of his American life, we have instead a haywire streak of writing which is precise in its delineation of certain events and details such as Pinkney's "red, fat face," but which doesn't show us a single person, a firm place, a national view. It evinces exactly that combination of precision and unloosed abstraction which was crucial to the criticism in the *North-American Review*.

In the preface to *Rachel Dyer*, Neal asserts that he was compelled to write because, "I was an American" (*R*, ix), a statement in which the personal and the national are utterly compatible. Not only is there no conflict between the particular "I" and the general "American," the categories appear naturally to reinforce one another, as if his identity and the nation's were continuous. In support of this sense of seamless connection of self to public, Neal boasts a lover's bond with his reader, who has "touch[ed] his heart with a naked hand" (*R*, xix–xx) and sensed its "pulsation." Dwelling on "the many tears, that you may have dropped over him" (*R*, xx), Neal imagines his reader as his soulmate. But over the course of Neal's preface, such symbiotic harmony is hard to come by. Far more typical than the congruence which "I was an American" claims are tortured pleadings with and renunciations of the reader. Indeed, the idea of novel-writing as personal revelation to a sympathetic audience ready with "many tears" is ultimately just a fantasy, for Neal is strikingly uncertain that he will interest anyone at all with personal and passionate material. His skepticism about his audience's sympathy may be a reaction to the scandals incited by his earlier novels' revelations about himself and others, scandals which led to his departure for England, where he wrote *Rachel Dyer*. But if the earlier problem had been public odium, in *Rachel Dyer* Neal now fears a reader whom he simply bores. Neal sternly chastises the reader for a cold indifference, as he laments that "ye *are* invisible to him" (*R*, xx), and in a fit of pique claims that because the reader is uncaring he has decided that *Rachel Dyer* will be "the very last [novel] I shall ever write." Ruefully certain that the announcement has failed to provoke the recalcitrant reader, Neal blusters, referring to himself in the third person, "Can it be that you feel no sort of emotion at hearing him say, Lo! I have finished the work – it is the last – no sensation of inquietude?" (*R*, vii). Even so, the assumed reader is still recalcitrant; he imagines that his reader "feel[s] no sort of emotion" at the news and is so utterly alienated that Neal must even ventriloquize the indifferent response: "Why should you feel any [emotion], you ask" (*R*, vii). Neal's wish had been sympathy for his personal revelations, and he had been met with outrage; but when outrage passes into no reaction at all the author despairs. The preface is, then, a drama of Neal's desire to convey affect to his reader and his frustration in doing so. What nationalism would portray as a necessary reflexivity between individual and generality is here an impossible ideal productive mainly of isolation and bitterness.

The disjunction between self and nation is such that Neal calls his struggle on its behalf "a secret" that "must not even be guessed at by another" (*R*, x). Waging war for the United States "alone," almost in a vacuum, Neal soliloquizes, "Shall I go forth said I, in the solitude of my own thought, and make way alone against the foe" (*R*, x). He in effect disavows his country (both "the Reviewers of America" [*R*, x] and "the opinion of the public" [*R*, xi]), in the name of defending it. To Neal, the imagination of a nation is disturbing precisely because there is no faith that the nation really exists beyond his mind. That's why the "insolent question" (*R*, ix) of Sydney Smith of the Edinburgh Review, "*Who reads an American Book*?" (*R*, x) unnerves and inflames Neal: if no one reads him, his nationalism is utterly solitary, without any general purchase or relevance. He displays his final inability to imagine who or what would be a satisfactory American reader by echoing in frustration Smith's dismissal of American literature and writes, "Let these words be engraven hereafter on my tomb-stone: 'Who reads an American Book?'" (*R*, xx). He also, here, takes recourse in a familiar type to elicit interest in his reader. Perhaps he cannot make any reader, and any American let alone America, interested in his novels or in his life. Yet in requoting "Who reads an American Book?" he takes his best chance at getting a response: Smith's question was an infamous statement, one that would be seen as entirely likely to provoke.

There is something odd about ending this tortured preface, with its claims of passion, grounded feeling, tears, etc., with that eternal refrain. For one thing, his gesture of insisting that his reader cares nothing for him, while saturating his writing with expressions of feeling, resembles the language about America as a barren rock. Is it actually a lament over the barrenness of the land, or is it that calling it barren allows one to begin to create associations with generalized inventions? Comparably, is Neal actually upset that he has no reader who is like a lover, meeting him in person outside the text, or is such a denial of his reader's interest a strategic lead-in to the refrain of "Who reads an American Book?" It seems that the profusion of Neal's language on this point indicates a freedom in renouncing the model of the reader-as-lover. His woeful abandonment by the uninterested reader allows him to address that general, hypothetical field of responses and ideas which does not require specific individuals. One *can* write an American book once the individual reader's existence is buried with ostentatious crocodile tears. The demise of the object world and the subject, again, allows an elaboration and extension of potential, impersonal experience to come into focus. "Who reads an American book?" then becomes a question like "Who has not felt it?" – in this case, the answer is no one and, as a consequence, anyone.

# CHAPTER 2

# Sensing Hawthorne: the figure of Hawthorne's affect

Hawthorne's writing, although polished and genteel, nevertheless approaches the reader in a particularly unsettling manner, as when he states in "The Custom-House" that "the reader may smile, but must not doubt," or allows, in "Young Goodman Brown," the reader to determine Brown's night only a dream, "if you will."[1] Although Hawthorne's approaches to the reader have most often been discussed as invitations to the reader to participate in the making of meaning, I argue that Hawthorne's engagement hinges, instead, on emblem-making.[2] Somewhat as in Neal, for Hawthorne this entails obscuring what is being represented (marginalizing rather than problematizing meaning) in order to raise questions about how the voice of a narrator solicits a certain affective experience. Experience is, furthermore, proposed out of the text's offer of conflicting vectors: reading along with the text, and taking images and ideas out and away from it. That figurative idea of a difference between moving along with and moving out and away from the text is the abstract, rather than personal, affect of Hawthorne.

I

The way emotion in Hawthorne emerges around the creation of emblems instead of around persons is particularly notable in "The Minister's Black Veil," a story that first appeared in the 1836 issue of *The Token*.[3] The story concerns Parson Hooper, who wears a black veil over his face, to the dismay of those who know him. The story begins with, and dwells upon, the effect of the veil upon his congregation:

"But what has good Parson Hooper got upon his face?" cried the sexton in astonishment.

   All within hearing immediately turned about, and beheld the semblance of Mr. Hooper, pacing slowly in his meditative way towards the meeting-house. With one accord they started, expressing more wonder than if some strange minister were coming to dust the cushions of Mr. Hooper's pulpit . . .

   The cause of so much amazement may appear sufficiently slight.[4]

The "slight" veil shocks the whole congregation, which is thrown into "astonishment . . . wonder . . . [and] amazement." But Hawthorne has not had enough; in a scene like Neal's courtroom full of bemused and befuddled voices over the entry of the minister George Burroughs, he narrates a panoply of responses:

"I can't really feel as if good Mr. Hooper's face was behind that piece of crape," said the sexton.

"I don't like it," muttered an old woman, as she hobbled into the meeting-house. "He has changed himself into something awful, only by hiding his face."

"Our parson has gone mad!" cried Goodman Gray, following him across the threshold.

A rumor of some unaccountable phenomenon had preceded Mr. Hooper into the meeting-house, and set all the congregation astir. Few could refrain from twisting their heads towards the door; many stood upright, and turned directly about; while several little boys clambered upon the seats, and came down again with a terrible racket. ("M," 372)

The veil has set everyone's minds whirring and their bodies on edge, with "a rustling of the women's gowns and shuffling of the men's feet" ("M," 372). The "mysterious emblem . . . shook with his measured breath as he gave out the psalm" ("M," 373), as an accompaniment to the words.

Hooper's preaching has never been "energetic," but by speaking through the veil a "subtle power was breathed into his words." The sermon, like a Hawthorne story, uses language that is unnervingly light to produce a shuddering affect: "There was nothing terrible in what Mr. Hooper said; at least, no violence; and yet, with every tremor of his melancholy voice, the hearers quaked" ("M," 373). If the language is simple – there's nothing "in" it which is "terrible" – its *effect* is terrible, and that terror emerges from the presence of the veil alongside the language. In religious instruction, ministers used emblems as a way to underscore a moral lesson: the combination of a written moral with a visual image drove home the point.[5] Hooper's moral words are similarly driven home through the appeal to the visual that the "mysterious emblem" provides: words and visual images teach more powerfully than mere analysis. One could also consider the veil, as an emblem accompanying language, to be a dramatization of the role of figurative language as an ornament apart from prosaic communication. In this sense the "emblem" is a sign of Hawthorne's imagery, "emblems" in words rather than in pictures, placed offsides from the narration and representation. The suggestion of "The Minister's Black Veil" is that the use of emblems, aside or above the meaning, ruins the immersion of character and narration and in so doing produces emotion. For the effect of the veil is to break off Hooper's engagement, which ruptures the life of Hooper as a plotted character and as a comprehensible psychological agent. We never find out why he acts as he does, and in essence nothing significant happens in the story once the veil is donned.

True, Hooper's sermon is on "secret sin, and those sad mysteries which we hide from our nearest and dearest" ("M," 373), but despite this and other misleading hints that at issue is what lies in the innermost, dark heart, the story homes in on the potency of the veil as a "mysterious emblem" ("M," 373) or, in Hooper's words, "a type and a symbol" ("M," 378). The emblem drives people to attempt to find out what it means and what is inside Hooper to make him act this way – is it "innocent sorrow" ("M," 378) or "secret sin" ("M," 379)? But Hawthorne never decides this question, and both what is inside Hooper and what the veil means are demonstrably immaterial to its emotional effect. So powerful is the emblem, it does not even need to be Hooper's particular "double fold of crape" ("M," 378): a little "wag[]" dons his own "black handkerchief" and in so doing terrifies his friends and himself ("M," 377). "The Minister's Black Veil" is about the triumphant creation of an emblem: a shred of fabric is employed to convey a meaning; but rather than conveying a moral as would a traditional emblem, it suggests an ambiguity about secret sin or sorrow, and that interpretive impasse is a watershed of common "quak[ing]" ("M," 381).

That the communication of feeling, rather than meaning, is the primary task of the veil is underscored by Hooper's conception of it as a reaction to secrecy among persons. On his deathbed he avers that what is at stake is neither sin nor sorrow, but that persons conceal things from one another:

> "When the friend shows his inmost heart to his friend; the lover to his best-beloved; when man does not vainly shrink from the eye of his Creator, loathsomely treasuring up the secret of his sin; then deem me a monster, for the symbol beneath which I have lived, and die!" ("M," 384)

The black veil is a symbol for the fact that "on every visage [there is] a Black Veil!" – that no one is entirely open in his presentation of himself to another. But Hooper's communication is not exactly about explaining one's distinct self to another's; it entails an absolute connection that occurs by replacing the self with the emblem. For even though the veil "hung between him and the world" ("M," 382), it connected Hooper to all the world, as an emblem to which everyone reacts. The terror of the story is its performance of how emotional connection emerges not out of interpersonal intimacy (such as his marriage to Elizabeth might provide, or a confession might forge) but out of a flight from the personality altogether, into confounding (interpretively perplexing and emotionally inflammatory) emblematicity.

In "The Minister's Black Veil," to show oneself to another person is to enter into unmediated emotional oneness, to lose any sense of personal distinction or of property in one's own affections. And because the emotional power of the veil can be so firmly felt even though its meaning is inscrutable, its emotional force exists independent of the human specificity of an intentional agent necessary to the creation of meaning. As Hooper puts it, he is able to "live[]" and "die" "beneath" the symbol, but not to convey his views through it. The point is that emotional intimacy emerges at the cost of the personality, of the self's coherence and ability to act in relationship to others, and to convey meaning to others.

This contention runs against the grain of a great deal of Hawthorne criticism, which has focused on the psychological subject and on its relation to others in the social world. For Gordon Hutner, Hawthorne's evasiveness about the reference of his tales, such as the obscurity about Hooper's motivation, encourages the reader to sympathetically intuit the secret truth and so to construct a shared world; for Jeffrey Steele, Hawthorne recognizes that "we do not exist in a vacuum as independent, self-reliant individuals" but rather are constituted "by our being for and with others."[6] In Lauren Berlant's analysis, Hawthorne perceives that national identity depends upon "writing to harness the libidinal energies of the American 'people' for the purposes of national fantasy," so that nationhood can be felt as "an intimate quality of identity, as intimate and inevitable as biologically-rooted affiliations through gender or the family," exemplifying the psychological process of building both personal and national identity.[7] The work of Joel Pfister and Gillian Brown stresses Hawthorne's engagement with the nineteenth-century construction of the conception of the individual. Even as criticism has shifted from truths of how the subject must exist in the social world to a concern with the subject as a historical formation intertwined with the conditions of nineteenth-century liberalism and capitalism, it has maintained a framing conception of the location of emotion and experience in the specificity of the subject and also in the actuality of the body, a specificity in various tensions with a world of social concerns alternately conceived of as deeply part of the subject, or as false fronts for that interior self.[8] Pfister points out that Hawthorne's account of the psychological is almost perfectly adapted to psychoanalytic readings, which for Pfister indicates that Hawthorne is engaged in creating the very account of the self that would make psychoanalysis possible. Yet the ease of such readings also points up that such accounts of emotion and its origin in the self offer

evasive recourse from the more moving and abstract affect to which the
subject is incidental. Understandings of the psyche as something to be read
into, expressed, and so on – all that Terada categorizes as the "ideology of
emotion" – are in Hawthorne's writing alternatives that would placate the
terrible evanescence of an affective experience unconnected from persons.
If Hawthorne can, as Sharon Cameron puts it, "reverse the conventional
notion that the soul is interior, private, and inaccessible," the sense that the
soul is outside the self is a primary condition to be at times staved off or
transformed into the more graspable notion that persons are distinct and
possess souls and feelings within them (as Georgina's birth-mark suggests
that her feelings and desires are inside her, to be represented on her face).[9]
Perhaps the frequently hateful quality in Hawthorne of persons and the
terms in which they represent and interpret themselves and others and
conduct their relations evinces some of this sense that people serve more
to obscure and to suppress affect than to experience it.

Still earlier Hawthorne criticism explored the contrast of his style's tissue-
like lightness and decorum to a current of intensity, usually conceived of
as a form of depth. Longfellow praised Hawthorne as a belletrist who "uses
words as mere stepping-stones, upon which, with a free and youthful bound,
his spirit crosses and recrosses the bright and rushing stream of thought,"
and Anne Abbott noted that while Hawthorne's "style may be compared to
a sheet of transparent water . . . in its clear yet mysterious depths we espy
rarer and stranger things, which we must dive for, if we would examine."[10]
Like Longfellow, Abbot stresses the invisibility and the movement of the
style, but her appreciation for the author's "continual flow of expression"
is set in tension with the notion of objects "we must dive for," as it suggests
that the forward flow and the transparency of the water conceal what's truly
going on beneath that surface.[11] The tension between flow and depth also
emerged in Evert Duyckinck's assessment that Hawthorne's style "flows on
pellucid as a mountain rivulet, and you feel in its refreshing purity that
it is fed by springs beneath."[12] Hawthorne's style, then, is termed lucid
and flowing, even as he is praised for a psychological depth that suggests a
perpendicular movement that dives downward rather than flows forward.
This depth is conceived through the figure of the stream, common to
Longfellow, Abbott, and Duyckinck, and this figuration pushes the matter
away from the ostensible subject of how the prose represents such depth and
evokes that process through a common, iterated image of surface and depth.

Melville's account of "Hawthorne and His Mosses" held that such
critics had mistaken Hawthorne for a light stylist, when in fact he was
"immeasurably deeper than the plummet of the mere critic."[13] Yet the

issue is not quite that other critics think that Hawthorne is superficial, while Melville sees that he is deep; the same contrast is, as we have just seen, present in the very critics whom Melville dismisses. But for Melville, Hawthorne's depth cannot be accessed through "the plummet" of critical attempts such as Duyckinck's or Abbot's to penetrate the prose; Melville's insight is in noting that the depth demanded a figurative rubbing of the text: "[Ye] cannot come to know greatness by inspecting it; there is no glimpse to be caught of it, except by intuition; you need not ring it, you but touch it, and you find it gold."[14] As a touchstone measures the quality of "gold" by the streak of metal left upon the stone, so too the reader might know Hawthorne's "greatness" by the author's effect upon the reader, an effect evidently of reams of images of streams and touchstones.

The question of how a playful lightness related to something stronger and darker continued to be formulated as a matter of a depth behind the superficial elegance of Hawthorne's style in criticism of the mid-twentieth century. For example, when in 1949 Philip Rahv celebrated Hawthorne's "submerged intensity and passion" and critiqued Hawthorne's submission to the "moribund religious tradition of old New England," its "submer[sion]" was both what hindered and what made powerful the author's "intensity and passion."[15] In Frederick Crews's *Sins of the Fathers* it is the very concealment of desire under the boot of the "tyrannical superego" that makes the novels rebuses of "sexual anxiety," waiting for the critic to delve in and uncover Hawthorne's "dwelling on powerful and 'ancestral' *tree-trunks*."[16] Such assessments identify the psychological perspicacity of Hawthorne's art as a result of its occlusion of desire: by covering over it, the art reveals it, which suggests both the possibility that psychological depth can be known only through its occlusion, and, more powerfully, that psychology only becomes deep – and hence, in this critical frame, authentic – through the distance that occlusion places between desire and our knowledge of it.

Trilling objected that critics such as Crews and Rahv shared a "belief in the magical force and authority of words and their arrangement, as in a charm or a spell, an expression of belief that literature characteristically makes its appeal to archaic human faculties which have been overlaid by civilization and deeply hidden."[17] But, Trilling countered, Hawthorne had only a "surface aesthetic" and his "charm and fragrance . . . may well be his essence."[18] And yet, there is something insufficient about this vapidly charming Hawthorne, in part because it is implausible that almost all his critics could be so grotesquely over-interpreting him. And even in his own account of Hawthorne's "charm and fragrance," it turns for Trilling into a personal matter: "[Henry] James was much engaged by the beauty of

Hawthorne's work, by its textures and hues, of which he speaks not so much with critical admiration as with personal delight."[19] Such delight is, writes Trilling, available to "whoever has first read Hawthorne in childhood" when, untrained in critical methods, he could still apprehend "something that spoke to him, and very movingly, before ever ambiguity was a word, some wind or music of unparticular significance."[20] Trilling renders the "charm and fragrance" of the "surface aesthetic" matter for either James's "personal" experience, or some "whoever['s]" memory of childhood reading. The personal reader is unconcerned with meaning and with pressure; his is a work of *sensing*, not of interpreting. Trilling engages such personal sensing, however, by means of another person (James) and a generic "whoever." That Hawthorne's surface aesthetic turns into a personal one for Trilling indicates that there is emotion here, but it's just that it is unfamiliar to think of superficiality as serious or passionate.

Trilling ended up suggesting that Hawthorne *does* push from superficial style into some dimensional reality; "he suggests to us the limits of art, and thus points to the stubborn core of actuality that is not to be overcome."[21] Thus Trilling's work was more to reverse than to abandon accounts such as Rahv's: Hawthorne still has a "core" apart from his style, but now it is not hidden in or behind but outside or in front of it. Still the ongoing teasing out of how such a style, such a "surface aesthetic," keeps pointing to some "core" or other indicates that these two things are not as distinct as critics have suggested. The oddity, the interest, is again that the intensity or presence is an illusion of a core that is projected by the light surface. When we enter into an affective relationship with Hawthorne's writing, it is precisely not an experience of finding some deep reality hidden in the language; neither is it to find some deep reality that has been obscured by the artifice of culture, conventions; nor is it to enter a realm of empty surface aesthetics. It is to echo Hawthorne, both in reading along with him and in moving, in one's attempt to analyze him, into the making of further images, from Longfellow's stream to Melville's touchstone to Trilling's fragrance.[22] This moving along with Hawthorne, moreover, yields the essential images of spatiality as movement along and also through the text that constitutes the space of affect in Hawthorne, in which perpendicular vectors yield images, and intimacy depends on this repetitive form rather than the mutual understanding of subjects.

II

"Out of the soil of New England he sprang – in a crevice of that immitigable granite he sprouted and bloomed."[23] James's return to the rock imagery of literary nationalism reminds us that Hawthorne at once exemplifies and solves the problem of producing American types and emblems. The apparent solution is continued attention to the problem, such that the making of emblems and types is what draws out the reader's experience. Renaissance emblem books, such as those by Francis Quarles, Henry Peacham, or Andrea Alciati (some of which were still in print in the nineteenth century), had also explored the rationale of the images they presented. Their emblems were generally composed of three parts: the legend (usually a biblical quotation), a visual image, and a verse explaining how the image illustrated the legend. The emblem form provokes reflection by explaining why they make sense – explication that is unnecessary for an arbitrary convention (because there is none) and a natural symbol (because it is innately self-evident). Reading an emblem, one is invited to think through the relationship between legend, verse, and image, a spatial relationship between three iterations of single idea. Because each says the same thing, they go nowhere: one contemplates the distance between them as an iterative extension precisely because there is no substantive difference between the different iterations (many of these books were also composed largely of emblems from previous emblem books). Hawthorne shares with the Renaissance emblem tradition a tendency to produce around the image an explication of its rationale that is also an indication of how one should interpret it. And most of all, what Hawthorne asks of his reader is to follow the analytic process of making a connection, marking a similitude, of literal and figurative meaning. As in the emblem books, this following along has a notably static quality that pushes against the iterative progression.

Whereas for Neal and the critics of the *North-American Review* producing emblems and types was a vexed enterprise, in Hawthorne it appears to be the easiest thing in the world. Consider the placidity with which he allows that the boy who frequents Hepzibah's cent-shop in *The House of the Seven Gables*, consuming ginger cookies in different shapes, is an emblem of Time:

This remarkable urchin, in truth, was the very emblem of old Father Time, both in respect of his all-devouring appetite for men and things, and because he, as well as Time, after engulfing thus much of creation, looked almost as youthful as if he had been just that moment made.[24]

Hawthorne claims that this character as he lives in nineteenth-century Salem is "in truth" an "emblem," an easy assertion of the non-invented, real connection between modern American boy and some greater significance. I say "some greater significance" because the boy is implicitly indicative of "Time," but directly said to be actually emblematic of "Father Time," a personification of the abstraction Time. And while the abstraction of time surely does devour (although only figuratively), only the personification of "Father Time" may be said to retain a look of youthfulness (it cannot even be a figurative youth that time per se would evince). So this young character is claimed to be an emblem, but only by way of being conceived as an emblem of another emblem. The ease in Hawthorne's emblems is directly connected to his reliance on the comparison to a preexisting emblem to make a transition from an emblem (Father Time) of an abstraction (time), and then suggest that the ordinary American boy is himself an emblem of the first emblem.

Consider the organ-grinder's monkey in *The House of the Seven Gables*:

The mean and low, yet strangely man-like expression of his wilted countenance; the prying and crafty glance, that showed him ready to gripe at every miserable advantage; his enormous tail, (too enormous to be decently concealed under his gabardine,) and the deviltry of nature which it betokened; – take this monkey just as he was, in short, and you could desire no better image of the Mammon of copper-coin, symbolizing the grossest form of the love of money. (*H*, 493)

As in the passage about the urchin, Hawthorne asserts the self-evidence of this emblem, and tells us things are emblematic of other emblems – of "Mammon," personification of greed. The "just as he was" monkey is connected to another materialized image of the abstraction of greed. Thus, although it seems that Hawthorne is telling us that the real monkey is innately emblematic of the abstraction greed, it turns out that he is narrating a logical if not temporal journey from abstraction (greed) to emblem (Mammon) to emblematic reality (monkey, "just as he was"). Although Hawthorne gracefully indicates that the ordinary people and things he finds in nineteenth-century Salem are naturally emblematic, he is in fact recounting a process of connections that begins in abstraction, proceeds to emblem, and finally to another, more detailed emblem – "just as he was" is the last stone lain, not instantly self-evident at all.

This narrated logic, in which abstraction precedes emblem, which leads to emblem with more full detail, is already present in *The American Notebooks*, a collection of observations and ideas. For example, Hawthorne speculates:

To make literal pictures of figurative expressions; – for instance, he burst into tears – a man suddenly turned into a shower of briny drops. An explosion of laughter – a man blowing up, and his fragments lying about on all sides. He cast his eyes upon the ground – a man standing eyeless, with his eyes on the ground, staring up at him in wonderment &c &c &c.[25]

In themselves, "figurative expressions" are already implicitly "literal pictures," because to say a person bursts into laughter or explodes into tears is to evoke a physical version of an emotional transition or expressive moment. For Hawthorne to further extend such implicit literalness is to do something like what he does with the monkey and the urchin: take an abstraction rendered into a more material image (personification in the first cases, figuration in the second one) and then put that back into a more fully material form. The movement from abstraction, to figuration, to realistic image is here a progressive expansion of the original combination of abstract and literal.[26] Because this is a repetitive expansion of the original notion, not a qualitative transition, the prospect of making emblems becomes a train of concatenations additively extended, "&c &c &c." Notwithstanding his assurances that emblems are self-evident, Hawthorne does not allow emblems to stand and serve as signs of abstractions, but rather repeats them and draws them out with analysis of their possible effects.

Back in the examples of the monkey and the urchin from *The House of the Seven Gables* Hawthorne is also dilatory about his emblems. He relates that the urchin is an emblem of Father Time because he devours everything and yet is always young. It is a process of consumption, as a whale-shaped cookie "began his progress down the same red pathway of fate, whither so varied a caravan had preceded him," including not just one material, indeed edible representation but also "Jim Crow, the elephant, the camel, the dromedaries, and the locomotive" (*H*, 451). With the monkey, Hawthorne enumerates the elements of greed, from the "mean and low, yet strangely man-like expression of his wilted countenance" and his "prying and crafty glance" to the indecent tail and "the deviltry of nature which it betokened" (*H*, 493). The monkey "just as he was" is not something seen in a single glimpse at all – he is a sequence of qualities. The passages follow along with the reason of the emblems, not how they were actually invented, and that rationale is a train of repetitive dilation, as in the case of Father Time who repeatedly devours "so varied a caravan." The making of emblems, in both *The House of the Seven Gables* and *The American Notebooks*, is a sequential process: each emblem rests on a procession from abstraction, to implicit figuration, to full figuration; the emblems are arranged in series which are implicitly infinite; and the series forecast literal renderings of the images.

Angus Fletcher argues that because the characters in allegorical narratives stand for abstractions – Patience, Virtue, Despair – they are incapable of change. Therefore nothing can happen to them as characters: they can only parade their natures, making an allegorized character "tantamount to an image."[27] In Hawthorne the issue is reversed: images act like allegorical characters, parading their nature rather than signifying their meaning. My point is that the stress is neither on the thematic investigation into how the metaphoric and the literal are related, nor on the meaning of the images, but on movement along a narrated intellectual transformation from abstraction, to emblem, to more fully literalized emblem. This narration of images raises questions about the status of narrative fiction in Hawthorne. By this I mean not the intra-fictional question of the difference between the novel and the romance, but the topic of "literary nonreferential narrative," in Dorrit Cohn's formulation.[28] For Hawthorne engages in a mode of telling that is not the same as the narration of invented stories experienced by characters, nor the explanation of the history of how an image was actually made, but a following along with the logic of images.

The narratives of Hawthorne's emblems refer to how the emblem has worked, and forecast how it may continue to work. This is not only to narrate allegory, in which true change is impossible, but also to imply that the process of ideas from author to reader could be a comparable train of extended instantiations. Hawthorne's gestures that the reader can "take" an image imply that those images, in the form of ideas, should be handed over from the author to the reader, somewhat as the young boy who sees the veil on Parson Hooper's face fashions his own version, and then frightens himself, or in which Channing approaches Brown's writing as putting the idea of a deserted house into the reader's or critic's mind, where it is then expanded. The stress on the process of these transformations, rather than on their thematic substance, educes reading as accompaniment and encourages the reader to ape the prose's unfolding. In this it is linked to the experience of reading as conceived in associationism, although we do not quite leave Hawthorne's writing for our own reverie of associations in the way that Alison and Kames theorized. Nevertheless, we also don't burrow into it, for the language glides past without demanding or acquiescing to a reader's gripping attentiveness, with just that sense of ease that accompanies his emblem-making.

The *Notebooks* offer ideas to the author himself, as their future reader; in the case of the fiction, images are offered to the reader with rhetorical gestures such as, "take this monkey." *The American Notebooks* seem to speak to the author as if he were not himself, the romances seem to speak to the reader as if he or she were in part responsible for the writing of the work. In so doing, Hawthorne would have his readers work as stages in an iteration of affective presence. While the narration of emblems urges that a reader merely follow the author's lead, consuming one idea after another, the gestures of proffering emblems suggest a counter-movement that would have to dispense with the text, either in occurring after its consumption, or in a moment in which reading stops and is replaced by the reader's more direct taking of ideas from the author (for in such a moment even an emblem or piece of rhetoric stands as an idea in the reader's mind). Something of this is also indicated in the way that the passages I have explored thus far turn on progressions which go nowhere: movement without progress indicates the possibility of a counter-trajectory of movement. Thus, in some places, the sense of Hawthorne might be construed as running parallel to the lines of the text, as a reader follows along with him; but at other moments, it appears to move away from that trajectory, either in being forecast as continuing on after the text is finished, or in being conceived of as occurring at moments when the narrative line is stopped or stalled. In each case, however, Hawthorne's emotional quality depends on a sense of depth or spatiality, a spatial figure that is variously constituted through author's and reader's speculations over the making of emblems.

To this point, I have spoken as if the monkey and the boy were real, when they are only denizens of a work of fiction. This conflation of the real within a fiction and the historical real (between the internal and external frame of reference) is encouraged by the allegorical relationship of abstractions to objects that can be conceived of as real (whether that reality be within or without the fictional). This last point will take some time to explain, but to begin with I shall point out that much the same approach to the monkey as innately emblematic occurs in the original description of the monkey Hawthorne and his daughter Una saw "In Boston," on "Collonade Row," as recorded in *The American Notebooks*.

While his master played on the organ, the monkey kept pulling off his hat, bowing and scraping to the spectators roundabout – sometimes, too, making a direct application to an individual – by all this dumb show, beseeching them to remunerate the organ-player. Whenever a coin was thrown on the ground, the monkey picked it up, clambered on his master's shoulder, and gave it into his keeping; then descended, and recommenced his pantomimic entreaties for more. His little, old, ugly, wrinkled face had an earnestness that looked just as if it came from the love of money deep within his soul; he peered round, looking for filthy lucre on all sides. With his tail and all, he might be taken for the Mammon of copper coin – a symbol of covetousness of small gains, the lowest form of the love of money. Doubtless, many a man passed by, whose moral being was not unfairly represented by this monkey. (*AN*, 271)

When we "go back" to the notebook, looking for the origins of the image in the novel, we don't find the monkey as mere observed animal. Hawthorne conceives of the original monkey's emblematicity as immanent in the actual scene, just as he does in the fictional scene. The monkey's face "looked just as if it" expressed avarice, and here he already "might be taken" as an emblem, as if that potential for interpretation is part of his appearance.[29]

The *Notebooks* are not a personal record of an actual life, not yet rendered into general or public form, nor do we have what look like mere notes for further use. As James observes, "They contain much that is too futile for things intended for publicity; whereas, on the other hand, as a receptacle of private impressions and opinions, they are curiously cold and empty."[30] The *Notebooks* seem resolutely finished, notwithstanding their fragmentary qualities, and this finished quality turns on the way potential, rather than achieved, emblems educe a sense of actuality that depends upon analytic recounting.

A walk yesterday through Dark Lane, and home through the village of Danvers. Landscape now wholly autumnal. Saw an elderly man with two dry, yellow, rustling bundles of Indian corn-stalks, – a good personification of Autumn. Another man hoeing up potatoes. White rows of cabbages lay ripening. Fields of dry Indian corn. The grass has still considerable greenness. Wild rose-bushes devoid of leaves, with their deep, bright red seed-vessels. Meeting-house in Danvers seen at a distance, with the sun shining through the windows of its belfry. Barberry-bushes, – the leaves now of a brown red, still juicy and healthy; very few berries remaining, mostly frost-bitten and wilted. All among the yet green grass, dry stalks of weeds. The down of thistles occasionally seen flying through the sunny air. (*AN*, 19–20)

Dated Tuesday, October 25, 1836, this passage embarks from the foundation of Hawthorne himself, taking a walk. That he does not say he took a walk is characteristic of the notebooks' prose: an "I" is implied, taking a walk, but what is actually written is like a checking off, a notation of "a walk," that such a thing as a walk has been – not been taken but just been. He then proceeds to generalize about the neighborhood: "Landscape now wholly autumnal." Insofar as now it is autumn and hence must earlier have been summer, the generalization implies seasonal progression. But it does so statically, for the emphasis on "now wholly autumnal" erases explicit mention of a change, thereby countering the temporality implicit in "yesterday." From the generalization – there was a walk, it was all autumnal – Hawthorne makes note of a particular sight, a man carrying stalks of Indian corn. Hawthorne's swooping in on this particular produces a shift from the common generality of "now wholly autumnal" into the more regimented generality of "Autumn": capitalized, abstract Autumn, rather than the specific autumn of "now," in October 1836. Training his eyes upon "an elderly man with two dry, yellow, rustling bundles," Hawthorne is highly specific – there are *two* bundles, and they are allotted three adjectives. But that specificity, that patient painterly eye of the author's, actually brings him to the notion of a way to personify the abstract "Autumn."

Hawthorne is not recording his own walk – so much is left out of this and many other entries – he is recording the objects seen on his walk as they are perceived. He writes, "The down of thistles occasionally seen flying through the air," not that he occasionally saw it, and not that it occasionally does so, just that thistles being seen occurs. The phrasing marks a deliberate divestiture of syntactical logic, in denying the combination of subject and verb. The effect of such controlled abjuring of the sentence form is of a perceiving of objects, with some locality – October, Danvers, "at a distance," – but also without personality. The same conception of objects seen, yet not of a person seeing them, is evident in "All among the yet green grass, dry stalks of weeds," in which a scrupulous attentiveness to things just as they are is evoked by the absence of the sentence form. The passage conveys a sense of immediacy because it has not added on the figure of the subject, the logic of narration of human action, or even the logic of allegorical interpretation.

Contemplation of the apprehension of objects is conjoined with a sense that such apprehensions are all potentially emblematic in the way that the first man explicitly is, insofar as things in themselves are perceptions of things in isolation from any setting, narrative, or subject. The absence of narrative and of personality from such a passage, its carving down to a static sequence of objects ("Wild rose-bushes devoid of leaves, with their deep, bright red seed-vessels"), possesses a spare certitude that counts as a form of highly engaged attention to what is, not of reduced abstraction from the panoply of manifest life. Hawthorne's concern with the emblematic and the analytic clearly distinguishes him from the empirical engagement in the marrow of things, even the phenomenological sense in which things are really things as they are known by consciousness.[31] His abstraction neither places him, as Stubbs has it, in the classic tradition of the romance that "order[s] the random happenings of experience so that the reader could *comprehend* the experience,"[32] nor as Lora Romero argues, in "a modernist aesthetic intent on distancing itself and its products from the trivialities and banalities of everyday life."[33] Instead, abstraction and the affect of presentness, of reality, each seem to increase upon contact with one another.

Indeed, it is the presentation of abstract morals that often produces the image of a body. It is in this manner that, in, *The House of the Seven Gables*, Hawthorne concludes his discussion of the organ-grinder, his monkey, and his little diorama of figurines that move in an endlessly repeated cycle.

Possibly, some cynic, at once merry and bitter, had desired to signify, in this pantomimic scene, that we mortals, whatever our business or amusement . . . bring nothing finally to pass . . . But, rather than swallow this last too acrid ingredient, we reject the whole moral of the show. (*H*, 492–93)

Hawthorne moves away from the set of figurines, which seem an allegory of allegory (the people just stand for someone's abstract "moral") and into the figurative illustration of what it would be to eat an idea: to "swallow" a moral, as if the body could ingest an abstraction. As the voice of the author figures itself as capable of physically tasting the "acrid" quality of the abstract moral, the notion of both physical and emotional sensation is raised specifically in the relation of the narrative voice to its figured body. The concern with how images could be eaten is a concern with what kind of experience reading his own concatenating images is: how it is like consuming an idea. Such moments in which emblems and ideas appear to effect the body pose questions about the relationship of the narrative voice to, on the one hand, characters and, on the other hand, readers – questions that I address over the rest of this chapter.

III

*The Scarlet Letter* is the work of Hawthorne's that would appear most profoundly to explore the isolation of human consciousness, and the problem of how an individual can be put somehow into intimate relation with others – to, in short, refute my argument. For example, there is Dimmesdale, on the scaffold at night, interpreting the A-shaped cloud in the sky as directed towards his own personal guilt:

It was, indeed, a majestic idea, that the destiny of nations should be revealed, in these awful hieroglyphics, on the cope of heaven . . . But what shall we say, when an individual discovers a revelation, addressed to himself alone, on the same vast sheet of record! In such a case, it could only be the symptom of a highly disordered mental state, when a man, rendered morbidly self-contemplative by long, intense, and secret pain, had extended his egotism over the whole expanse of nature, until the firmament itself should appear no more than a fitting page for his soul's history and fate. (*S*, 252)

The passage clearly poses the alternative of the communal views of Puritan typology, in which the fate of the community is written in the sky, to the privacy of Dimmesdale's view of the apparition and the work of a "morbidly self-contemplative" soul.

However, this thematic concern, and the basic scene in which it is brought up, reworks a scene from Lydia Maria Child's *Hobomok*, published in 1824. In *Hobomok*, a cloud shaped like a ship appears in the sky; the main character, Mary, takes it as a portent "meant for herself only" and about her "lover," while to the rest of the community it has a general meaning (that "some mishap" was "about to befall the shipping which is coming hither").[34] This concern was explicitly about the making of literary images in America; *Hobomok*'s preface avows that "barren and uninteresting as New England history is . . . there is enough connected with it, to rouse the dormant energies of [the author's] soul."[35] In the passages about the clouds, Child suggests the equally implausible ways that Mary's personal imagination and the Puritans' superstitions interpret the cloud, only to conclude that such interpretation is inevitable and to proceed with the conviction that associations need not be convincing or true in order to be moving, and even to become accepted as true.

In *The Scarlet Letter*, the ostensible problem of subjective perception – "the disease in his own eye and heart" – accompanies the conventional assertion that the mind makes what it will of the world around it:

We impute it, therefore, solely to the disease in his own eye and heart, that the minister, looking upward to the zenith, beheld there the appearance of an immense letter, – the letter A, – marked out in lines of dull red light. Not but the meteor may have shown itself at that point, burning duskily through a veil of cloud; but with no such shape as his guilty imagination gave it; or, at least, with so little definiteness, that another's guilt might have seen another symbol in it. (*S*, 252)

Thus the very idea of a concern with the "disease[d]" and isolated mind in relation to a set of public interpretations of the world repeats a theme from not only Child's but also Neal's uses of the Puritans to pose, and then to dismiss, questions about how individual experiences of the world relate to communal ones. Hawthorne's apparently quite deliberate reiteration of the convention of posing the question has the effect not quite of making us think about the thematic concern of how individual perceptions relate to those of others, but of making us hover over a question that is evidently now a conventional locus of interest.

Hawthorne even uses his own work as if it were a set of conventions: for instance, he writes in "The Minister's Black Veil" of "that saddest of all prisons, his own heart" ("M," 382); years later, in *The House of the Seven Gables*, he writes, "what other dungeon is so dark as one's own heart! What jailor so inexorable as one's self!" (*H*, 498). This repetition of his own image occurs as Hawthorne asserts the unassailability of the interior self. To repeat both himself and others in discussing the inviolable interiority of the self points up the conventionality of that which seems most subjective and most interior, and thereby to undercut its very isolation: if all are prisons, what makes us any different from one another? The contrasting possibilities of deep isolation and the utter lack of individuality each emerge, in Hawthorne, around the repetition that makes emblems; each is displaced by an attendance to the relationship of author to reader, in which subjectivity and publicity appear more as a set of comforting, albeit evidently corrupt or unconvincing, escapes from a more primary sense that affect emerges over the work of the emblem and the relationship of the speaker to the audience, as in exclamations such as, "What shall we say."

As with the language of "what shall we say" or "what other jailor," the prose foists its concerns onto the reader in the intimate, urgent conversation between Hester and Dimmesdale in the forest, as they plan to run away together. Hester urges Dimmesdale to

"Leave this wreck and ruin here where it hath happened! Meddle no more with it! Begin all anew! . . . Why shouldst thou tarry so much as one other day in the torments that have so gnawed into thy life! – that have made thee feeble to will and to do! – that will leave thee powerless even to repent! Up, and away!"

"O Hester! cried Arthur Dimmesdale, in whose eyes a fitful light, kindled by her enthusiasm, flashed up and died away, "thou tellest of running a race to a man whose knees are tottering beneath him! I must die here. There is not the strength or courage left me to venture into the wide, strange, difficult world, alone!"

It was the last expression of the despondency of a broken spirit. He lacked energy to grasp the better fortune that seemed within his reach.

He repeated the word.

"Alone, Hester!"

"Thou shalt not go alone!" answered she, in a deep whisper.

Then, all was spoken! (*S*, 288–89)

Hester has just told Dimmesdale that Roger Chillingworth has been the watcher and prier into "this exposure of a sick and guilty heart" (*S*, 285). As Dimmesdale understands it, while Chillingworth "has violated, in cold blood, the sanctity of a human heart," he and Hester "never did so" (*S*, 286). What kind of intimacy do Hester and Dimmesdale possess, if not that of knowing the secret heart of another? It is an intimacy in which "Thou shalt not go alone!": in which one proceeds, but not as a separate person. As Hawthorne writes earlier in this same chapter, these two would "throw open the doors of intercourse, so that their real thoughts might be led across the threshold" (*S*, 282). Allowing thoughts to move "across the threshold" of a figurative space is necessary for this intimacy which no longer seems to merit the name, since in it thoughts move together across a boundary while Hester and Dimmesdale as characters are left behind. We might think of this as a moving across the threshold of a home, as a bride and groom do, but that threshold is also the spot at which Hooper appeared with his veil, and the spot at which the narrative of the *Scarlet Letter* pauses over a rose (as I discuss shortly). It is moving across a threshold, "throw[ing] open the doors of intercourse," that Hawthorne urges in concluding the conversation, "Then, all was spoken!" What is the temporality of that "Then"? Everything has been spoken, everything is about to be spoken, or everything has been spoken without actually being said, only implied? Such ambiguity leaves the absolute intimacy between Hester and Dimmesdale in a state between having occurred and about to occur: a threshold at which consummation is both memory and anticipation.

Consummation, physically speaking, has already been achieved, and visible in Pearl:

> In her was visible the tie that united them. She had been offered to the world, these seven years past, as the living hieroglyphic, in which was revealed the secret they so darkly sought to hide, – all written in this symbol, – all plainly manifest, – had there been a prophet or magician skilled to read the character of flame! And Pearl was the oneness of their being . . . how could they doubt that their earthly lives and future destinies were conjoined, when they beheld at once the material union, and the spiritual idea, in whom they met, and were to dwell immortally together? Thoughts like these – and perhaps other thoughts, which they did not care to acknowledge or define – threw an awe about the child, as she came onward. (*S*, 296)

Hawthorne doesn't describe Pearl as the result of their union, but as constituting it: "Pearl was the oneness of their being." Such "union" is alienated from Hester and Dimmesdale themselves and made as Pearl, whom they "beheld . . . together," as she "came onward." Pearl is an emblem, hovering between "material" and "spiritual" ("now like a real child, now like a child's spirit" [*S*, 294]), and constituting an intimacy between Hester and Dimmesdale outside their individual distinctness; their thoughts move out of their minds, across a threshold, and in essence become Pearl. Hester and Dimmesdale's adultery is not a sexual act between bodies and persons whose representation is made only indirectly, it is a gesture projected "Up, and away!" from the trajectory of the novel. It is made within neither the diegetic world, nor the actual world of Hawthorne and his real reader, but as an idea of space that passes from one mind to another, as when Hawthorne passes the line "Then, all was spoken!" onto the reader. Insofar as Pearl is this idea of space, it is notable that Hawthorne writes of "an awe about the child," which suggests that her parents, as both authors and readers of her being, see her effect as only something "about" her "as she came onward" – as space hanging about her progression.[36]

In the first chapter of *The Scarlet Letter*, Hawthorne relates that in front of the prison door is "a grass-plot, much overgrown with burdock, pig-weed, apple-peru, and such unsightly vegetation, which evidently found something congenial in the soil that had so early borne the black flower of civilized society, a prison" (*S*, 158). The detail with which he lists the types of weeds before the door calls to mind the excessive material detail that Fletcher catalogued as a characteristic of allegorical form, but here the weeds do not stand for anything. They do, however, prepare the way for the metaphor of "the black flower" of the prison, for there is an implicit comparison of prison to weed: natural but ugly. Rather than let weed stand for prison, Hawthorne has his weeds stand "Before this ugly edifice," both in his scene and in his telling, as an implicit metonymic image of the prison. The weeds are recalled when Hawthorne turns to metaphor: "the black flower" is, after all, "borne" out of the same "congenial . . . soil" that the weeds enjoy, as the implied metonymy is followed by the metaphor. We might be counted on to know the prison is the "black flower of civilized society," but Hawthorne adds "a prison," thereby preempting the work of interpretation (what does it mean? A prison).

Much as we saw above in passages from *The House of the Seven Gables* and *The American Notebooks*, Hawthorne proceeds through the stages of the image rather than let it signify, and how we are to follow that making is the key issue, rather than how to interpret the image. The transfer of the stages of the image to the reader is, here, suggested with the mention of how the flowers "might be imagined." Along with the weeds and the prison, there is

a wild rose-bush, covered, in this month of June, with its delicate gems, which might be imagined to offer their fragrance and fragile beauty to the prisoner as he went in, and to the condemned criminal as he came forth to his doom, in token that the deep heart of Nature could pity and be kind to him. (*S*, 158)

The passage intimates the ways that the flowers, metaphorized as gems, might be inhabited by agency, in that they "offer" themselves "to the prisoner." As an emissary or even an allegorical representation of "Nature," this rose-bush offers its flowers to the prisoner. As immediately before Hawthorne undid his "black flower," here he suggests ways that the metaphor of "gem" might be extended and added onto until it becomes allegorical, not in the sense that it means nature, but in the sense that it acts on Nature's behalf.

The rose which, in Hawthorne's words, "may serve, let us hope, to symbolize some sweet moral blossom, that may be found along the track, or to relieve the darkening close of a tale of human frailty and sorrow" (*S*, 159), is for Bercovitch "a virtuoso performance of multiple choice that is meant to preclude choice . . . for it instructs us *not* to choose between" the meanings offered.[37] The rose passage is central to Bercovitch's account of *The Scarlet Letter* as both an expression and an instrument of liberal ideology, for it sacrifices absolute liberty (it could mean anything) for the prospective unity of pluralism (it should mean a limited number of things at once, although how these conflicting meanings can be accommodated remains beyond reach as yet).[38] In contrast, I have been indicating that what is at issue in this passage is neither the meaning of the rose as a symbol – not even one whose meaning is processual, as Bercovitch observes – nor the interpellation of the reader into a state of belief in the value of multiple meanings. The passage uses the idea that the rose could be a symbol as one note in a chain of proximate connections as one thing gives way to another, as, for instance, the weeds are near the prison (in the world depicted), and near the "black flower," in the order of the passage.[39] What is most prominent in this passage is how the reader is being urged to follow along the story-less, character-less narration of processes of literality and figuration, of union, proximity, and extension.

The passage's leading on of the reader comes to a halt with the offer of a rose, approached through the statement, "This rose-bush, by a strange chance, has been kept alive in history" (*S*, 159). The statement that the setting of the novel (the imagined world in which characters could move) is the world of "history" gestures toward the claim that this is a novel set in the real world, such that a plant growing in Hester's time could be construed as growing in the historical, as opposed to fictional, world. This in itself is not remarkable, insofar as most fiction takes place within actual places, as the fictional Hester inhabits the city of Boston. But because we don't normally bother to designate inconsequential objects such as a rose as real or fictional, commenting on the rose's movement through fictional to historical world spotlights how fiction blurs the difference between those worlds.

The questions about how a rose could exist in such worlds consecutively are multiplied to include concerns about narrator and reader by the observation that follows:

Finding it so directly on the threshold of our narrative, which is now about to issue from that inauspicious portal, we could hardly do otherwise than pluck one of its flowers and present it to the reader. (*S*, 159)

When Hawthorne offers an object from the world represented in the novel to the reader, he violates the presumption of fiction, that we are, as Edgar Dryden phrases it, "participating in the lives of other people."[40] Hawthorne does so by proposing a relationship of author to reader, founded on the offering of the rose, which takes attention away from both plot and character. Leaving Hester and the narrative alike, Hawthorne suggests a contrary direction of the image of the rose from narrator to reader, as if the telling of the image process – through literal, metaphorical, metonymic states, and through the mind of the author, the narrator, and the reader – were the main subject of the passage. The offer of the rose does not disturb the presumption that we are reading about a world as real as our own just because the narrative voice speaks to the reader, for such addresses to the reader are common enough. What is unusual is the indication that the narrator could touch the rose, as if his hand could reach into the scene and pull the rose out of it, and the implicit transfer of an object from the novel's world into that of the reader by a narrator capable of touching, in addition to speaking of, objects, and of offering things to, in addition to speaking to, the reader.

Now, on a primary level the plucking and presenting is figurative, but because Hawthorne has just averred that "this" rose-bush still exists in the world of "history," the figurative expression seems to perform the action of proffering a rose to his reader, both an image of the rose and a real rose. The proffering, in between achieved delivery of a representation of a rose and promised delivery of an actual rose, and in between figurative expression for offering an idea and literal idea of presenting an object, explicitly raises the relationship between author and reader in such a way as to show it turning on series of literalizations and abstractions. The process of image-making – connecting ideas of abstractions to ideas about entities – expands to a process of connecting author to reader, a connection also of how ideas are related to things, specifically to bodies.

The plucking, in which the narrator can physically interact with the rose that is, as we have been made unusually aware, real as well as fictional, raises the image in the reader's mind of the narrator's hand, much as, in *The House of the Seven Gables*, the narrator raised the idea of his tongue when he tasted the moral of the organ-grinder's figures. We can read the rose passage by assuming that the speaker is Hawthorne himself, and thereby normalize the idea of the narrator offering an object to the reader, insofar as an actual reader and Hawthorne are both real people who, notwithstanding their temporal and spatial distance, inhabit the same human world. But to read the speaker as Hawthorne the person is to resist the most immediate effect of the sentence, which is to assert that the rhetorical position of narrator also exists within the world that is common to both fiction and the historical real (such as, Boston), that the narrator lives in the same world as Hester and the reader. In exaggerating the status of narration as the placement of ideas and images in the mind of a reader, the sentence accents how fiction supplies trains of thought to a reader through a disembodied voice (which is, arguably, even stranger than making up stories about imaginary people).

When he himself conflates narratorial and authorial voices in "The Custom-House," Hawthorne simultaneously raises the issue of how fiction provides images to the reader. Writing about his real life as inspector of customs, Hawthorne adds the fiction that he found an actual scarlet letter. The transition into fiction emerges around the literary nationalist problem of trying to find something of interest to the "fancy" in the history of the Custom-House. The interest begins to emerge with the accident of contact with the physical world, as he "chanced to lay [his] hand on a small package, carefully done up in a piece of ancient yellow parchment" (*S*, 144), and intensifies with the draw of "a certain affair of fine red cloth" (*S*, 145). Thus instead of reading through "documents" and intentionally trying to summon the imagination, Hawthorne lets himself be moved by the package's "yellow parchment" and the "fine red cloth" of the letter. Because the embroidery is "greatly frayed and defaced" and "time, and wear, and a sacrilegious moth, had reduced it to little other than a rag," to look at its material is to look at its age. This marking of age on the fabric puts the fabric on the cusp of losing all material presence, as it is "little other than a rag." Just as the scrap is about to vanish, it "assumed the shape of a letter" (*S*, 145).The overture's process from conventions and stale effort into contact with materiality is, in summation, succeeded by attention to how materiality signifies temporality, and then into the impending loss of materiality that accompanies the transformation of the rag into a letter.

The next chance encounter with the object, when he "happened to place [the letter] on [his] breast" (*S*, 146), extends the fiction of finding the "A" into the almost supernatural fiction that the letter physically burnt him:

It seemed to me, – the reader may smile, but must not doubt my word, – it seemed to me, then, that I experienced a sensation not altogether physical, yet almost so, as of burning heat; and as if the letter were not of red cloth, but red-hot iron. (*S*, 146)

The claim that we are not allowed to "doubt" isn't equivalent to an injunction to believe Hawthorne was actually burned, nor even to believe that he actually felt burned. Rather, what we "must not doubt" is that "it seemed to" Hawthorne that he had a "sensation not altogether physical, yet almost so." "Almost" and "not altogether" physical: this form of feeling is defined in terms of its proximity to but nonidentity with physical sensation, and also in terms of its partial rather than total physicality. Hawthorne's perception of heat is attended in the passage by the idea that the letter's material reality might be figuratively transformed, "as if the letter were not of red cloth, but red-hot iron." If the branding scarlet letter carries a force as of "red-hot iron," it is that figurative heat (not the literal color) that Hawthorne feels "not altogether physical[ly]." The letter's tactility becomes scorching as its conception becomes more distanced from the physical object, ever closer to an emblem. This legend of the A's genesis narrates the creation of an affective response that is linked to contemplation of an emblem moving at the juncture of the material and the meaningful. The burn made by the thing turning into an emblem is framed as the basis of our relationship to Hawthorne, who asserts "the reader may smile, but must not doubt." The point of not being allowed to doubt what is obviously a highly dubious assertion is exactly that we are now reading fiction, that form of discourse which, as Cohn points out, is immune to judgments of truth and falsehood. The weirdness of the passage is that in it Hawthorne points out that reading fiction is to take the narrator's images with something of the passive and quasi-physical excitement that Hawthorne depicts his narrative self experiencing in response to the scarlet letter.

The passage's ambiguity about the nature of the burn might appear to exemplify the literary interest Knapp defines, one of wondering over how we will choose to interpret a text. In this respect, Knapp's account would emphasize the same moment of hovering over the possible multiplicity of choices available that Bercovitch emphasizes.[41] But in contrast to either way of reading, each of which would hinge on interpretation of meaning, I have been arguing that in these relations of images, the concerns that generate emotional agitation are how the abstract and the literal are related, how the author and reader are related, and, finally, how the two relationships can be mapped onto one another. The last point may be further illustrated in the conclusion of "Young Goodman Brown," which hinges on undecidability about whether Faith is really a witch or not. But the narrator doesn't even care about this matter, as he dispassionately allows, "Be it so, if you will."

Had Goodman Brown fallen asleep in the forest, and only dreamed a wild dream of a witch-meeting?
    Be it so, if you will.[42]

To actually wonder, was it a dream or wasn't it? would be to miss the point of the story, which hinges on the not-knowing, as Brown watches and wonders for the entire rest of his life. What we get at the end of "Young Goodman Brown" is the affect of presentness which results when interpretation has been mooted (as in "The Minister's Black Veil"). If interpretation of what an author means is void, one is left with the experience of reading, and this is what Young Goodman Brown is thrust into: his fascination with eyeing his wife depends upon knowing that he'll never know what is in her heart. The story leaves an echoing sense of presence produced out of Brown's skepticism – not knowing is a condition of connection. Additionally, Hawthorne again takes a question about interpretation – what happened? – and turns it into a moment about how the author addresses the reader, as in his indifferent "Be it so, if you will."

The apparent epistemological question – how do you know if it is a dream or a memory – is also, especially as Hawthorne points up the presence of his voice as that of the storyteller, asking if it was all a dream or not, more fundamentally an ontological question about the difference between dreams and reality. And that question, within the realm of fiction, is without consequence: whether Brown really saw a witches' coven, or only dreamt it, in each case the events are really the invention of an author. In that sense, there is nothing at stake, for both dream and reality are fiction. The expostulation, "Be it so, if you will," also suggests that the author is not describing something with an existence outside his own invention, and betrays that our interest in and concern with what really happened is an interest in nothing, as if the world and characters he represents are irrelevant ciphers. The point is not so much that we can't decide what is true, or know what is true, about Brown, but that Brown, and the world and the characters of fiction are nothing in the face of this voice and the "you" whom it addresses. These gestures place a new light on moments such as the proffering of the rose or the injunction not to doubt, for if on the one hand they could be explained away as entirely diegetic phenomena, when that diegetic world is defined as immaterial, the relation of actual persons to the text is heaved into sudden urgency.

The experience of Hawthorne's emblems has been extensively analyzed in both the formalist and the deconstructive treatments of Hawthorne. In *Symbolism and American Literature*, Charles Feidelson defines symbolism as a single process of perception in which actual experience and its representation are indistinguishable: "the real world is known in symbolic form . . . to know is to symbolize."[43] New Critical accounts of the same era share with Feidelson a commitment to the concept of the symbol as a mode of turning language and real experience into a single entity, either because symbols are already extant in the world in a fundamentally mythic sense or because the artist is capable of creating symbols. But, as Feidelson and Hawthorne's New Critical readers themselves saw quite accurately, Hawthorne repeatedly missed such a benchmark of great art. Thus it was that deconstruction seemed especially appropriate to explain Hawthorne, asserting that the connection of reality to representation through symbols was not the point for Hawthorne. Jonathan Arac wrote that Hawthorne's work "*undoes* meaning, leaching traditional significance and function from old forms and techniques. His allegory is the ghost of allegory; its substance has been rendered intangible."[44] Meaning has been undone, leached out of the form; but meaning is also the substance of the form, that which was tangible. Such mournfulness also marks Evan Carton's account, in which Hawthorne wants to be a symbolist, but finds himself on the verge of a deconstructive writing only and all about language.[45] Thus deconstructive accounts show a Hawthorne who mourns for and, as Arac's account of Hawthorne as uncanny suggests, tries to resuscitate a union of the signifier with the body/signified, a union that it nevertheless declares impossible.

The answer to this bleak impasse of lost illusions is a new account of how we still can reach an immersion in language which is also an immersion in human life. In Carton's view:

experience is always allegorical, self-divided, at once intimate and abstract, a representation of itself . . . [This makes allegory] the medium of experience itself, a medium that holds word and thing, spirit and matter, self and other in mutual indebtedness but not in synthesis.[46]

For Carton, both language and experience are "self-divided, at once intimate and abstract, a representation of itself," and thus there is no substantive difference between the two, because each is constitutively a differential relationship of itself and its image (incidentally, the force of Terada's account of deconstruction as a theory of experience is evident here). Carton's claim is an example of a broader way that deconstruction shares with formalism an imperative that representation and being be reconciled. For formalism, they become the same thing; for deconstruction, both life and art turn out to be iterations of the eternal, true difference between being and representation.

Yet the more important question for Hawthorne is that posed in the moments when the narrative voice would put images of its body in the reader's mind, posed as a question about the relationship of abstraction to the material, as when the A almost burns Hawthorne. Together these concerns pursue the question of how an idea can be exciting, and how emotion can be construed through the figure of a space around the text. That relationship, in the allegorical form, can be thought of as entailing representation: how does a material thing stand for an abstraction? But this question of representation, even in Hawthorne's allegory, is subordinated to the question of how the abstract relates to the literal per se, as a relationship that, although it may be thought of as one of representation, is neither always nor necessarily such a problem. Allegory suits the problem of how the abstract and the material comport insofar as its constitutive relationship is between an abstract meaning and a literal meaning, not between a meaning and the manner of its representation.[47] One can read Christian's journey in *Pilgrim's Progress* as a travel narrative, but it also can be read as a transformation undertaken by the soul of the believer. What makes it allegory is that the literal and the abstract meanings are each complete on their own. And although these two meanings share the same signifier, this does not necessarily mean that allegory incurs meditation upon the relationship of the signifier to the signified, or even on the nature of signification per se. It allows Hawthorne to assert the relative inconsequentiality of the signifier (since it is arbitrary) and of questions of representation in general. Why focus on a way of representing either an abstract idea or a literal entity, when there is no essential – no true or telling – tie between the representation and the object (abstract or literal though it may be)? Rather, focus upon the relationship between the meanings, between those things that are represented: the literal, a world of things conceivable as evident to the senses, and a world of things that are conceivable only as abstractions.

This allegorical relationship is one of things to ideas but, insofar as thing and idea are both the meaning of a single set of images in allegory, this is not a question about representation. And in Hawthorne's hands, this reflection upon the relationship between the thing and the idea that are signified by the same words is a reflection upon the relationship between the author and the reader, each of whom seem of course to be both embodied and disembodied, insofar as author and reader are only rhetorical poses adopted and proposed or hypothesized by the text, but also presume and tend to seep or collapse into the notion of an actual person. But, as in the case of Hester and Dimmesdale, whose intimacy consists in their stepping out of their characterizations and into a space that moves forward, in Hawthorne the text evokes an affect of intimacy that depends upon, precisely, the notion of a domain of experience that is performed in the accompanying of author and reader in reading – of our taking the images from the speaker, as he suggests himself in tasting his own moral or in offering us a rose. Thus, while the transition from *The Scarlet Letter* into *The House of the Seven Gables* can seem like a letdown, I think it shows an intensification of this projected accompaniment of the author and the reader around the emblem.

IV

In chapter 2 of *The House of the Seven Gables*, "The Little Shop-Window," the action, such as it is, begins with Hepzibah Pyncheon waking to begin "what it would be mockery to term the adornment of her person" (*H*, 377). To say this is to hazard a way of describing the action – "to term [it] the adornment of her person" – but still not to do so. Hawthorne entertains the possibility of so describing things, and thus implicitly lets the things themselves begin to exist as though apart from his words for them. This disarticulation of the words and the things described is extended in Hawthorne's next sentence, which gasps, "Far from us be the indecorum of assisting, even in imagination, at a maiden lady's toilet!" (*H*, 377). This continues the approach toward and retreat from indecency seen in the previous sentence, and it also seems, with the exclamation mark, to be generating an excessive excitement over the relationship of seeing and imagining seeing a lady.

Hawthorne transforms associationist theory's manner of posing inquiries regarding normal feelings about possible scenarios (such as, what does a man feel when looking at a garden?) into a narrative mode, as when he asserts that "Individuals, whose affairs have reached an utterly desperate crisis, almost invariably keep themselves alive with hopes" and then brings in Hepzibah as an example of that principle: "Thus, all the while Hepzibah . . . had cherished an unacknowledged idea that some harlequin-trick of fortune would intervene, in her favor" (*H*, 407). But Hawthorne's Scottish mode becomes a meditation on deferred, possible action, as when he suggests that "Not with such fervor prays the torpid recluse, looking forward to the cold, sunless, stagnant calm of a day that is to be like innumerable yesterdays!" (*H*, 377). Wondering, "Will she now issue forth over the threshold of our story?" only to immediately follow, "Not yet, by many moments" (*H*, 377), narration through general possibility opens out onto a state of never-quite narrating, rather than leading to a fully specified example.

Amid this frozen state of possibility, the narrative voice annexes to itself some of the status of a character. Hawthorne writes as if the narrator were in the house, only "suspect[ing]" what his characters are doing, and then reacts to those possible actions:

We suspect Miss Hepzibah, moreover, of taking a step upward into a chair, in order to give heedful regard to her appearance, on all sides, and at full length, in the oval, dingy-framed toilet-glass, that hangs above her table. Truly! Well, indeed! Who would have thought it! (*H*, 378)

The voice is explicitly not that of an omniscient narrator, since he tells us he cannot see through the door to tell what Hepzibah is doing. Yet neither is the narrator a character, as he is never depicted as being an actual person within the world. The narrative voice's ontological peculiarity is further indicated with the sentence, "Our story must therefore await Miss Hepzibah at the threshold of her chamber." Insofar as the voice can refer to "our story," it cannot be equivalent to that story; insofar as the story has to wait for the characters, it appears to be (like the narrator) defined as if it were subject to the conditions of the world that it should define. And because Hawthorne also imagines his story as the place in which Hepzibah moves, "Will she [Hepzibah] now issue forth over the threshold of our story?" (*H*, 377), he insists too on the separability of the character from the story, for the story becomes a space in which she moves. The more that nothing happens, the more that Hawthorne won't just do his job and tell us what Hepzibah does, and the more that Hepzibah resists entering into life – his not-narrating pries apart the narrative voice, the characters, and their actions. That picking apart of person, place, story, voice and body, is posed around the familiar question of making literary interest out of American life in all its purported blandness: "We have stolen upon Miss Hepzibah Pyncheon, too irreverently, at the instant of time when the patrician lady is to be transformed into the plebeian woman" (*H*, 383).

Hepzibah has previously come with a load of paraphernalia ("antique portraits, pedigrees, coats of arms, records, and traditions"), which sounds like a trove of literary conventions even before the lost inheritance is thrown in. Now, Hawthorne uses an emphatic colloquialism to describe what she has become: "hucksteress of a cent-shop!" (*H*, 384). Hepzibah's transformation from lady to plebeian is a transformation from old-world literary type into the kind of challenging subject for American fiction we have seen discussed at length in earlier criticism:

How can we elevate our history of retribution for the sin of long ago, when, as one of our most prominent figures, we are compelled to introduce – not a young and lovely woman, nor even the stately remains of beauty, storm-shattered by affliction – but a gaunt, sallow, rusty-jointed maiden, in a long-waisted silk gown, and with the strange horror of a turban on her head! (*H*, 386)

While the voice began the chapter as if waiting outside Hepzibah's door, through posing her as a conventional literary problem Hawthorne places her at a qualitative in addition to a spatial remove. The chapter begins by keeping Hepzibah from acting, and ends by keeping her from being even a character; it moves ever further from the work of narrating the character's actions, and places ever more emphasis on the animation of the voice which is so peculiarly defined in relation to the prospect of this typified character.

Nothing much happens for most of *The House of the Seven Gables*, and this entrenches the inherently stalled nature of allegory. Through that stasis, this novel increases Hawthorne's tendencies to break off from both narrative and character, and to replace questions about how characters feel and act (questions that concern the world inside a novel) with questions about the narrator's and reader's shared attention to emblems. The immobility of *The House of the Seven Gables* has been discussed as a part of an attempt to idealize and to control the reality of a profusion of activity and uncertainty in American labor.[48] But in terms of Hepzibah's appearance as a "plebeian" American rather than an aristocrat as a central character in fiction, making "tradition" out of "change" is to construct a stable literary type that would be capable of possessing emotional interest. And we could also say that the problem of being interested in the new is, in *The House of the Seven Gables*, profitable as a way to produce extended interest or curiosity in a subject – that extension of curiosity being not a resistance to change but a way to become interested in the new by making it lasting. Another way to put this is that what looks like death, denial, and idealization to previous critics is Hawthorne's form of engagement and intimacy.

After all, the chapter about the dead Judge Pyncheon is one of the most arresting – both in the sense of stopping, pausing, and also of charging or exaggerating – in the entire novel. Judge Pyncheon will never turn into "Governor Pyncheon," for he has died before attending the banquet that would have launched his campaign. As the chapter's title misnames its character, the chapter as a whole refuses to acknowledge that it is lavishing its time over a corpse. The narrator addresses the body as if it could stir: "Pray, pray, Judge Pyncheon, look at our watch, now! What, not a glance?" (*H*, 586), but in the second paragraph of the chapter has let drop that Jaffrey's "breath you do not hear" and that he "cannot be asleep" (*H*, 582). Under the pretense of such ignorance over the Judge's death, the chapter goads him to various exploits, with addresses such as, "may the peaches be luscious in your mouth, Judge Pyncheon!" (*H*, 585). In stressing Pyncheon's "sensual" appetites and urging him to indulge them, listing the "Turtle, salmon, tautog, woodcock" and other foods to be served at the banquet

(*H*, 589), while knowing full well he cannot do so, Hawthorne returns to the taunting of characters for their inability to have physical lives present in his earlier remarks on "maiden" Hepzibah's virginity.

Taking that denial of character still further, Hawthorne stages an apocalypse of the novel's world. A shadow passes over the moon, and

There is no window! There is no face! An infinite, inscrutable blackness has annihilated sight! Where is our universe? All crumbled away from us; and we, adrift in chaos, may hearken to the gusts of homeless wind, that go sighing, and murmuring about, in quest of what was once a world! (*H*, 589)

In blotting out not only Jaffrey's face but also "our universe," Hawthorne refuses his reader the respite of grasping onto the imagined reality of the novel's world. Such vacuity demands a confrontation with the status of what it is that we are reading, for if "There is no face!" there is the statement, "There is no face!" This exclamation, like the rose offered in *The Scarlet Letter*, indicates an excitation that depends upon violation of the convention that a narrator represents and describes a diegetic world to the reader, and a resulting confusion about the nature of the prose, which appears at such moments to make assertions that there is nothing to be represented (a stepping up of the stakes of "Be it so, if you will" or "Then, all was spoken!") and yet to presume a transfer of excitement from the author, whose exclamation points signal his agitation, and encourage ours.

The assertion, "There is no face!" is made in an insouciant voice, which, having destroyed the world it depicted as if kicking over a sandcastle, then throws down the "ridiculous legend" of Pyncheon ghosts and coyly confesses, "We are tempted to make a little sport with the idea" (*H*, 591). The flirtatiousness is no accident; the idea that the author could speak to the reader without the pretense of a believable narrative world is the condition of an exposure of the narrative voice to the reader. Hawthorne waits upon a procession of ghosts as if in an allegorical train: "First comes the ancestor [old Jaffrey Pyncheon] himself" who gazes on his portrait (*H*, 591); then, "the whole tribe" (*H*, 592); finally the arrival of supposedly living characters, Judge Pyncheon and his son. In conclusion, Hawthorne reminds us outright that "The fantastic scene, just hinted at, must by no means be considered as forming an actual portion of our story" (*H*, 593). Thus the narrative voice can speak of things within its story, and of things without it. Such powers assert that voice's nonidentity with the story it tells, which allows the voice to enter inside the world it depicts at key moments. One was when the voice waited in the hall for Hepzibah; another is here, when it turns out the voice (which had, in the Hepzibah passage, figured itself as a ghost) has been waiting through an entire night along with the corpse: "We needed relief . . . from our too long and exclusive contemplation of that figure in the chair . . . Thank Heaven, the night is well-nigh past!" (*H*, 593). But as the vigil at Hepzibah's side ended in a journey out into theorizing, rather than narrating the character's action, here as well the vigil over Judge Pyncheon has let the character wither on the vine. When "The watch has at least ceased to tick; for the Judge's forgetful fingers neglected to wind it up," the voice is still inhabiting the room, but not the character, as if the narrator had replaced the character as the denizen of the fictional setting (*H*, 593–94).

The moment in which it is allowed that the voice is here but the Judge is not yields a barrage of inquiries, as the narration-as-asking moves with increasing haste:

> Will Judge Pyncheon now rise up from his chair? Will he go forth, and receive the early sunbeams on his brow? Will he begin this new day . . . with better purposes than the many that have been spent amiss? Or are all the deep-laid schemes of yesterday as stubborn in his heart, and as busy in his brain, as ever? (*H*, 594)

To whom is the narrator speaking at this point? To the reader, himself, to Jaffrey? Jaffrey finally fails to move even as he is berated by the narrative voice – "What! Thou are not stirred by this last appeal?" As the narrative voice borders on apoplexy, it hones in on the corpse as such:

> one of your common household flies . . . has smelt out Governor Pyncheon, and alights now on his forehead, now on his chin, and now, Heaven help us, is creeping over the bridge of his nose, towards the would-be chief-magistrate's wide-open eyes! Canst thou not brush the fly away? . . . Not brush away a fly! Nay, then, we give thee up. (*H*, 595)

Throughout the chapter on "Governor Pyncheon," the voice repeatedly addresses the Judge as if he were capable of responding to it. It appears as if Hawthorne were confused about the difference between characters that are invented and represented by the voice, and readers who hear and are affected by that voice. In a sense, "Governor Pyncheon" treats its character as a reader, and duly berates him for his unresponsiveness in a manner that recalls Neal's taking his reader to task for failing to shed a tear over him. The salutation of the Judge with, "may the peaches be luscious in your mouth" also recalls Hawthorne's directions that the reader "may choose" or may imagine the scarlet letter. As much as Hawthorne treats Jaffrey as if he were a character, then, he also treats the reader as if he or she were a character relying upon authorial direction. But here Hawthorne's voice has learned that Jaffrey is just a body: not that he is real and material, but that he has no agency and can take no direction. It is precisely such passages that have led critics to analyses of Hawthorne's interest in the relationship of the abstraction of the self from the body as an exposure of the desire for such an abstraction but also of its inevitable failure and the demand – either in Hawthorne, or of Hawthorne – to come back to earth and to the body. Yet I find that Hawthorne in effect perceives that what we call human connection occurs at a remove from the person, as when the narrative voice seems to stand alone in a fictional room, exposing itself to the reader.

Passages such as "There is no face!" or the offer of the plucking and proffering of a rose, or the extended address to the Judge's corpse should register as obscene insofar as they raise the concept of intimacies both emotional and physical in such a way as to deny the integrity of the persons who might be involved. They do so largely in insinuating that a narrative voice might be capable of touching objects in the world of the characters and of the reader, and of putting the idea of an object (including a body part) into the reader's mind. By extension, this would be a voice capable of touching the characters, and even of touching the readers. It would do so, though, by presenting the idea of parts of its body, which is to suggest the interest of that body not as the condition of a human being – as this narrator never turns into a character, or into Hawthorne himself – but as parts that appear capable of performing a single, signal act that is their nature. In violating the disembodiment of the narrative voice and asserting its capacity to exist both within and outside the novel, such moments hinge on a curiosity about possible actions of body parts that is quietly obscene. But that obscenity is grounded in Hawthorne's proffering of such potential actions as transgressions of the boundary between the abstract and the literal that would disintegrate character, author, and reader.

From the Judge's corpse to Phoebe's virginal bosom, to Hepzibah, who never "knew, by her own experience, what love technically means" (*H*, 378), to Clifford who "had never quaffed the cup of passionate love" (*H*, 473), Hawthorne seems most interested in this novel in how affect can be removed from both the physical object and the body of the one said to experience it. I take the disarticulation of emotion and intimacy both from characters, and from readers' identification and sympathy with those characters, to be at stake in the expulsion of the characters from the House of the Seven Gables. Leaving the novel and the house at one and the same time, Hawthorne proposes a happy consummation of his plot and in particular of the relationship between Holgrave and Phoebe. But such heterosexual connection is quite expressly performed by their banishment from the house, which in effect stands, holding the scene as an object of fascination – after all, what could be less interesting than the idea of Holgrave and Phoebe's wedding night? The repeated moments throughout his work when Hawthorne entertains the veiling of faces, from "The Minister's Black Veil" to the veiled lady in *The Blithedale Romance* to the moment when Jaffrey's face is literally blotted out, imply precisely that whereas we would think emotion would be most powerfully written in the face, where body and feeling most fully reside, Hawthorne conceives rather of not just obscuring, but vacating the face altogether, and with it the union of body and feeling it seems to not only exemplify but to incarnate as actually a way to evoke emotion. What results, when the presence of a represented world between reader and author is like the face blotted out, is a consciousness that the feeling of the tale exists in the relationship of author to reader that is indicated by the text, although each is by definition absent from that text. The tale's affect rests, that is, in the idea of a relationship only as it is projected out of the ideas conveyed by, but not the world depicted by, the text (like, in other words, Hester and Dimmesdale's flight, "Up, and away!").

Once the characters have left – finally done something and gone somewhere – the novel can claim a vector of zero in returning to its own title, "The House of the Seven Gables," but now with the addition of the exclamation mark.

And wise Uncle Venner, passing slowly from the ruinous porch, seemed to hear a strain of music, and fancied that sweet Alice Pyncheon – after witnessing these deeds, this by-gone woe, and this present happiness of her kindred mortals – had given her one farewell touch of a spirit's joy upon her harpsichord, as she floated heavenward from the House of the Seven Gables!

THE END          (H, 626–27)

In having a zero vector – however many pages it travels, it returns to where it began – the novel must be seen as again distinguishing between its own trajectory and that of its story. Its trajectory is of movement without progress: going and staying in place at once. This is to write a novel with the structure of an emblem: a repetitive assertion and extension of a single idea, one that makes a space without difference or change. But it also seems to be a reflection on the peculiar way that writing, particularly but not solely fiction, constitutes a form of linear progression, from chapter to chapter and so on and so forth, but yet we do think of books as containing a set of ideas and images which persist in the mind once reading is over. My point is that even the closest reader – one most scrupulous in ever-returning to the text – has to stop reading, stop following the process of the novel's sentences, in order to think about it, to know it or to "digest" what he or she has read, like the boy with his cookies. In that sense, the space of a novel is not just the linear extension of its sentences and of its plot, but also the reflective space in which a reader stalls and, as Hawthorne puts it, "takes" the ideas conveyed into his or her own mind. In many instances, this reflection would be reflection over what it all meant – but I have been suggesting that in Hawthorne it is reflection over what has been felt and, more particularly, how that feeling has been effected. Indeed, how feeling is effected, out of the presentation of a space constituted by two opposite directions of movement, would constitute the question, and also the solution: feeling is effected through thinking about the figures of spatiality that effect it.

In conclusion, I want to return to a set of terms discussed in the introduction. There, we saw the apparent opposition of two ways of thinking about literature: either as meaning what the author intends, in which case our experience of it is irrelevant, or as meaning our experience, which would entail either being committed to all our subjective experience and the death of meaning, or being committed to a certain intertwining of subjective experience with meaning (which latter position appeared to share a great deal with New Criticism's commitment to joining meaning to experience through metaphor). In the case of Hawthorne, I have argued that the meaning is not destroyed, or shown to be in some important and variously conceived connection to our experience or its manner of expression, but is beside the point of the experience of reading Hawthorne. And yet, I have also argued that the experience of reading Hawthorne has little truck with character, psychological motivation, and physical life. Hawthorne both figures and asks his reader to figure an experience of affect that is essentially an abstraction, a space construed out of movement that goes nowhere. Thus, Hawthorne produces some of that hovering fascination identified with literary interest, yet not as a hovering of the particular subject over its relation to the abstract, but rather as an abstract structure that is, in effect, the property of neither the text nor the reader, but projected between them.

Hawthorne's life may show the success of marriage and his and Sophia's apparently great love for one another, and his disillusionment with the Transcendental idea that even work and dirt and the body could be spiritualized. But his writing remains quite Transcendentalist in its solicitation of an experience – of essentially sexual, if intellectual, excitement – by movement through emblems, not through the narration of characters' own experiences. The writing shows an excitement that is formed in the making of emblems through extended narrations of their analysis, and I think it is in part for this reason that virgins such as Phoebe, Clifford, and Hepzibah interest him. Emblem-making is the locus of an affect which depends on disregarding the distinctions and embodiments of actual persons and proposing abstractions of movements and spaces. The houses, graves, and other substitutions for living bodies, animated by integral selves, are evidence of the structures of spatiality constructed out of the conflicting vectors of movement forward and movement through, of accompaniment and interpretation, that the prose reader must engage; it is the haunting of affect in such figures of spatiality and movement that constitutes Hawthorne's engaging vacancy.

# CHAPTER 3

# "Life is an ecstasy": Ralph Waldo Emerson and A. Bronson Alcott

"Life is an ecstasy,"[1] writes Emerson, at once celebrating life and rendering irrelevant all the specific characteristics of any actual experience. Similar neglect of the very lived experience he is calling magnificent colors the end of "The Poet":

Wherever snow falls, or water flows, or birds fly, wherever day and night meet in twilight, wherever the blue heaven is hung by clouds, or sown with stars, wherever are forms with transparent boundaries, wherever are outlets into celestial space, wherever is danger, and awe, and love, there is Beauty, plenteous as rain, shed for thee, and though thou shouldest walk the world over, thou shalt not be able to find a condition inopportune or ignoble.[2]

As these quotations indicate, experience is newly valued in Transcendentalism, but this value depends upon a certain indifference to the quality of such experience. This is part of Transcendentalism's rejection of Lockean empiricism, particularly the account of experience as the objective process in which a blank subject takes in knowledge of the concrete world.[3] Yet the reaction isn't exactly to embrace the subject, either in the sense of the all-important ego identified with Emerson's "Self-Reliance," or even in a more immanent interaction of self and world, for Transcendentalism explicitly rejected the definition of the subjective as the personal. In this regard, Christopher Newfield's objection, "Why do we call this self-reliance?" is accurate – although I would add that it isn't self-submission either.[4] As Richard Poirier observed, Emerson's "concept of 'individuality' is unrecognizable in . . . the ordinary sense of the term," for it is "achieved by the surrender of those features which define the individual as a social or psychological entity" and is, therefore, a kind of "anonymity."[5] For self in the individual sense – the sense which concerns criticism about Emersonian individualism – is not what Emerson is often speaking of.[6] As Emerson wrote: "A man may say *I*, and never refer to himself as an individual . . . The great man, even whilst he relates a private fact personal to him, is really leading us away from him to an universal experience."[7]

In *At Emerson's Tomb*, John Carlos Rowe charges that Emerson's Transcendentalism is "practically useless," and presents Emerson as the founding figure in an American "separation between literature and life [that] has made the voice of the intellectual sound distant and hollow."[8] Jay Grossman urges Americanists to resist "the persistent Emersonian pressure" of abstraction from practical reality.[9] Yet while these critics attack Emerson for his blindness to life, others have sought to revive him for his pragmatist account of how beliefs and ideals are made through the very stuff of life. Jonathan Levin, arguing for the importance of both ideals and the aesthetic to pragmatism, uses Emerson's "conception of the sacred and the ideal . . . tied to human experience in this world" as a primary example.[10] Extending Levin's pragmatist account, Gregg Crane argues that Emerson sees "higher law" as "a mutable human creation, an ongoing attempt to put moral inspiration into political dialogue and legal practice."[11] Thus, there is a critical disagreement about whether Emersonian idealism represents execrable abstraction from experience or a profound articulation of the ideal as formed through actual experience. This, in itself, is not surprising, for Emerson appears both to celebrate and to ignore life; yet each side of this disagreement over Emerson is mistaken in conceiving of experience in Emerson as subjective. And if, as I argue, experience in Emerson is already "universal" and utterly different from the grain of human experience, not only are the attacks on Emerson for ignoring the contingent mistaken, so too are the pragmatist revivals of Emerson.

The issue is not simply the concept of experience as a universal in Emerson; it is also how such universal experience is conceived in relation to language. In Emerson writing and reading count as the practice which would evoke universal experience – a life without characteristics, an experience apart from the conditions of subject and object. This entails an attempt to imagine experience as something moving through subjects and objects in a manner analogous to but not identical with the way that meaning passes through signs. Emerson's belief in the possibility of an experience so alienated from the individual, and his use of writing to produce it, resembles nationalist fiction's premise of writing to prompt the reader to an experience which is the typical product of cultural associations and ideas. And although his use of the essay, rather than fiction, marks an important distinction between Emerson and the fictions of Neal and Hawthorne, his work shares with those figures an abiding concern with emblem-making and prose analysis as a way to provoke and to shape such universal experience, rather than representing or arguing for it. I take this project to differ from a representation of such experience, an argument for it, or for a linguistic embodiment of it, terms in which it has been explored previously.[12] Emerson's writing aims to produce universal experience – experience which does not depend upon the physical senses or even upon the human subject. Not just the essays but all the world exists, in Emerson's account, in order to make the universal experience that is moving awareness possible, for such experience occurs by means of phenomena (both the phenomena of our minds and bodies and the other phenomena which make up the world as we know it).

I

With observations such as, "The senses interfere everywhere, and mix their own structure with all they report of" ("I," 942), the essay "Illlusions" can certainly look like a discourse on the kind of epistemological concerns driving pragmatist recuperations of Emerson. But in "Illusions," Emerson invokes the epistemological problem that we only know objects through our subjective apprehension, not to solve it or to work within its terms, but instead to point out that it suggests that we can see our vision. That, in other words, our experience is something we can actually perceive, precisely as it becomes intertwined with the things we are trying to know through it. "In admiring the sunset, we do not yet deduct the rounding, coordinating, pictorial powers of the eye" ("I," 942) – not yet, but Emerson is beginning to think of what it would be to see vision. His very concern with how particularity compromises objective perception – with what he calls "interference from our organization" – becomes a positive interest in seeing perception, the powers of the eye. For when a cloud blocks our view of the sun, that cloud becomes visible.

Life is sweet as nitrous oxide; and the fisherman dripping all day over a cold pond, the switchman at the railway intersection, the farmer in the field, the negro in the rice-swamp, the fop in the street, the hunter in the woods, the barrister with the jury, the belle at the ball, all ascribe a certain pleasure to their employment, which they themselves give it. ("I," 942)

At the opening of the paragraph, it sounds as if human sensations are a cloudy nuisance, keeping us from the "ecstasy" of unadulterated life, with which the senses "interfere." But in fact it is the very mistaken perception of the world, that condition of subjective human experience, which is "sweet as nitrous oxide." Even the experience of tasting food is pleasurable as an experience of our own senses, not of the sugar in itself: "Health and appetite impart the sweetness to sugar, bread, and meat" ("I," 942). Thus, gaining a form for knowing objects is itself the condition of "ecstasy," as if the knowing or registering of an object were in itself sweet. And when registering an object is declared in itself sweet, it begins to seem that what interests Emerson is apprehension itself.

The opening of "Illusions" contrasts the apprehension of objects to the apprehension of apprehension, so to speak. In a brief allegorical narrative, Emerson imagines apprehension as a light, thrown by viewers onto the objects they see. He proposes two ways in which this illuminating light interacts with objects. In the first, it simply throws them into relief, as would a harsh spotlight:

We shot Bengal lights into the vaults and groins of the sparry cathedrals, and examined all the masterpieces which the four combined engineers, water, limestone, gravitation, and time, could make in the dark. ("I," 941)

The very force with which the viewers must shoot flares to make the cave visible makes clear the firm distinction between them and the objects they see. The cave is complete in itself before the viewers intrude, as natural elements make fine "masterpieces . . . in the dark." Those natural objects may be masterpieces of some kind, but they don't mean anything. They resemble other objects, as nature "mimetic[ally] . . . mak[es] night to mimic day" ("I," 941). But mimesis here does not entail representation of one thing by another, only the mutual resemblance of two things.

In contrast to such apprehension, Emerson proposes that "the best thing which the cave had to offer was an illusion" ("I," 941).

On arriving at what is called the "Star-Chamber," our lamps were taken from us by the guide, and extinguished or put aside, and, on looking upwards, I saw or seemed to see the night heaven thick with stars glimmering more or less brightly over our heads, and even what seemed a comet flaming among them . . . Some crystal specks in the black ceiling high overhead, reflecting the light of a half-hid lamp, yielded this magnificent effect. ("I," 941–42)

While in the first instance the rocks resembled but did not represent other objects, here the rocks are representations, as they depict a starry sky. This is to say that the rocks are worth looking at not as something interesting in themselves, like the complete natural masterpiece, but as a way to see something else which is absent. In this second instance, the lights carried by the viewers, which are symbolic of their faculty of perception, change hands. Furthermore, the light itself isn't here to make it possible to see an already complete natural wonder; the illusion isn't finished until the light is supplied to reflect off the stones, making them look like stars. In other words, the viewers in this cave see a light, which had been their own means of seeing, as something which does not belong to them, but is rather displayed to them. And this display of their own, now alienated, perception, has been made possible by representation. In the passage, then, objects which are signs remove subjective experience (figured in the lamps) from the person, as lamps are "put aside," but then made visible as a represented perception. In the Star-Chamber people read a perception which is no longer their own, and they look at objects (stars) which are not actually there.

For Emerson, when we read objects in addition to seeing them – when we see objects as representations of objects that are not there – we grasp our apprehension or our experience in itself. Such experience, or apprehension, no longer inheres in the objects or the subjects present in the moment and place. This makes experience or apprehension a distinct entity unto itself, performed through persons and objects – dependent on them but not conditioned by them. As such, any particular qualities of objects are simply irrelevant: "There is no need for foolish amateurs to fetch me to admire a garden of flowers, or a sun-gilt cloud, or a waterfall, when I cannot look without seeing splendour and grace."[13] The reason Emerson sees only splendor and grace is not that he has forgotten that death, misery, and the like are ugly and painful. It's that "looking," a conscious mind seeing, is itself splendid and graceful regardless of what it sees. The point is like Kames's and Alison's view that experience is pleasurable as long as it is coherent, organized, and interconnected moment to moment – even if it is an experience of pain, sorrow, or terror.

"Illusions," a mid-career essay, illustrates Emerson's belief about experience, a belief which underlies his better and more baffling earlier writing. One might say that the earlier Emerson was writing to transform experience, while the later Emerson uses writing to illustrate the transformation of experience, except that illustration and analogy are indispensable to the universal experience which the earlier Emerson's writing would produce.[14] It is to this use of the image to provoke a transformation of experience, in which the writing serves the function of the Star-Chamber, that I turn now.

The opening sentence of "Circles" suggests an analogy of abstract idea to concrete image which is never allowed to cohere into metaphor: "The eye is the first circle; the horizon which it forms is the second; and throughout nature this primary figure is repeated without end."[15] Emerson suggests that the jump from experience to abstraction is analogous to the jump from immediate to distant experience by asking us to know what is right here (in "the eye"), then to know the limit of our experience ("the horizon"), and finally to know an abstraction (infinity). The structure of analogy is also present in the assertion that "the eye is the first circle," which compares a body part to a geometric shape. An analogy is implied, but it is not quite finished, in part because Emerson has not said that the eye is like a circle, but that it is one. Emerson draws our attention towards thinking of the eyeball as an object by invoking the shape of the circle, which is analogous to a round eyeball. But he does not quite reach the complete analogy, in part because the circle is two-dimensional, while the eyeball is three-dimensional. The analogy Emerson seems to make between the distance from body to horizon and the distance from extension to infinity is similarly jeopardized. He appears to compare an empirical to an abstract relation, but from the beginning the empirical example is somewhat abstracted: what is going on between eye and horizon is not vision but the obscure formation of the horizon by the eye. And the eye does not quite count as our experience in the body, but rather as our subjective perception of an object outside us, while the horizon can't count as an outside object, since now its only existence is in the eye – the entire thing swims before the mind.

So we try again: Emerson's image implies a subject in a landscape perceiving a distant object. This we may take as an illustration (if not the clearest) of philosophical questions about the relationship of subject and object. Emerson also proposes a scheme of circles, each one larger than the last. These may be concentric, but they may also be imagined serially, as if set next to one another, because they are numbered first and second. Therefore in one sentence Emerson suggests first a philosophical problem, then a representational image to illustrate that problem, and finally a completely schematic image of it. We could think of the two images, representational and schematic, as two ways of illustrating the philosophical problem, but we could also think of the schematic design as that which makes possible the analogy of the representational image to the philosophical problem. Having suggested these three components all at once and so raised the question of their relation to one another, the sentence begins to alter each illustration of the philosophical problem rather than clarifying their relationship. The concrete image of the eye and horizon, as we have seen, already seemed to mutate into a comment on the formation of the horizon by an eye, losing its clear specificity as something we might experience. And the schematic design itself changes: first it is just one circle, then it is the movement from one circle to a larger one, then it is that additive movement taken to infinity. In this way, despite the essay's superficial suggestion of one primary figure underlying everything, the effort to pin down a particular "primary figure" in the sentence, be it an image, a problem, or a design, is blocked as Emerson suggests more and more possible figures.

The constant mutation of the figures makes it too obscure to think of them as incidental illustrations of a philosophical point. In "Circles" the reader's attention is distracted from the philosophical questions and forced onto the figures which had seemed mere illustrations of them. Furthermore, the misfit of the schematic images of subject and object distracts us from the topic, and makes us look at its abstract form: we forget to ponder the question, and instead begin to ponder the principle (circle, series) which makes the illustration possible. It is as if in pondering a love triangle we were to forget to think about the persons involved, or the psychological dynamics, and become entranced with the pure shape of the triangle. In this sense, we are now looking at the form by which we are able to conceive of the problem. Hence the philosophical question of how a subject sees an object becomes the occasion for an attempt to see a subject's perception, by seeing the forms that thinking employs. There is an added twist: unlike the case of a triangle, here the form by which we think of the problem is not static; it is plural, changing, and growing. The ideas and images seem to move in a line, pulsing forward, as "step by step we scale this mysterious ladder" ("C," 405); but then they also seem to expand from the center, as if it is a single form which is growing, as when "around every circle another can be drawn" ("C," 403). In the end, the only commonality between the different images is that the reader has seen each one turn into the next. We see our frustrated reading occur, from one idea to the next (from number, to extension, to infinity), and from one figure to the next (from eye to circle to horizon to planet) precisely because the reading never lets us see anything else – never lets us finish or comprehend. To see one's thinking in this way is to perceive from outside subjects and objects, and, in "Circles," the apparent existence of experience unconditioned by both persons and things is as an abstract movement or gesture. For movement, "sliding," is precisely what Emerson reads in common objects. As Emerson writes, "the meaning of the very furniture, of cup and saucer, of chair and clock and tester, is manifest" not as a lesson or truth but as "shak[ing]" and "rattl[ing]" and even "danc[ing]" ("C," 408). Stripping experience and awareness of all phenomenal attributes, Emerson ends up with an abstraction rendered in the successive agitation of forms: in essence, a movement.

Conclusions such as Crane's, that "Circles" is evidence of how literature "intrud[es] on our habitual ways of thinking about and experiencing the world" and in so doing "opens new perspectives on fundamental concepts such as beauty and justice" suggest too straightforward a sense of the essay as about the need to repeatedly open up and then redefine our ideas.[16] Levin also takes this route, perceiving Emerson's account of the circle as a model of pragmatist epistemology: "The circle is Emerson's figure of figures, collapsing the eye and its horizon, a life and the world that includes it."[17] The same can even be said of Cavell's assertions in "Finding as Founding" that Emerson is suggesting a new formal category, an addition to Kant's, of "finding" – for even as an attempt to reckon with Emerson's restless motion, this is to decide it is a basic conception of finding as a way of producing knowledge, something we can grasp and use to make our experience and our knowledge possible. Notwithstanding their recognition of changeability in the circle, these accounts still read the circle as an allegorical illustration of an idea (even if that idea is of the ongoing negotiation of image and idea). They read it, if you will, as I read the cave in "Illusions" – as a picture of an idea – when this image of the circle operates in a more unsettling way. Packer was right to point out that Emerson's images never produced that New Critical fusion of idea and image, writing that "the notion that idea and image either can or should be fused into 'inseparable unity' (that God-term of formalist criticism) is exactly what Emerson denies."[18] And her point could be extended to apply to the subsequent pragmatist accounts of Emerson, in which belief is in ongoing negotiation with his images: the fusion of belief and experience is also one he denies. Nevertheless, the reason the possibility comes up at all is that his imagery, and even his language, does seem somehow to matter, to intrude; thus I turn next to the question of language in Emerson.

   Although famous for the grandiose claims it makes for poetry, in some sense "The Poet" is an essay *against* poetry: against interest in "metre" ("P," 450), and against "the fancy" ("P," 447). It dismisses the fretting labor of artistic skill as an unpleasant "cant of materialism" ("P," 449), interested in superfluous "rules and particulars" ("P," 447). Emerson compares one poet to "a fowl or a flying fish, a little way from the ground or the water," who ludicrously tries to pass off this ponderous flight as a journey into the "all-piercing, all-feeding, and ocular air of heaven" ("P," 452), intimating that claiming to tell a reader about divine apprehension is absurd. The essay is particularly critical of instantiating thought in a symbol, as Emerson criticizes the way Swedenborg "nails a symbol to one sense, which was a true sense for a moment, but soon becomes old and false" ("P," 463). Emerson also writes that "all religious error consisted in making the symbol too stark and solid" ("P," 464), returning to his point from the "Divinity School Address" that "Historical Christianity" was mistakenly attached to Jesus's "tropes."[19] In all these ways, then – for its fiddling with language, its absurd pretension to tell people of divine truth, and its unhealthy drive to embalm truth in metaphor – "The Poet" is an essay against poetry.

Of course, "The Poet" is a work that elevates and praises poetry, even if its definition of it does away with many of the standard claims of poetry's power. It begins to explain the value of poetry by establishing that all persons have a poetic relationship to the world. The ordinary "hunter" values his "horses, and dogs" for a "living power" they convey to him, not for their "superficial qualities" ("P," 453). "There is no man who does not perceive a supersensual utility in the sun, and stars, earth and water" ("P," 448), as even the most average person hears "primal warblings" ("P," 449) animating the objects around him, from the "sun, and stars" to a crude flag "on an old rag of bunting" ("P," 454), which "shall make the blood tingle under the rudest, or the most conventional exterior" ("P," 454). This universal capacity to sense the "supersensual utility" of objects means, writes Emerson, that "the people . . . are all poets and mystics!" ("P," 454). In this respect, then, poetry is a common property of "the people," and it is a way of seeing something in objects that is not identified with their objecthood.[20]

Although all men can read the divine in the world around them, "there is some obstruction, or some excess of phlegm in our constitution," which makes it impossible for most men to "utter" what they see, to "report the conversation they have had with nature" ("P," 448). Men are "mutes" who, when they try to put into words what they have perceived, find they "miswrite the poem" ("P," 448, 449). In contrast, the poet is an "utterer" who can "write down these cadences more faithfully" than the average man ("P," 450, 449). The poet, then, is the man who not only can see but can say what he has seen – who can both "receive" *and* "impart" ("P," 448). If it is already poetic for the hunter to see the power in horses, why is there any need for the poet to return? Why is there a drive to put this intimation into language? Perceiving that which transcends objecthood automatically produces an urge to transmit it – as if one were to catch a hot object and need instantly to toss it to another's hands – but most people fail to do so and instead hold on tight. For Emerson says that "wherever the life is, [the Universe] . . . bursts into appearance around it" ("P," 453), very much as though when one perceives the universe or soul in a form, such soul begs to be put in yet another form.

Although objects "arise and walk before him as exponent of his meaning" ("P," 467) this "he" is all but inhuman – devoid of all personality, he has flung open "his human doors" and allowed "the ethereal tides to roll and circulate through him," and is "caught up into the life of the Universe"

("P," 459). It then must be that the essential thing about the poet is that he shows that universal experience can be put repeatedly into objects and persons, that the process is not finite but can be reenacted over and over again. Thus, although universal experience is conveyed, like meaning, through arbitrary forms, unlike meaning it is no particular subject's intention. As sounds or marks might be said to shelter or entertain meaning (and thereby become words), phenomena in general are a medium in which universal experience is suspended. In the "instant dependence of form upon soul" ("P," 447), each "instant," in each moment, spirit re-takes form. And, as meaning does not inhere in words, universal experience moves through phenomena but does not inhere in them: Emerson contrasts "the stability of the thought" with "the accidency and fugacity of the symbol" or form that conveys the thought ("P," 456). Emerson insists that, though spirit may take form in every moment, nonetheless it is "independen[t]" ("P," 456). The essential way that the poetry Emerson describes fails to be a union or a negotiation of experience with meaning, or a transformation of experience into meaning, is that it is no subject's intention.

Emerson's own writing does not really seem to express an individual authorial intention, as several critics have contended – which would, of course, raise a concern as to whether it is writing at all.[21] A certain assault upon his own intentionality is evident in his repetitiousness, as Oscar Firkins noted of one paragraph of Emerson's: "At the end of the first sentence, the ratio of thoughts to words is one to six; at the end of the passage it is one to twenty-eight."[22] The attempt to reduce authorial intention's presence in language has struck Stanley Cavell as part of an attempt to locate truth and meaning within the structure of language. To Cavell, Emerson is engaged in a project of leading words back to their natural, inherent state, as if the conventions of speech in a community were a "home" of truth.[23] But the role language plays in Emerson is of unconditioning language, emptying it out rather than finding what really lies within it. Emerson seems to think that words can be repeated so often, and ideas reworked over and over, until they lose their odious association with one single, fossilized meaning. Thus they are worn into universality like the Bible, "played upon by the devotion of thousands of years, until every word and particle is public and tunable."[24] In this sense the essays are all essentially repetitions of one another, which "play[ ] upon" and revise similar ideas and images until they too are "public" like the Bible. Drawing ideas and signs out over time is for Emerson a means of stripping words of their fixed meaning, making them symbols not of a particular person's intention but chutes for an abstract experience to rush through.

Repetition, reworking, and the slow drift in significance they bring about deliver language into a fresh state, free from associations, akin to that it originally had. When coined, "each word was at first a stroke of genius . . . because for the moment it symbolized the world to the first speaker and to the hearer" ("P," 457). This instant connection is "poetic," writes Emerson, for here language serves as "images, or tropes," and not in its "secondary use" as a shorthand or substitute for life ("P," 457). Emerson calls this secondhand linguistic function "a cant of materialism," precisely what it was to Kames and Alison: an understanding of writing as a handicraft, the ingenious arrangement of words entailing "some study of rules and particulars, or some limited judgment of color or form, which is exercised for amusement or for show" ("P," 449, 447). Materialism assumes that the meaning of a word resides in the word itself, without any call for an injection of meaning or individual experience by the author – as if language were a set of tiles, painted with images, which the writer would simply set in a pattern. In contrast, poetry is "naming a thing because he sees it," simply attaching a form to an idea ("P," 457). So while the stripping away of associations might seem to be the very opposite of the creation of associations that earlier nationalists had discussed, in fact the idea is that language would somehow deliver an experience that was no person's subjective experience or property in a way that shares basic tenets with the nationalists.

In Emerson universal experience is, like meaning, carried by arbitrary signifiers. These signs of the spirit are at times characterized as straightforward manifestations, either as simple consequences or demonstrations of the ideal, or as literal presentations of it, but at other times they appear importantly figurative, as they indirectly work a transformation in what they seem at other times simply to depict or communicate. In those cases objects and words denote spirit in a manner more metaphorical than literal, for the ideal is altered, inflected and brought into focus through the form of the sign. Metaphor is invoked, struggled with, and yields to the reader's experience of the very forms of his cognition, from a suddenly impersonal, universal perspective. That constitutes Emerson's actual delivery of the universal, abstract experience he never quite describes or symbolizes, and constitutes his most complex extension of the nationalist literary project. For as that discourse wished to make American lives into something compelling and, in a somewhat more limited way, universal through a combination of realism and imagination, such an aspiration is also held by the Transcendentalist: to make fantastic images serve as literal accounts or, more strongly, as deliveries of truth. (One might think of this as like Hawthorne's wish to provide his reader not just with an image of a rose, or the meaning 'rose,' but with a rose.) Emerson's work is another instance of how American prose works to produce impersonal, abstract experience through extended trains of images. Whether it is possible or not, this is the ambition of Emerson's essays. Emerson sometimes tries to represent or illustrate such universal experience, but in the essays that make him famous, he more strikingly writes as if his writing could make experience universal, independent of the qualities of persons, things, and even words.

Because the essays seek to produce universal experience, how we actually do experience them might seem to be a particular issue in criticism. Packer observes that Emerson's sentences are "charged terminals that the reader must take the risk of connecting; the latter's reward is a certain electric tingle."[25] Schirmeister asserts "Emersonian reading cannot get distance on itself. It occurs precisely as a kind of auto-enactment of the subject," and Levin explains, "While I hardly plan to suspend my own professional authority in what follows, I hope at least to recover the profound and liberating sense of uncertainty located . . . at the leading edge of a transitional margin" in Emerson's prose and others in the pragmatic tradition.[26] To become susceptible to Emerson's writing would certainly be, as Levin notes, a step outside the bounds of professional authority; for this reason Schirmeister insists on "a detour through another discourse external to it."[27] A gleeful instance of becoming susceptible to Emerson is Cavell's account of himself as the child of Emerson's hysterical male pregnancy: "Found for philosophy, I clasp my hands in infantine joy."[28] The abandonment of professionalism that Emerson solicits is, in these quotations, one of admitting one's personal susceptibility to Emerson – to admit feeling the pull of his rhetoric, of being moved by his prose. Yet being personally moved by Emerson, and being drawn into a sense of filial connection to Emerson, are not entirely accurate to that universal experience toward which Emerson's prose labors. To read Emerson's essays is to find identity – not just one's professional identity, but one's very subjectivity, and one's sense of oneself as part of a tradition – pulled out from under our feet. In this sense, responses to Emerson of hysterical identification and liberated self-empowerment, are reactions against – refusals of – his relentless commitment to the nonessential quality of subjectivity and human tradition.

I noted, in opening this chapter, that a shared misunderstanding of experience as it works in Emerson is particularly evident in critical disputes over Emerson, which are often not about Emerson, but about over who owns Emerson and over what Emerson's place in American literature and, by extension, in current American culture should be. For Emerson is a paradigmatic founding figure in American literature, and as such he appears to stand as an incarnation of American national identity. That is what Cornel West means when he describes Emerson as a "freedom fighter" – someone for whom democracy is an identity, not a set of beliefs (this is underscored by West's commitment to "being a democrat," an identity linked to how you feel "in your skin").[29] West's sense that what is at stake in talking about Emerson is what it is to *be* an American is rampant in Emerson criticism; that is why even though Rowe wants Americans to get over Emerson for good in *At Emerson's Tomb*, he does so by figuring Emerson as a dead parent rather than a mistaken author. And it is also why Grossman thinks that even though Emerson is deeply mistaken, even ethically reprehensible, we need to reassert Emerson's place in a "genealogical" literary history in which what matters is what Emerson "inherited from his father[ ]" in terms of beliefs, and what Emerson "bequeaths to . . . American literary history" – why, even, he thinks it is necessary to *Reconstitut[e] the American Renaissance*.[30] Whether they want to revive or to bury Emerson, both sides of this critical debate agree that Emerson matters because he is part of an American tradition, and we either have to strive somehow to wrest ourselves away from his inheritance or reclaim it anew. Why else should George Kateb think it matters for his own account of the theory of democratic individualism that Emerson's individualism appears to depend on God, unless democratic individualism is tied in some deep way to Emerson?[31]

As Charles Mitchell observes, "the contemporary debate over the meaning of individualism in America is, in effect, a debate over the meaning of Emerson."[32] This appears to say that if we knew what Emerson meant – if we could get that hermeneutic question right – we would know what American individualism is. (This actually seems to me to be Newfield's point: once he has construed Emerson's liberalism as authoritarianism, he suspects this means that liberalism is authoritarianism too.) But Mitchell's point is, somewhat differently, that claims about what Emerson meant are really claims about what account of American individualism you want to hold. For in fact, Emerson appears to provide a hermeneutic problem that cannot be solved: "the meaning of Emerson's individualism has always been contested."[33] Rather than argue for one interpretation of Emerson over another, in these accounts of American individualism as an identity, what Emerson stands for is more important than whatever inscrutable notion Emerson meant; Crane, for example, lays claim to Emerson "with a bit of judicious tinkering."[34] Such debates are not about what Emerson meant (as he seems to mean anything, everything, and nothing) but about Emerson as father of a genealogy of Americanness: about how, in essence, to experience and identify with Emerson. Thus Mitchell explores Emerson by exploring how later authors "appropriated" him.

This is what we see in Newfield's writing of an entire book about *The Emerson Effect*: the experience of reading Emerson, and the effect of Emerson on succeeding generations of Americans and readers. Newfield's concern is, in large part, the feeling Emerson produces, "the political sensibility that allows its loss of both private autonomy and public sovereignty to *feel OK*."[35] This focus on the experience of Emerson is pointedly opposed to a focus on what Emerson meant: "*without necessarily intending to* he contributed to a perennial American 'democracy and free-markets' nationalism that harbors a seemingly unlimited faith in freedom through hierarchy."[36] The attack on Emerson is an attack not on what Emerson's writings mean, nor even on what Emerson meant to do; it is on the "effect" of Emerson, the feelings that he has produced in his readers. And because Newfield is so committed to the idea that, regardless of his intentions, Emerson is to be identified with the effect he has had, he will not say that Emerson was wrong and so are those who agree with him, and that we should reject his account of liberalism, or even that we should reject liberalism. Instead, even Newfield – a great Emerson hater – proposes we continue to experience Emerson, but that we extend his effect in a different direction. Thus he locates "radical democracy" among the weeds of Emerson's authoritarian liberalism, and hopes to develop this alternative Emerson.[37] Newfield concludes with another way to take Emerson up, to keep him as our own, as we "overcom[e] his submissive individualism" in order "to follow his advice."[38]

The struggles over the Emersonian inheritance – and those who argue for and against Emerson are essentially arguing about how to experience and to identify with Emerson – are about how to see him as part of an American tradition and identity. That is why these critics keep locating whatever beliefs they hold in Emerson and why somehow it matters for those beliefs about American literature and liberalism that Emerson be assimilable to them, thought of as their founding father. But the commitment to experience as identity does not match up with the universal experience with which Emerson is most concerned. Emerson is not trying to meld meaning or belief with experience, or meaning with language, in the various ways that poststructuralist and antifoundationalist critics have suggested, and that have led them to *need* the authority of Emersonianism to underwrite accounts of democracy and selfhood for which they cannot just argue. Nevertheless, experience is clearly involved in Emerson's writing: it's just that the way it is involved is misunderstood. I have argued that Emerson's practice is built on the premise that universal experience is passed through words, things, and persons in a manner analogous to the way meaning moves through words – and yet such experience is no one's intention or meaning.

As is evident in "The American Scholar," Emerson's version of literary nationalism is ultimately not about joining subjective experience into overarching traditions. Reprising the wish to make types out of American subject matter, Emerson blasts, "I ask not for the great, the remote, the romantic; what is doing in Italy or Arabia; what is Greek art, or Provençal minstrelsy." He sounds the literary merit of exploring and poetizing "the philosophy of the street, the meaning of household life," and disavows the European preference for "the sublime and the beautiful."[39] Like the ranks of other speakers and writers on American intellectual life, Emerson wants American subjects to be made interesting by revealing a universal relevance in them, and he hopes to see "the ultimate reason in these matters" of American daily life. In that spirit, he notes that the American experience must not be germane to some "single person," but must speak of that single person only as "inspired by the Divine Soul which also inspires all men" ("AS," 70–71).

The ordinary and the personal must open out onto the universal and the timeless, by means of loud, unstilted announcements of universality and strings of piecemeal objects:

What would we really know the meaning of? The meal in the firkin; the milk in the pan; the ballad in the street; the news of the boat; the glance of the eye; the form and the gait of the body; – show me the ultimate reason of these matters; show me the sublime presence of the highest spiritual cause lurking, as it always does lurk, in these suburbs and extremities of nature; let me see every trifle bristling with the polarity that ranges it instantly on an eternal law; and the shop, the plough, and the leger, referred to the like cause by which light undulates and poets sing; – and the world lies no longer a dull miscellany and lumber-room, but has form and order; there is no trifle; there is no puzzle; but one design unites and animates the farthest pinnacle and the lowest trench. ("AS," 69)

This is a paragraph which in saying that ordinary life and average people matter actually loses sight of them. The ordinary is eclipsed because it is whipped up into the abstraction of "the farthest pinnacle and the lowest trench." The passage refuses to say anything (even anything invented) about what "the meal in the firkin" looks or smells like, how the "milk in the pan" tastes; it places no person in "the shop," or at "the plough." Having no scene in which these tokens of American life reside, it also has no plot or story around them.[40] Emerson would suggest the universal import of local subjects by stepping back from them and asserting that one spirit ranges through each terse and keen example.

In "The Poet," Emerson's nationalism consists in the premise that any shape, including ones identified with America, can hold "Being" or "power": "Our logrolling, our stumps and their politics, our fisheries, our Negroes, and Indians, our boasts, and our repudiations, the wrath of rogues, and the pusillanimity of honest men, the northern trade, the southern planting, the western clearing, Oregon, and Texas" are symbols like water, the sun, or the stars ("P," 465). In a magnificent turn on the lament of American dullness, for Emerson it is that very dullness that proves that any form whatsoever can carry divinity, and that finally the very taking form of spirit is what really counts as beauty. To be "tipsy with water," to see no "condition inopportune or ignoble" is to see anything – a pine tree, a Quaker, a drunk or a businessman as "divinity transmuted," and, therefore, as magnificent ("P," 461, 468, 447). Thus Emerson's entire process of making "logrolling" and the like into compelling types of the divine involves taking everything local, personal – and American – out of them. He writes that "the poorest experience is rich enough for all the purposes of expressing thought" ("P," 455), and seems to believe even more strongly that the experience should be as blanched and dried as possible. "The meaner the type by which a law is expressed, the more pungent it is . . . just as we choose the smallest box, or case, in which any needful utensil can be carried" ("P," 454–55). Emerson notes that "bare lists of words are found suggestive," and indeed he takes American images and strips them down into "bare lists": "the northern trade, the southern planting, the western clearing, Oregon, and Texas" ("P," 465).

Emerson's claim – which I take as the essence of Transcendentalism – that life is ecstasy is driven by the belief that just looking at it can transform it. As Emerson puts it in "The American Scholar," the power to "alter matter" is superseded by and absorbed into the power to "alter my state of mind": one looks at nature to see the soul, but the soul can change nature. Thus, "the ancient precept, 'Know thyself,' and the modern precept, 'Study nature,' become at last one maxim" ("AS," 65, 56). For all that one reaches out to the external world as a key to oneself, because nature's "laws are the laws of his own mind" ("AS," 56), it is also true that such reaching out, such knowing of the world, utterly transforms and remakes that world. A person who studies nature "vanquishe[s]" and "plant[s]" the "wilderness" ("AS," 60), until, finally, "the firmament flows before him and takes his signet and form" ("AS," 65). Such an aggressive approach to the world would wrench out of, or else force into, it a significance above and beyond the shape of a leaf or the expression on a face, insisting on an uncompromised brilliance that might be either revealed in or expressed through a Massachusetts backwater.[41]

The glance that can change the world brings back, for us (not for Emerson), Robert Smithson's commitment to the idea that art could be made with a look. As Michaels wrote, "The glance leaves the shape of the ground – its topography – untouched but utterly alters its ontology; it is the difference between the infinite and a map of the infinite, between a thing and a thing that represents."[42] Emerson's glance would work like Smithson's, insofar as it too takes the object and turns it into something other than an object of the subject's experience, into something more like a meaning. That is why Jehlen sees Emerson as fusing the intention a writer would express with the thing that the land just is. For Emerson, writes Jehlen, "nature functions linguistically quite directly, not needing, except as a recorder, the intermediation of man."[43] In Jehlen's analysis, what Emerson does is turn what one person means into the same thing as what the land (object) is. This is what makes Emerson central to the identity of America as nation which, in Jehlen's account, has as its signal quality the "incarnation" of belief in liberalism as the identity of the literal ground of the country. So it makes total sense, for her, that Emerson should think that nature is language, and that all a person speaking or writing does is repeat – "record" – what nature says or, in other words, is.[44] But what happens in Emerson's investigation of how words are like things is different from the fusion that Jehlen imagines, *and* from the diametrical opposition in Michaels's theory, where a thing has to be turned into a representation, experience replaced by meaning. What Emerson envisions is the proposition that experience could be something that did not inhere in the condition of subject and object. In that, it would certainly be *like* meaning, but yet it would still not *be* meaning, insofar as it is not the intention of any subject. Still less would it be the substance of an American experience to be inherited.

II

Emerson has little relation to the conceptions of identity, experience, and tradition that he has frequently been folded into. The concerns about what a tradition is (about, in particular, how ideas pass from one person to another), which structure the attempts both to throw off and to claim Emerson's inheritance, are misunderstandings of how these concerns about intellectual ownership function not only for Emerson but also in the teaching and conversation of Bronson Alcott, and, indeed, in the relation of Emerson to Alcott as fellow Transcendentalists. Alcott's writings were not

successful, but his primary focus was on works of direct engagement with
other people, which he called "humane work" or "Human Culture," in the
sense of human cultivation. He saw his work as "the art of moulding man –
of planting the new Eden – of founding the new institutions."[45] The difference between Emerson's media and Alcott's was a source of some friction
between the two. In his journal, Emerson wrote that "Alcott want[ed] a historical record of [their] conversations," but that he himself preferred writing
which "never names, or gives you the gloom of a recent date or relation, but
hangs there in the heaven of letters, unrelated, untimed, a joy & a sign, an
autumnal star."[46] Alcott was suspicious in turn that Emerson's commitment
to writing was an excessive attachment to the "historical"; in "Days from a
Diary," Alcott had specifically advocated "CONVERSATION" as a practice
of making "souls . . . meet" and contended that while Emerson's essays were
"truly noble," ultimately "all expression, save action, is falsehood fabling
in the ciphers of truth."[47] The difference between Alcott's commitment to
conversations and Emerson's commitment to essays is somewhat petty –
each is concerned that the other's practice is too focused on the contingency
of subjective experience and historical ground. But, as Emerson's writing
engaged in a passing through images that would yield universal experience,
Alcott's conversations focused upon reading texts and producing series of
images, with, again, a commitment to the universal experience this would
yield, rather than to the meaning of the images or to their symbolic aptness.

One of Alcott's most successful projects was the Temple School, located
in downtown Boston, which he opened in 1834. Alcott saw the job of the
teacher to be assisting the child in realizing the knowledge, particularly
spiritual knowledge, that was innate in the mind. To bring out this inborn
wisdom, Alcott would read stories and inquire about "the feelings which
had been called forth," have the students write journals, and engage them
in moral discussion.[48] Such pedagogical innovations, spelled out in *Record
of a School*, Elizabeth Peabody's essays on the school's principles and her
transcripts of discussions at the school, were received fairly well. But when
Peabody's transcripts of Alcott's *Conversations with Children on the Gospels*
were published in 1836, a scandal erupted over the sexual frankness of the
discussions, in which Alcott invited children to speculate about conception
and childbirth. In the face of public scandal, many students withdrew and
the school closed soon thereafter.[49]

The *Conversations* is a series of discussions, each beginning with a reading
from the gospel and proceeding with a discussion of that reading. From
class to class, the selected gospel passages move sequentially through Jesus's
conception, infancy, and youth. Insofar as Jesus's life is studied as a model

for the students' own development, this is fairly traditional Bible study: Jesus is an object of both worship and emulation.

MR. ALCOTT. Such of you as think that Jesus had something within him which
   you have not in you, may rise.
   *(Ellen and Corinna rose.)*
   Do the rest think you have all the faculties that he had?
   *(They assented.)*                                                   (*C,* 1: 200)

Here, Jesus is beside the point: he is an occasion to develop the manifestation of spirit, not a unique union of the two. And the students are also beside the point. Here, they are barely allowed to speak; but throughout the conversations, more subtly, the development of children into perfect beings is forged by an examination of the self, which aims at eradicating all that is particular to that self.[50]

One becomes perfect, it appears in the *Conversations,* through the medium of emblems. Although Jesus is the central emblem being investigated in the course, specific classes entertain a wide variety of other emblems. And, much as there is no qualitative difference between Jesus and other people, and between one person and another, for Alcott there is no serious difference between using one emblem or another.

MR. ALCOTT. Suppose you had the thought of innocence in your mind, and you
   wanted other people to think of it with pleasure, how could you represent all
   you felt about it in one word of an emblematic character?
ANDREW. I could think of a spring of fresh water.
ANOTHER. I should say a little lamb.                                    (*C,* 1: 179)

Both "fresh water" and "a little lamb" are acceptable emblems of "innocence." There is a striking fluidity in the association of spiritual idea with concrete emblem. Granted, objections are voiced: when Augustine avers that "Blue is an emblem of faith" Alcott challenges the child: "Is not green like faith?" Nonetheless, when Augustine returns, "No; green is more like fear" (*C,* 1: 76), that is the end of the matter. There is a slight suspicion that it is important that one's emblems be right in an objective sense, but a much stronger conviction of the intuitive rightness of the emblem based on the individual's internal barometer. If a child is certain that blue is the right color for faith, that vision will not be argued away from him. As a result, the book contains many emblems, each one proper to the student in the moment, and no final lexicon of the spirit. This is even true at the theoretical level. Discussing a moment when the Bible uses an emblem of a "shoe-latchet," Alcott asks, "What is that mode of expression called?" He receives the following responses:

EDWARD J. A parable.
ELLEN. An allegory.
FRANKLIN. An emblem.
LUCIA. A figurative expression.
CHARLES. Stopping to unloose a shoe-latchet expresses feeling lowly in com-
parison, unworthy, humble.                                             (*C*, I: 175)

Just as there is no final adjudication about which images are the correct
ones, there is no final adjudication about what term is the correct one for
these images: "parable," "allegory," "emblem," "figurative expression," or
Charles's description of what the image means instead of what it is. The
multiplicity of emblems – the offering of a series of answers to questions
like, "What is a net an emblem of?" (*C*, II: 126) – is an end in itself.

The commitment to seriality rather than to individual accuracy is also
evident when Alcott asks for pictures of a biblical passage he has read aloud.
This task, of offering a picture of the reading, is effectively another version of
the offering of emblems: the pictures are outward signs of the meaning of the
text. In a typical class, after his reading Alcott poses the question, "Now what
came into your minds while I was reading?" and these are the responses:

JOSIAH. The deserts seemed to me a great space covered with sand, like that in
the hour-glass. The sun was shining on it, and making it sparkle. There were
no trees. John was there alone.
EDWARD J. I thought the deserts meant woods, with paths here and there.
LUCY. I thought of a space covered with grass and some wild flowers, and John
walking about.
CHARLES. I thought of a prairie.
ALEXANDER. I thought of a rocky country.
AUGUSTINE. I thought of a few trees scattered over the country, with bees in the
trunks.
GEORGE K. I thought of a place without houses, excepting John's; and flowers,
trees, and bee-hives.
MR. ALCOTT. I should like to hear all your pictures, but . . . I have not time.
(*C*, I: 61–62)

Alcott is not concerned about whether the passage actually describes a
"prairie," "woods" or "a rocky country," or whether there are "bee-hives"
or "wild flowers" in the desert. What he *does* care about is just the speaking
and the hearing of the pictures.

To say that the objective correctness of the individual image (or, the
accuracy of the connection between the image and the idea) is not important
is not to imply that the giving of images is arbitrary. Their validity is
based on the way that they are developed and imagined. Alcott is adamant

that at certain points the students cross the line over into promiscuous invention. Edward knows to confess, after describing angels with "feathers and diamonds on their heads," that he "made up some of this while I was telling it. I did not think it all while you were reading" (*C*, I: 78). The pictures may be imaginary, but they must be directly in reaction to the idea or to the text: they are an intuitive response, not an invention. So Alcott "urge[s the students] seriously and honestly to tell their real image and not invent one" (*C*, II: 135).

One student, Josiah, draws sharp censure from Alcott for "fancies . . . to which there is no end" (*C*, I: 96), among them that during the nativity Jesus had "a star" in the middle of his forehead (*C*, I: 95) and that "God sent down a box, and the angels opened it, and a sweet perfume of incense came out" (*C*, I: 96). Josiah's mistake is even more than that his images are invented. It is that he is excessively interested in the details of his images, of the box with its perfume or the image of "a bow and arrow which came down out of heaven, without any body to hold them, and the bow shot the arrow out of itself, and the arrow flew above the clouds" (*C*, I: 96). Josiah does try to return to the spiritual: the bow and arrow, he avers, "is a sign of the spirit of Jesus, which goes higher than all things," but Alcott exclaims, "That is enough, Josiah" because it is clear that Josiah's real interest here is in the intricacy and originality of his own image (*C*, I: 96). The teacher "check[s] Josiah" because, as Charles notes, Josiah "was going into outward things so much" (*C*, I: 245, n. 117). Correct imagining is the standard of judging the emblems: based on intuition rather than invention, and never losing sight of the meaning and straying into outward details.

Correct imagining is, in essence, a process of producing an image which represents a single, abstract idea:

MR. ALCOTT. I wish you would all of you give me an emblem of Creation.
HERBERT. A little child beginning to speak.
MARTHA. A little child.
SAMUEL R. A bud beginning to open.
GEORGE B. A plant coming out of the ground.
ELLEN. A little child beginning to exist. *Mr. Alcott spoke of Incarnation generally.*
(*C*, I: 199)

Alcott begins with an abstract idea, "Creation," and then asks the students to produce external images which correspond to it. He does this over and over in his conversations, asking for "an emblem of love," "an emblem of anger," and so on (*C*, II: 297). Imagining must never be carried too far afield because it is fundamentally about the connection of idea to image. But one doesn't want to say that this is allegory, for no action occurs in the outward images, no characters or plots develop; and, no theory is ever articulated through them. Consider the following exchange:

MR. ALCOTT. What does an acorn prophesy, or intimate?
ALL. An oak.
MR. ALCOTT. What does a child suggest?
SEVERAL. A man.
MR. ALCOTT. What does a caterpillar foretell?
ALL. A butterfly.                                                    (*C*, 1: 33)

The toggling between image and abstraction (Alcott will ask both what images signify and how ideas might be represented in images – moving from image to idea and back again) suggests that the meeting point of the image and the idea is the crux of value. Development of the image or the argument is not important; the instantaneous contact of idea and image is paramount.

As a result – because time does go forward – the *Conversations* reveal series of such instants, series of such contacts between idea and image, principle and picture. In this sense, the *Conversations* depend on temporality per se, if not on temporal specificity: on the form of connection and extension of time. The forward movement of seriality is implicit in the way that Alcott in the above passage imagines emblems to be the fulfillment of a spiritual idea, not simply the representation of one: hence his stress on the notion of "prophesy, or intimate" and "foretell." But it is also foretold in the teacher's quick movement from question to question: "What does an acorn . . . what does a child . . . what does a caterpillar foretell?" There's a rhythmic movement from topic to topic, forward through the conversation. Such interest in temporal movement is apparent in the way Alcott will sometimes let the students offer series of emblems, one after the other: they answer, "A little child beginning to speak . . . A little child . . . A bud beginning to open . . . A plant coming out of the ground . . . A little child beginning to exist." Such a string of images, one after another, does not elaborate upon the notion of "creation" in any allegorical, let alone metaphorical, sense. Here the *Conversations* parade partially or momentarily intuited images of some idea, each one a spontaneous reaction. Temporal extension works in tandem with spiritual animation, running through individuals like a ghost's hands on a harp.

Packer writes that the *Conversations* sound like the work of "a particularly relentless dramatist of the absurd," as the students – "all empiricists" – are

egged on by Alcott to abstract spiritual verities they "stubbornly resist."[51]
What is particularly true about that characterization is that the transition
between the emblem or the picture and the abstract spiritual reflection
is obscure in most of the conversations. The form of teacher asking and
student answering can sometimes seem in this school to be stripped entirely
of content, with only a rule for the derivation of and attachment to answers,
not any standard for judging their truth or meaning. However, I see this
less as a matter of Alcott's manipulative idealism clashing with students'
empiricism than of a necessary occlusion in Alcott's use of the emblem to
connect the concrete to the abstract. He summons emblems at the opening
of each conversation, but then jumps to abstraction rather than leads to it,
as he almost never discusses the particulars of any of the images the students
produce for him.

MR. ALCOTT. Which has most meaning, a bud or a flower?
SEVERAL. A flower.
SUSAN. A bud, because it is going to be a flower, and makes you think of it.
EDWARD J. Perhaps the bud will be picked.
MR. ALCOTT. Accidents are always excepted. (*He then asked like questions about
    many things . . . He remarked that their answers showed which minds were
    historical and which were analytic . . .*)                          (*C*, 1: 13)

What is being discussed is the idea of a bud; the historical contingency or
"accident" is irrelevant, excised from the discussion. What matters, then, is
not the thinking, which is "historical" (what happened to a specific flower?)
but "analytic" (what does the idea of a bud signify?). Such signification,
moreover, entails an element of the prophetic: to mean something is also
to forerun it, as the bud means and predates the flower. In conversation
after conversation, Alcott's "like questions about many things" drive at
the elaboration of an analytic account of isolated images. These images
represent abstractions, but also are themselves abstract emblems ("a bud"
rather than "that pink rosebud") that are unsusceptible to plucking or
accident. Consequently, the images are foundational and yet unexamined,
as Alcott clearly finds these images to be an indispensable starting point even
though he never seems to really build on them. Phenomena are necessary
for the approach to the ideal, but yet nothing about them matters except
that they are directly given by the spirit: not invented by the fancy, and not
taken to have any inherent value.

The conversations themselves are driven by Alcott in such a way that
Edward's suggestion of the historical accident of picking the bud is
"excepted." Also excepted is any description of an emblem which, like

Josiah's image of the "bow and arrow," which I discussed above, extends too much into the visible and material world.

M R.   A L C O T T.   Those who think there is a place called hell, where there is fire like
    that in the grate, hold up your hands.
    (*Not one.*)
  Now those who think this word . . . is the sign of a state of mind, signify it.
    (*All rose.*)
J O S I A H.   Hell is a valley, I think, where they breathe evil spirits and writhe.
M R.   A L C O T T.   An outward valley, or – ?                                        (*C*, 1: 82)

And just as hell can be conceived *through* the idea of "an outward valley," but not conceived of *as* such a valley, Alcott teaches that the sky can be an emblem of heaven, but it cannot be imagined as heaven. Charles complains to Alcott, "I wish you would let me say that God is up in the sky; for I like to think of God up there, though I know he is my thought and inspires it." But Alcott resists: "there is danger of mistaking the forms for the thoughts themselves." Alcott seems unwilling to acknowledge (if not simply unable to grasp) the distinction between metaphoric and literal expression: to say hell is a valley has to be to literally say it. Charles maintains a difference between metaphoric identity ("hell is a valley" as a metaphoric expression) and literal identity ("An outward valley"). But to Alcott even to say metaphorically that "hell is a valley" is to have made a bond of the idea and the literal, outward form of the idea. It is not that he doesn't see the difference between metaphor and literality, then, but that the way that metaphor unites the idea of hell with the idea of the place of a valley is, already, to have put too much stress on the "outward." Figurative images are just as much of the world as are literal images or even things themselves.

Alcott shares the contradictory investment in and evident neglect of life that Emerson betrayed in announcing that "life is an ecstasy." For example, he is capable of speaking of "this exile in Flesh"[52] as well as of "a sense in which the body may be called God" (*C*, 1: 237). The body is both irrelevant, other to spirit, and yet also somehow identical to it, in "a sense" a part of its being. This is perhaps most clear in the aspect of the *Conversations* that caused a scandal, Alcott's discussions about "birth of spirit in the flesh" (*C*, 1: 66). Alcott envisions this as the spontaneous material expression of the soul. He asks, "What does love make?" and answers, "Does it not make something to love?" (*C*, 1: 57). The directive, "these sacred events . . . ought never to be thought of except with reverence" (*C*, 1: 63) may have seemed a meager caveat at the time, but Alcott really does seem interested in sexual reproduction as spiritual process. As he puts it, "Faith brings out what is planted in the spirit into the external world" (*C*, 1: 57), framing the very action of spirit as that of making itself a form. To give a picture of "Creation" or "innocence" would be precisely the same kind of making, in Alcott's mind, as conceiving a child. For Alcott, the body is a form, and materiality is the domain of forms. This domain of forms is one Alcott is both intimately engaged in, as necessary to the bringing out of spirit, and utterly resistant to seeing as an end in itself, or in any way bondable to spirit.

In discussing "the coming of a spirit," he asks the children, "What is meant by 'delivered'?" (*C*, 1: 63). None of them knows, or at least none of them is willing to say if they do. William thinks it means that the mother gave the child to its father, some that it means God gave the child to her, and Charles hopes that when the child "was fairly born she was delivered from the anxiety of the thought" (*C*, 1: 63). Rather than explain it to them, Alcott asserts that "the physiological facts, sometimes referred to, are only a sign of the spiritual birth" (*C*, 1: 63) – and so the actual event remains unseen. Going on, Alcott asks the students to give "emblems of birth," and they answer "rain," or "the rising light of the sun" (*C*, 1: 63). Yet he brusquely replies, "There is no adequate sign of birth in the outward world, except the physiological facts that attend it, with which you are not acquainted" (*C*, 1: 64). Spiritual birth is instantiated in a material form which is invisible and unspoken: "God draws a veil over these sacred events" (*C*, 1: 63). This might seem to be merely the demand of nineteenth-century propriety, but Alcott had already violated those demands. It seems more seriously due to his insistence on the analysis of the abstract idea of an object, not on its accidental specifics. His pedagogy consists in asking for pictures and emblems with which no one is to become fully "acquainted," even that essential coming into being of the body which most emblematizes his entire practice, giving a form to a spiritual idea. Alcott's apparent tone deafness to his language about making love – his inability to hear that as dirty – actually makes sense as something more than just naïveté. Sex mattered to him because of the life that emerged from it – because really of *conception* as the taking of form, and pleasure and desire between bodies and between persons were as irrelevant to the issue as was Charles's image of the sky or the feathers Josiah wanted to put on the heads of angels in his own images. The fact that Fruitlands, the utopian community that Alcott led with Charles Lane, disintegrated in part because Lane insisted on celibacy, and Alcott refused it, then seems to have little to do with Alcott's desire somehow getting in the way of what was otherwise a rigorous asceticism of cold baths and vegetarianism.[53] Sexuality, far from being the sign of materiality and physicality, was to Alcott the greatest case of how human experience, embodied life, was evidently an ongoing transition from one form to another, rather than the possession of an inviolable self. And while on the one hand his account of sex as reproduction seems strictly religious and heterosexual, on the other hand insofar as his understanding of this is so abstract that a bud, a shoe-latchet, or a conversation can also count as spirit taking shape – in which conceiving a child is not only like, it is the same as, conceiving an idea or an image – it is as if everything is this sexual making-shape. In this Alcott is quite a bit like Hawthorne, for in each sexuality is thought of as a making of images apart from the body and the person, with the result not of its repression but of its being everywhere in abundance.

Alcott's real understanding of how life is perfect is, then, not that it is devoid of suffering, sickness, and death; it is that it is always making instantaneous connection to the spirit, no matter what form it takes. In Alcott's understanding, all of life – *any* external fact whatsoever – works as a flash-point emblem of the spirit. He lectures his students, "Matter is like a great sea; and the moving of matter – its universal changes – is produced by a living Spirit which pervades it" (*C*, II: 27). Jesus, then, is simply a very good example of what the entire world and every being in it is: a piece of "matter" which has been moved, animated, by "a living Spirit." Such a spirit would seem to exist only insofar as it moves this material world: without matter to animate, where or what is it? In this sense, the *Conversations* are most basically about the touch of spirit to matter; and the particularities of "creation" versus "innocence," "a bud" versus "a net," or George K. versus Charles, are largely irrelevant.

MR. ALCOTT.  Are there *outward evidences* of Spirit?
CHARLES.  Actions, any actions, outward actions, an earthquake, the creeping of a worm.
GEORGE K.  Moving, the creeping of a baby.
LEMUEL.  The moving of a leaf, lightning.
ANDREW.  A waterfall, a rose.
FRANK.  Walking.
      . . .
MR. ALCOTT.  You perceive then what I mean by outward evidence of spirit?
CHARLES.  Things, external nature.                          (*C*, I: II)

Any piece of the world – "Things," as Charles sums it up – can be "outward evidence of spirit," whose course seems traceable in the movement of ideas from student to student. Charles's "creeping of a worm" becomes George's "creeping of a baby"; George's "moving" becomes Lemuel's "moving of a leaf"; a notion of progressive, developing movement animates "the creeping of a baby," "the moving of a leaf," "a waterfall," and "walking." Conducting the conversations results in a gradual permutation and shifting of the emblems which evokes Alcott's understanding of how "Spirit acts on and through matter." For Alcott suggests that "matter is . . . soft, yielding, fluid, easily moved, continually affected by the spirit that stirs in it, and shapes it to our senses." The very variability of responses is a sign of how the classroom is itself shifting, "continually affected by the spirit that stirs in it" (*C*, 1: 135). Person to person, each voice serves, in turn, as a fraction of matter "yielding" to the pressure of spirit.

Emerson's torrents of images are, like Alcott's, constantly altering, transforming emblems of the spirit. That spirit, I would now say, becomes a term indistinguishable from a universal experience or animate awareness – a life not identified with persons, and also not identified with a particular divine figure. Each man is not only producing series of images that respond to "the highest spiritual cause," but also searching for signs of such animation in purposefully inauspicious and ignominious objects. "Suburbs and extremities" such as the "shop," and also such as Lemuel and Ellen, are compelling tokens of the divine in part *because* they are so drab. Also like Alcott, Emerson seems to hold ultimately to a faith in the external world as something constantly "animate[d]" – moved and brought to life by a propulsive spirit ("AS," 69).

Emerson avers in "Circles" that movement, such as "sliding," is the "meaning" one reads in ordinary things. Thus, he specifically describes the shaking and dancing of "the very furniture" including "cup and saucer" and "chair and clock and tester" ("C," 408–9). Alcott, in his classroom, also investigates the meaning of "the very furniture" as precisely one of movement: he asks his class,

Is any piece of matter in the same state that it was an hour ago?
  *(They instanced pieces of furniture.)*
    . . .
Not only the whole universe is in motion, but every thing is in a state of change within it. There are sciences, which teach how the particles of bodies are mingled together . . . and that changes in their relative positions and proportions are constantly going on; that all things which seem to be solid are continually wasting and becoming air; and that the visible air is at all times being absorbed into solid bodies, and becoming visible. (*C*, 1: 135–36)

Movement, in both Alcott and Emerson, is the spirit's energy ruffling and remaking the "furniture" of the material world. I suggested just above that in the classroom the transformation of the images from student to student is a version of this spiritual transformation of matter; now, we are in a position to see that the classes are like Emerson essays (despite the ways that Emerson and Alcott each thought essay writing and conversation recording to be deeply different projects), in that they present image after image, never stopping to really investigate either the image or the idea.

The repetition of the discussion of the animation of furniture from Alcott's classroom and Emerson's essay shows the way that the Transcendental movement takes form as still another series or chain of images, of external manifestations and transformations of the spirit. Just as Charles's "creeping of a worm" becomes George's "creeping of a baby," Alcott's discussion of the animation of furniture becomes Emerson's discussion of the dancing "chair and clock and tester." Thus in its noncommittal offer of several emblems, Charles's answer seems an exemplary (exemplary partially because nonessential) instance of the Transcendental practice of expressing the spirit in emblems: "Actions, any actions, outward actions, an earthquake, the creeping of a worm." These events, authors, and persons are all occurring beside one another (in and around Boston), and one after another in a period of roughly two decades. Yet they do not quite occur together, or as one: they are adjacent, sequential, and equivalent exclamations. The movement has the shape of a roll call as individuals respond to the spirit, 'here,' 'here,' 'present' – "(*Several rose*)"; "(*Martha, Andrew, Lemuel*)"; "(*Some held up hands*)"; "(*Lucia, Ellen, Susan, George B. held up hands . . .*)" (*C* ii: 220, 176, 120, 193).

When Alcott and Emerson each discuss the moving of furniture – one in print, one in class – we note a resemblance, perhaps a causal connection, but not a union of the two images. Instead, distinct things are made to touch – an idea and an image, and a thought and a practice. What compels about the repetition in the movement is the firm sense of the fine, little differences between each particular, between George K. and Emerson's "autumnal star," and of the fact that every single different thing, and every different kind of thing reflects the same spirit or universal experience. The commitment is to nonessential, even trivial instantiations of the spirit, such as the peculiar and charming students at the Temple School, and the chain of emblems, "A little child beginning to speak . . . A little child . . . A bud beginning to open . . . A plant coming out of the ground . . . A little child beginning to exist."

Transcendentalism was resistant to New Critical formalism because the quintessential Transcendental move is to abandon metaphor and, more broadly, because its interest in the qualities of writing and action is so subsidiary to its interest in the spiritual. If New Critical formalism centers on the belief that the contingency of human experience can be rendered into lasting universality through its transformation into metaphor, Transcendentalism sees spiritual experience standing in immutable ideality outside the text or the form through which it becomes visible. It is the ugliness, the smallness, and the unimportance of experience, seen as one person's swatch of life, that New Critical formalism wanted to see articulated, expanded, and made resonant through the intervention of literary representation. And, it is a similar view of life as broken and contingent which new historicism wants to use literature to bring into language – just not into universality. But, it is the beauty and enormity of experience, seen as any person's full revelation, which Alcott would push toward through a student-centered pedagogy that is largely uninterested in students as individuals and which Emerson would bring out through his essays' hurtling claims and images. So Transcendentalism is incompatible with both New Criticism and new historicism, because each critical practice reads for moments when literature merges with experience, where representation is entwined with being (either to reveal the contingency of the past, or to render it universal). The interest in experience that we see in Transcendentalism is precisely not an interest in the particular, the contingent, but is rather an interest in the abstract and the universal. While it emerges along with a national commitment to a typical experience, using its techniques and premises (that reading is to evoke an impersonal experience, and that this depends upon emblematic and typified images as something to be used, analyzed, and run through), it pushes it much further to suggest an experience that is not typical or normal but universal. Poirier argued that the attempt to posit a "world elsewhere" through style could be likened to religious experience, as if literature delivered us into a transcendent aesthetic realm that was irreconcilable to our ordinary existence in the world. In contrast, I think that for Emerson and Alcott writing and conversation are exemplary of all forms of experience: abstract, animate gestures moving through words, persons, and things.[54]

# CHAPTER 4

# Laws of experience: truth and feeling
## in Harriet Beecher Stowe

Reading *Uncle Tom's Cabin* in 1853, Charles Briggs found a rejoinder to the question that once preoccupied John Neal: "Who reads an American book, did you inquire, Mr. Smith? Who does not?" Continued Briggs, "Apart from all considerations of the subject, or motive, of *Uncle Tom's Cabin*, the great success of the book shows what may be accomplished by American authors who exercise their genius upon American subjects."[1] *Uncle Tom* obviously mustered forceful emotional responses; in so doing, it performed the task that literary nationalism had demanded. In part by recalling the way *Uncle Tom's Cabin* seemed to fulfill the demand of literary nationalism, in this chapter I challenge both the view that Stowe's work is merely a contraption of stereotype and convention, and the view that it is a conduit of physically immanent emotion, all but unmediated by language. But of course Stowe herself suggested the latter notion, that *Uncle Tom's Cabin* facilitates a transparent exchange of authentic, subjective experience. In its final chapter Stowe wrote, "The separate incidents that compose the narrative are, to a very great extent, authentic, occurring, many of them, either under her own observation, or that of her personal friends."[2] This claim was underscored by the appearance of *The Key to Uncle Tom's Cabin* shortly after the novel, in which Stowe reasserts that *Uncle Tom's Cabin* was not her own artistic invention but "a collection and arrangement of real incidents, – of actions really performed, of words and expressions really uttered."[3] Thus *Uncle Tom's Cabin* is, Stowe maintains in the *Key*, not even quite rightly designated a "work of fiction," or is at the very border of fiction and document in its fealty to "really performed" and "really uttered" scenes. This claim to derivation from actual experience and specific observations looks quite different from that distaste for individual experience that we have seen previously, but in Stowe's initial understanding writing from experience consists in conceiving the world in abstract terms and, subsequently, fleshing out the details indicated by such terms. However, whereas nationalist literature had been concerned only with interesting its reader, Stowe's purpose was also to make readers change their minds about slavery. And because the experience that the text projects – that hypothetical experience to which it appeals – is, particularly in the aftermath of publication, increasingly subjected to tests of veracity, Stowe comes to abandon this entire understanding of literary experience in *Dred*. If, on the one hand, the rebuttal of *Uncle Tom's Cabin* with proslavery novels such as *Aunt Phillis's Cabin* suggests a persistent belief in projected experience, on the other hand the appeal to specific factual instances in the *Key* and in *Dred* suggests that around the use of literary experience as a tool in the abolitionist movement – the attempt, in other words, to use literature to prove something about the world – there emerged a differing standard of literary experience, closer to the current one of authentic experience.[4]

I

"With wild cries and desperate energy she leaped to another and still another cake; – stumbling – leaping – slipping – springing upwards again! Her shoes are gone – her stockings cut from her feet – while blood marked every step" (*UTC*, 65). The famous passage's close focus on Eliza's feet, shift into the present tense, and even the way the impatient and disjointed phrase "stumbling – leaping – slipping" mimics Eliza's awkward movement all help make this an absorbing moment. Eliza struggles across the icy Ohio river, and the novel's grip on the reader is at its height. Yet Stowe encourages her reader to be aware of her separation from the characters, even in sympathizing with them. We are led to feel as if we were right there, in other words, by being explicitly reminded that we are not:

If it were *your* Harry, mother, or your Willie, that were going to be torn from you by a brutal trader, to-morrow morning . . . – how fast could *you* walk? How many miles could you make in those few brief hours, with the darling at your bosom, – the little sleepy head on your shoulder, – the small, soft arms trustingly holding on to your neck? (*UTC*, 55)

The direct turn to the reader, in which Stowe addresses us in the second person and encourages us to recall our own "bosom," "shoulder," and "neck," brings out the distinction between, as the comparability of, the reader and Eliza. Being addressed as "you" reminds readers that they are not Eliza, and that despite their different situations, they would probably feel and act as Eliza does in her situation. Situation is critical to feeling here – persons can put themselves into external sets of conditions in such a way that their individual subjectivity is never at issue.

Stowe is rather restrained in comparison to other sentimental novels of the time, such as Susan Warner's *The Wide, Wide World*. In that novel, separation is almost unbearable: in the opening chapter, Warner describes how Ellen and her mother repeatedly "clasped each other in a convulsive embrace, while tears fell like rain," and there is a similar urge to fuse in Ellen's relationship with Alice Humphreys.[5] It makes perfect sense that Ellen's first friend of her own age is also named Ellen, and that no one bothers to figure out "which is which."[6] *The Wide, Wide World* also encourages a collapse of the reader and the character. Ellen is present in almost every moment, and the narration holds tightly to her emotional life, recording shameful reflections such as, "in her inmost heart she knew this was a duty she shrank from," or Ellen's description of an illness in which she watches "that crack in the door at the foot of my bed" and "all the little ins and outs in the crack."[7] There are almost no moments of editorial commentary, narrative speculation, or addresses to the reader, as Warner cleaves to the close focus of each scene.

In contrast, Stowe's narration upholds the distinction between the reader and the character with phrases such as, "Miss Ophelia, as you now behold her, stands before you" (*UTC*, 164). Stowe repeatedly uses this deictic strategy to figure experiences as at once engaging and distanced. Sometimes the narrator serves the deictic function, standing outside the scene and drawing our attention to an individual within it (as in the above quotation), while at other times she uses a character to present the scene. When Eva begins to convert Topsy to Christianity, it is shown through the frame of St. Clare and Ophelia's observation of it. And they, too, view Eva and Topsy through a frame:

advancing on tiptoe, he lifted up a curtain that covered the glass-door, and looked in. In a moment, laying his finger on his lips, he made a silent gesture to Miss Ophelia to come and look. There sat the two children on the floor, with their side faces towards them. (*UTC*, 289)

We approach the conversation of Eva and Topsy by the double mediation of Ophelia and St. Clare, and the curtain. After the climax of the scene, in which Topsy decides to try to be good, we retreat back out of the intimacy. "St. Clare, at this instant, dropped the curtain" (*UTC*, 290), and Stowe provides us with his and Ophelia's discussion of what they have witnessed. We are in the room with Topsy and Eva only for a moment before being drawn back out to view their interaction from a distance and ponder it, closing with St. Clare's observation, "It wouldn't be the first time a little child had been used to instruct an old disciple" (*UTC*, 291). To read *Uncle Tom's*

*Cabin*, then, is to be drawn close to characters while being held a certain distance from them. It is to be drawn into the observation of Eliza's bleeding feet, but also to be returned to the sphere of our armchair and our own children's arms around our necks; to be shown an intimate conversation through a doorway, as a mediating figure holds up the curtain for us to see. Experience is seen to follow from schematic situations that are completely reducible to concepts – like a theater's stage sets, ready to be packed up and reassembled in another state, inhabited by a different group of actors. Incidentally, this makes some sense of why Stowe thought that Southerners would be moved by her representations of the reality of slavery, when they were obviously not so moved by their experiences of it in their lives.

This matters, in part, because so much has been written about the claims to the sharability of experience in sympathy and sentimentality, and the ethics of how subjectivity is constructed in relation to the other in these closely related psychological processes. Both sympathy and sentimentality operate on a structure of identification. Sympathetic identification maintains an understanding that the spectator and sufferer are distinct persons, whereas in sentimental identification the spectator (or reader) psychologically fuses with the object of his empathy, so much as even to obliterate the consciousness of that person as other.[8] In essence, the critical questions turn on whether experience can be shared or not, and thus whether the claims of sympathy are those of genuine understanding of the other or of a dehumanizing cooptation of that other's experience and subjectivity as indistinguishable from one's own.[9] Most recently, scholars have suggested that both sympathy and sentimentality are more intersubjective, and some have even investigated the possibility that experience really can move between persons.[10] And yet even these revisions of the criticism of sympathy, along with the defense and the critique of its humanizing operations, retain crucial understandings of experience as that which has happened to a person, and then consider the ways that for one person to share another's experience can be theorized and assessed ethically and politically. Yet as Stowe writes about the experience of slavery, even as she works with the terms of sympathy, she is also thinking very much about the typical experience that literature would draw upon and produce. Another way to put this is that the reason experience seems so strange in Stowe is that it is precisely not what one person has undergone and can remember or narrate; it is, instead, the likely or normal response imagined to come from certain identifiable situations.

On one level, what I have suggested might be that Stowe is more strictly sympathetic than empathic and sentimental.[11] But even the sympathetic model does not encompass the working of Stowe's fiction and the way that it would elicit experience. For whereas the stress in the discourse of sympathy is on the psychological specificity of the subjects concerned (is, that is to say, a model of subjectivity focused upon how one's mind and heart responds to the appearance of another person's suffering), in Stowe the mechanism of that representation is shown as exterior to the subject. Her work continually calls attention to its own mechanics, so much so that Stowe tends toward an identification not of persons through the structure of the psyche or the text, but of persons with the text.

The infamous creakiness of Stowe's writing keeps one aware of the artifice of fiction, as if putting the architecture of the text into the foreground. At the end of the chapter "Topsy," Stowe writes that the girl has been "fairly introduced into our *corps de ballet*, and will figure, from time to time, in her turn, with other performers" (*UTC*, 260), thereby presenting the character as a discrete figure on a stage. She is almost eager to break the illusion of the scene and the continuity of the plot to highlight the artificiality of the novel's construction. The casual ease with which she observes, at the opening of another chapter, "A quiet scene now rises before us" (*UTC*, 139), tells of how little the novelist is invested in seamlessly presenting a self-enclosed world. She seems rather to be producing a puppet show, with "performers" deposited in "scene" after scene, wherever and whenever the author wishes. The break of continuity in location, character, and voice keeps readers aware that they are reading a fiction and being presented a privileged, bird's eye view encompassing a range of lives and places that no one person's story could provide.

Furthermore, the constant addresses to the reader also push the novel's characters away from the reader and refuse to let him or her lapse into identification with the characters; they are presented to us as ideas or types for us to examine and assess. This comes out especially in the novel's voluminous debates. For example, the chapter on Senator Bird contains extensive arguments between the couple: it isn't just that Eliza shows up and the Senator magically and instantaneously can't help feeling for her. Prior to that, Senator Bird asserts that "there are great public interests involved" while his wife counters, "would *you* turn away a poor, shivering, hungry creature from your door?" (*UTC*, 85). Eliza's actual arrival does not so much serve to refute the Senator's argument as it serves as both consequence and exemplification of Mrs. Bird's argument that in such an instance her husband would take in the fugitive. And the passages at St. Clare's often seem to be nothing but debates between Augustine, Ophelia, and Marie; the novel's arguments, both represented and conducted, are presented always as connected to the scenes it depicts. And although *Uncle Tom's Cabin's* scenes partake of a certain theatricality inherent to sympathy, this theatricality is front and center in such a way that identification of the reader with either the characters or the author is consistently revealed as possessing a structure dependent on the separation of persons – meaning that our response is not to what Stowe calls the real presence of persons in distress but to the denouement of diagrammatic scenes that present such events. What happens in Stowe is not even so much the identification of the reader with the analytic and ironic speaking voice of the novel (as Berlant argues is the case with Fanny Fern), but a quite explicit awareness of the way that topics are being presented in scenarios for a process that is at once imaginative (what story will play out?) and analytic (how should we judge the issues at stake?).[12]

*The Key to Uncle Tom's Cabin* presents itself as proof that the novel was taken from life – both Stowe's own life, and that of others whose testimony it includes. This essential understanding of the *Key* as proof of the truth of the novel has generally been upheld by criticism that deals with the *Key*.[13] For instance, Cindy Weinstein stresses that the *Key* uses facts to demonstrate that right feeling was grounded in truth, and she argues that Stowe's point was largely that she, unlike proslavery writers, understood the difference between fact and fiction.[14] Yet it is in the *Key* that the relationship between fact and fiction is, first of all, revealed to be utterly different from taking some actual events and making a novel out of them in the model of fictionalized history, and, second, is increasingly undone through the work of writing the *Key* (this second point I discuss in the next section of this chapter).

Even the subtitle's mention of "facts and documents" steps away from the claim that the novel is drawn "from her own experience," suggesting the importance of a generalized testimony rather than a personal one. When Stowe does describe her own experience in the *Key*, it is importantly impersonal. Moreover, although the *Key* compares events and persons in the novel to those in real instances, and sometimes makes a genetic connection between them, Stowe does not make a claim that the material or historical real is in some sense *more* real, or that it is ontologically in addition to temporally prior to the fictional. In one passage, the novelist tells us that Eliza is based on an actual woman whom Stowe says she observed "in Kentucky" as "she attended church in a small country town" (*K*, 22). But it appears that the character has superseded its original when Stowe remarks, "The description of Eliza may suffice for a description of her." Despite the reminder that she "stated in her book that Eliza was a portrait drawn from life" (*K*, 21), here the "original" (*K*, 22) is presented after the portrait, and need be described in no terms other than those given the fictional character. Indeed, she is taking her claim in the novel that the character was drawn from life now to bolster her claim that this actual woman was the original, and in the process Stowe reverses the very train of origins she ostensibly had been tracing. In addition, Stowe's experience of the "original" is limited to a glimpse, and what really animates Stowe is talking about the woman once she is no longer present: "The idea that this girl was a slave struck a chill to her heart, and she said, earnestly, 'O, I hope they treat her kindly'" (*K*, 22). Stowe speaks of herself in the third person and converts the condition of the "original" into an "idea": she presents persons as objects she observes and, more strongly, as ideas she entertains. Insofar as Eliza is taken from life, the process does not move in the conventional manner, in which a real person is refined into a fictional character. Instead the process is as follows: a real person is perceived as already a type or sketchy idea, which idea is then reflected and built up into a character, which character is finally and retroactively employed as the means of perceiving and conceiving the supposed original woman.

In addition to establishing such one-to-one links between character and "original," Stowe maintains that her characters and incidents are realistic because they are typical. To establish such typicality, she makes two moves: she indicates that comparable incidents and persons do exist, and that they are likely to exist. Take the example of Eliza's husband, George Harris. He is not "a purely exceptional case"; he is of a piece with the general character of "half-breeds" (*K*, 13). George is a fictional member of a class of persons of which Frederick Douglass is also "a very fair average specimen" (*K*, 19). That is not the same as saying that George is modeled on Douglass; rather, it is to say that a person and a character are equivalent examples of a class. Stowe combines literal reality with probable reality, declaring not just that a George-like character exists, but that one does and many others are likely to. Her method of indicating that order of likelihood is frequently to provide a string of examples, drawn from antislavery tracts and sources including conversations, newspapers, and letters. In the chapter on George, along with the example of Douglass, she includes two groups of advertisements for runaways which describe similar gentlemanly former slaves, excerpts from slave narratives, and "a specimen . . . related to the author by a lady in Boston" (*K*, 19), all to suggest that George is not an exception but a norm. Without citing a very great range of examples, Stowe lets a handful portend a myriad waiting in the wings: "These few quoted incidents will show that the case of George Harris is by no means so uncommon as might be supposed" (*K*, 19). Still, the potential for an exhaustive count is kept in range, as when she writes, "Now, let any one learn the private history of seven hundred blacks" (*K*, 42), gesturing toward an ideal encyclopedia of 700 "private histor[ies]." She has no actual ambition to present this complete record; the handfuls of examples suggest both the actual and the potential existence of many others. The work is, therefore, suspended between a present-moment documentary realism, and an imagining of what slavery must be like, which is oriented into a hypothetical future.

That imagining is, in the *Key*, repeatedly presented as a reading practice. The *Key* is rife with comments such as, "And, lo! in the same paper" (*K*, 141); "But let us open two South Carolina papers" (*K*, 134); and "before we recover from our astonishment on reading this, we take up the *Natchez Courier*" (*K*, 138), as if Stowe is at her desk, shuffling these papers around, picking up first one then another. Her comments can even be ironic riffs: she cites an advertisement that "TWENTY DOLLARS REWARD / Will be paid for the delivery of the boy WALKER, aged about 28 years" only to joke that "Walker has walked off, it seems" (*K*, 177). Furthermore, Stowe attends to the printer's presentation of each document, pondering the juxtaposition of slave advertisements with a Southern newspaper's "motto: 'RESISTANCE TO TYRANTS IS OBEDIENCE TO GOD'" (*K*, 176). The casual commentary only almost coheres into a narrative of Stowe herself reading; she prefers an open-ended "we" to the first person. The exhortations and commentary are examples of how anyone would respond – indeed, they are responses which we are encouraged to model. "We ask you, Christian reader, we beg you to think, what sort of scenes are going on in Virginia under these advertisements?" (*K*, 146). As *Uncle Tom's Cabin* depicted scenes interspersed with commentary and reflections, Stowe here characterizes both that novel's depictions and its arguments as the normal consequence of reading documents of slavery.

Although the opposition between their views on the politics of sentimental fiction is familiar in Stowe scholarship, Ann Douglas and Jane Tompkins agreed on one thing, which was that the novel was by no means realistic. The novel, in each critic's view, looked to an imagined world in which women wielded power; Douglas claimed this was ideological self-congratulation at the expense of realistic labor for change, while Tompkins countered that it was the progressive imagination of "a basis for remaking the social and political order."[15] I would contend at this point that the opposition the critics agreed upon – a difference between present-moment realistic depiction of the way things are, and an imaginary and future-oriented projection of how things might be – is inaccurate to Stowe. Presenting not just actual but probable types of persons, and providing situations and types to be pondered by the reader, is in Stowe a way to depict a reality which is of a different order from one person's experience or observation. *Uncle Tom's Cabin*'s unreal quality is the condition of its claim to truth to life.[16]

Stowe proceeds in the mode of George Lippard's Devil-Bug from *The Quaker City*, which was, alongside *The Wide, Wide World* and *Uncle Tom's Cabin*, one of the major bestsellers of the century. Devil-Bug, the dwarfed, one-eyed son of a prostitute, rules over Monk Hall, an upper-class den of iniquity. In that capacity he sets up occasions for dastardly events to occur, and then stands back and mutters from behind a curtain, or peeping through a secret window, "I wonder how *that'ill work!*"[17] Devil-Bug is the agent in these scenes – he sets up a trap so that a man will be murdered, for instance – but understands the crime he in effect commits as a drama unfolding under the sway of circumstances, which he watches powerlessly. Stowe too writes in the mode of "I wonder how *that'ill work!*" – constructing a model on the terms she sees laid out in slavery as an institution, she invites us to consider how events would then transpire. Such consideration entails both an analysis of the situations themselves and a curious projection of the events they would be likely to yield – a labor of fictive imagination and/as analysis. Thus, although on the one hand Stowe suggests a certain identification with the structure of the text, this structure is one that also still pushes attention away from itself, into the controlled projection of imagination and analysis.

The double gesture of sentimentality is that in the very process of realizing others as human, it obscures them by framing them only as versions of the self. In Berlant's words: sentimentality "has been deployed mainly by the culturally privileged to humanize those very subjects who are also, and at the same time, reduced to cliché."[18] For Crane, Stowe's "tableaux" of images evoke sympathy in the reader for "the legal claims of black Americans to simple justice and citizenship," but he also objects that their very typicality renders them of limited use, for they demand that others resemble us if we are to grant them human and moral agency.[19] The concerns, here, are how models of a purely formal politics can accommodate the claims of identity. In a way, we might say what was once a question about genre (realist or sentimental?) is extended into a question about politics (identitarian or universalist?)? That alignment of realism with identity and sentimentality with universality was made by Kenneth Warren in *Black and White Strangers*. Warren argues there that realism maintains the connection of persons to, and even their determination by, not only their present conditions but those they have passed through. In contrast, he observes that in sentimental fiction characters can "function as exceptions to the laws governing those who surround them," as figures such as Eva or Tom transcend the determinative conditions, both material and abstract, of their worlds.[20]

But insofar as Stowe can speak both of Rachel Halliday, "a woman with a bright tin pan in her lap, into which she was carefully sorting some dried peaches" (*UTC*, 139), and of slaves who "sobbed, and prayed, and kissed the hem of [Little Eva's] garment . . . after the manner of their susceptible race" (*UTC*, 297), it's hard to say that she really believes in either sentimental transcendence or realist determinism. It is Stowe's uneven relation to categories such as mimetic or stereotypical, grounded or transcendent, that makes Crane interested in Stowe but also frustrated by her limited commitment to the particularity of persons' differences. It also seems to be that unevenness in Stowe that prompts Karen Sánchez-Eppler's assertion that even though Stowe, in seeking to depict a black hero, is so hemmed in by the conventions of sentimental fiction that she must "erase his flesh" and "obliterate blackness," nevertheless, "antislavery fiction's recourse to the obliteration of black bodies as the only solution to the problem of slavery actually confirms the ways in which feminist-abolitionist projects of liberation forced a recognition of the bodiliness of personhood."[21] What is at stake here is the goal of locating a subjectivity and a citizenship capable of recognizing the specificity of the person, either in the form of the raced or sexed body or in the broader form of a recognition of racial and sexual difference and of the histories of specific experiences that affect persons' participation in the social and political spheres. What is perplexing, for any critic with that goal, is that Stowe both imagines such a more fully embodied account of the subject and citizen and shies away from it, as she once seemed to critics to alternate between realism and sentimentalism. I want to suggest here, as I have sought to throughout, that the problem lies with the critical frame of authentic, real persons, and experience in opposition to their abstracted transcendence. *Uncle Tom's Cabin* presents *as* real experience something that is run on the principles of using types to produce unowned experience, something projected out of the text rather than carefully drawn from life in the way we would understand such a term today.

II

*Uncle Tom's Cabin* long seemed, as Eric Sundquist observes, "a work that helped instigate the Civil War and then ceased to have value once its purpose had been accomplished."[22] Because her novel was so strongly identified with its effects (both its actual effects in the world, and its commitment to the reader's experience), it was also judged to lack any inherent value as a literary artwork.[23] Yet in writing a novel that is eclipsed by its effects, Stowe hews to Kames's and Alison's theory that the crux of art is the reader's experience. Both her faith in her own reactions as typical, and her commitment to the responses her work provoked rather than to the work as a self-enclosed project, follow out that associationist concept that a reader's experience of a book would be shaped by that book and would, in fact, be the author's real work. Indeed, her understanding in the *Key* that experience is comprised of ideas and scenarios as they are followed out in the imagination suggests that she was imbued with associationist interest in experience as a sequence of responses, which are impersonal and intellectual rather than embodied.

However, where Kames and Alison focused on emotions and ideas without worrying – or in order to avoid worrying – over their accuracy, as I noted at the opening of this chapter for Stowe (and for her readers) the accuracy was forcibly harnessed back in: it mattered above all that these reactions be true in the strongest sense of the word. She turns to the typical, projected reading experience for testimony and thereby demands that it provide truth that is closer to that of other modes of empirical discourse. One of Stowe's reactions to this pressure is to put the responses she wants to elicit *into* her writing, presenting on paper virtually all the views anyone might express and experiences they might have. Stowe's recording of responses and comments makes the novel somewhat hermetic – notwithstanding its effects in the outside world – because potential responses to it are already incorporated into it. In that sense, Stowe is relatively uninterested in the experience of her reader as it might move on and away from her work; she is, rather, committed to experience, not just as the effect the text aims to yield, as the art it would produce, but also as the analysis and imagination of narration that is, increasingly, written in the text. The infamous affective or experiential power of *Uncle Tom's Cabin*, then, neither derives from nor projects the contingent, subjective experiences of individuals: it projects a typical, standard experience on the basis of conditions, which it also makes available to its reader. Its sense of immediacy, of reality, even, is fundamentally connected to its investment in and presentation of sets of conditions, scenarios for analysis and projection. In other words, it is not that we share slaves' experiences by reading *Uncle Tom's Cabin*, but that experience as such – as something to appeal to or enter into – exists only as that which we would think of as following from certain conditions, not as the property of individual persons at all. But in contrast to the authors of other works I have discussed that share this notion, Stowe is newly committed to the truth of those responses, and thus, in writing them into her prose, she starts to collapse the difference between the text and the experience of it.[24] These concerns transform markedly in her readings of the slave codes in both the *Key* and in *Dred*.

For antislavery activists, the central legal issues were the position of the Constitution on slavery and the relationship of federal to state law, issues at the core of, respectively, the Dred Scott case and the Fugitive Slave Law.[25] However, antislavery literature did also consider the state slave codes, both statute laws and cases, primarily for evidence about the institution. The analysis of the slave codes brought up specific evidentiary issues, among them whether the code's prohibitions demonstrated what did or did not occur in slave states. For example, in *Uncle Tom's Cabin* Stowe wrote of a baby being sold away from his mother. As she notes in the *Key*, proslavery authors had objected that this could never happen because in "the statute-book of Louisiana . . . Every person is expressly prohibited from selling separately from their mothers *the children who shall not have attained the full age of ten years*" (*K*, 67, original emphasis). Finding "a charming freshness" in the notion that "A thing could not have happened in a certain state, because there is a law against it!" (*K*, 92), Stowe argues the reverse: the existence of laws prohibiting actions proves that those actions have indeed occurred. But this question of whether laws showed what did, or did not, happen in slave states is less central to Stowe's reading than is another way of interpreting the codes, which depends upon picturing the results that the laws themselves seem to proffer, as if a whole world could be extrapolated from their terms.

The latter mode of reading, using the laws to project the experience of slavery, is central to the abolitionist William Goodell's *The American Slave Code in Theory and Practice*. Goodell's book, to which the *Key* refers repeatedly, was published in the same year as the *Key*, with a prefatory letter asserting it, too, would prove *Uncle Tom's Cabin* was an accurate picture of slavery.[26] As Goodell labors "to show what 'the legal relation' is; what the usages of slaveholders generally are; and the natural and necessary correspondence between them," he argues that law leads inevitably to practice (*ASC*, 5). Their "necessary correspondence" is one of "cause and effect," and throughout the book Goodell insists that every facet of the slave code, and every bitter aspect of its practice, follows logically from the "axiom" that a man can be legally defined as property. Other antislavery works, including Lydia Maria Child's *Appeal in Favor of that Class of Americans Called Africans* and the *Narrative* of William Wells Brown, present compendiums of slave codes to the reader with minimal commentary in the expectation that the reader will infer that which the codes suggest.[27] Goodell made the turn to an audience's discerning power explicit: "The intelligent and reflecting reader will be compelled, if we mistake not," to see the cause and effect relation of theory and practice (*ASC*, 5). So an implicit analogy characterizes Goodell's book: the slave codes cause cruel actions, and they likewise cause readers to perceive that cruelty. In other words, cruel acts and the picturing of those acts are equally normal results of one statute. For Goodell, there is a firm distinction between this reference to the law – in which cruelty and the perception of cruelty are alike results of the slave code – and the abolitionist refusal to obey the law and campaign to repeal the law. In fact, Goodell was committed to the belief that laws should either be obeyed or broken depending on their morality: he avows that an immoral law is "void," for "the 'law of sin and death' is not obligatory" (*ASC*, 5–6). Thus one should interpret the codes loyally – obey them – to represent slavery, but one should disobey them in combating slavery by, for example, aiding fugitive slaves.

In the *Key*, Stowe continues her previously established mode of representing experience as the likely result of a set of conditions or a situation, evident in *Uncle Tom's Cabin*, and combines this with Goodell's suggestion that reading the law causes such imaginations. Her readings are both interpretations of the law and followings-out of the actions and events that the laws themselves proscribe, such that Stowe's own reading is an enactment of what is encrypted in the premises of the codes. Stowe tends first to excerpt paragraphs from laws, then to isolate and highlight phrases from them. From those phrases she draws an imaginary narrative, and then circles back to re-quote the phrase. For example: she takes up "the Revised Statutes of North Carolina, chap. cxi, sec. 22," which states that when a slave may "*run away and lie out, hid and lurking in swamps, woods, and other obscure places* . . . it shall be lawful for any person or persons whatsoever to kill and destroy such slave or slaves by *such ways and means as he shall think fit!*" (*K*, 83, original emphasis). Fascinated by the potential of the law's wording, Stowe remarks, "What awful possibilities rise to the imagination under the fearfully suggestive clause '*by such ways and means as he shall think fit!*'"

Musing that the Revised Statutes of North Carolina, chap. cxi, sec. 22 is "terribly suggestive to the imagination," she takes up the suggestion herself:

Let us suppose a little melodrama quite possible to have occurred under this act of legislature. Suppose some luckless Prue or Peg, as in the case we have just quoted, in State *v.* Mann, getting tired of the discipline of whipping, breaks from the overseer, clears the dogs, and gets into the swamp, and there "lies out" as the act above graphically says. (*K*, 84)

Combining the Revised Statutes with the case of *State* v. *Mann,* Stowe
ponders a hypothetical character, who gradually resolves from a vague "Prue
or Peg" into the fully specified "Prue." As she works up the scene of Prue's
lying out in an increasing detail of "alligators and moccasin vines," Stowe
keeps returning to the talismanic quotation from the statute ("lie out"),
linking the imagined scene back to the law's wording:

> We all know what fascinating places to "lie out" in these Southern swamps are.
> What with the alligators and moccasin snakes, mud and water, and poisonous
> vines, one would be apt to think the situation not particularly eligible; but still,
> Prue "lies out" there. (*K*, 84)

The passage persists in linking the scene back to the original phrase as the
"melodrama" continues:

> Suppose that, hearing the yelping of the dogs and the proclamation of the sheriff
> mingled together, and the shouts of Loker, Marks, Sambo and Quimbo, and other
> such posse . . . Prue only runs deeper into the swamp, and continues obstinately
> "lying out," as aforesaid; – now she is by act of the assembly *outlawed,* and, in
> the astounding words of the act, "it shall be lawful for any person or persons
> whatsoever to kill and destroy her, by such ways and means as he shall think fit,
> without accusation or impeachment of any crime for the same." (*K*, 84)

The drama culminates in the quotation from the law, which describes the
very killing it causes. Stowe's repetitive quoting throughout the narrative
highlights the sense that the killing she describes springs from the law, so
much so that its very wording can describe the murder of Prue. While
"all the defenders of slavery start from the point that this legal condition
is not *of itself* a cruelty" (*K*, 126), Stowe asserts that slavery is cruel and
violent by definition, and thus imagines the law as a weapon and even as a
murderer. She continually returns to the very words of the code, to insist
that the scene she has imagined is directed not by her but by the letter of the
law.

Insisting upon the causal responsibility of the law in the violence occurring in slave states was, in abolitionist discourse, a rebuttal of the proslavery
position that such violence was only an "abuse" of the system. The question
of abuses was of whether cruel actions committed by slaveholders upon their
slaves were criminal transgressions of the system – "abuses" – or inevitable
expressions of slavery's very nature. Another way to state this point is to
say that the proslavery authors thought of violence as the act of individual
agents, but abolitionists argued that it was inherent in the form of slavery itself. This was a line of reasoning Stowe had already noted in *Uncle
Tom's Cabin,* as Augustine St. Clare exclaims, "Talk of the *abuses* of slavery!

Humbug! The *thing itself* is the essence of all abuse!" (*UTC*, 230). It was also central to Goodell, who argued, "The hair-splitters in logic will never-theless persist in admonishing us to distinguish between the 'relation' and its 'abuse.' But what, we demand, must be the nature of a 'relation' that is constantly producing such fruits?" (*ASC*, 105). For Goodell *State* v. *Mann* – the case that Stowe is reading in the passage about "Prue or Peg" – is an important piece of evidence against the claim of abuses. In this case, the defendant was prosecuted for "assault and battery on a hired slave, named Lydia," only to be acquitted on appeal (*ASC*, 18). Goodell comments on this case at several points, stressing that the decision of Judge Ruffin, who presided over *State* v. *Mann*, revealed "the necessity of absolute power in the master over the slave, and the impossibility of any legal protection to the slave from that power, while the slave-system continues" (*ASC*, 18, 19). Goodell goes on to quote Ruffin to the effect that

"The power of the master must be absolute, to render the submission of the slave perfect. It would not do to allow the rights of the master to be brought into discussion in the courts of justice. The slave, to REMAIN a slave, must be sensible that there is NO APPEAL from his master." (2 Devereaux's N. Carolina Rep., 263). This justifies our statement that "the legal relation of master and slave" is responsible for all this despotic power. (*ASC*, 110–11)

Goodell's position is twofold: slavery, as an institution, is the cause of acts of violence ("responsible for all this despotic power"), so that the responsi-bility for them lies not with the slaveholders but in the law; but, because the institution of slavery is wrong, it is the responsibility of individuals to resist it. The individual's moral responsibility to fight slavery is, that is to say, predicated in Goodell on a belief in the responsibility of the system of slavery for the acts of violence that occurred under it. Extending that dual move, in which slaveholders are not personally responsible for its wrongs because the system is itself the perpetrator of the wrong, but in which per-sons are compelled to resist precisely that system on the basis of their moral conscience, Stowe has praise for both Judge Ruffin, who executes the letter of the slave code, and for judges who would resist that law and heed their consciences. She classes Ruffin with "men of honor, men of humanity, men of kindest and gentlest feelings," and twice describes him as "obliged" to pronounce his decision with "inflexible severity" (*K*, 71); she also praises judges who "listen to the voice of their more honorable nature, and by favorable interpretations" aim to "soften" the code's cruelties. "All we wish is that there were more of them" (*K*, 72).

But there is something new about the duality as it surfaces in this passage in the *Key*, which is that Stowe lauds judges who do two completely opposite things, in the exact same situation. That she does so around the position of the judge draws into play a conflict in the law of the time over how judges should interpret the law: on the basis of the letter (legal formalism) or on the basis of the judge's sense of right (moral law). Her equivocation over *State* v. *Mann*, in which she has praise both for the moral judges and for the formalist Judge Ruffin, thus seems to point right to a substantive concern on Stowe's part about the conflict between moral law and legal formalism, and critics have discussed from different angles the extent to which Stowe depends either upon pure law or upon a law guided by moral conscience.[28] This concern is evident in Goodell, and indeed in abolitionist thought in general, but in these passages it is caught up with the relationship of asserting that a true picture of slavery comes from faithfully following out the consequences of the letter of the law to asserting that the result of that would be a moral injunction to work to both resist and destroy the institution. And insofar as I have argued that Stowe's fictional practice is to insist upon following out the consequences of sets of conditions (something she drew out in the *Key* through her adaptation of Goodell's method of reading the law), her writing serves as the inevitable effect of those laws and suggests that her reader must follow suit as well. But, especially insofar as she begins to write such responses back into the novel, this suggests that Stowe's understanding of fiction as evinced in *Uncle Tom's Cabin* is so committed to perceiving the experience of a text as determined by that text as to be indistinguishable from it. Consequently the agency to change that Goodell presumes to come after picturing the world the codes project disappears. Collapsing the experience of the text into the text as fully as she had begun to do in *Uncle Tom's Cabin* – moving towards that New Critical model in which the experience became not just the effect of, but indistinguishable from, the text – meant that there was no longer room for the concept of the reader's additional, active response to the inevitable picturing of slavery.

That something in her reading of *State* v. *Mann* in the *Key* unsettled Stowe's understanding of her own fictional practice is supported by the fact that the case became a central part of her next novel *Dred*, in which her method is drastically altered by the sundering of fact and fiction. *Dred's* preface is blunt about the difference between art and evidence:

if the writer's only object had been the production of a work of art, she would have felt justified in not turning aside from that mine whose inexhaustible stores have but begun to be developed.

But this object, however legitimate, was not the only nor the highest one. It is the moral bearings of the subject involved which have had the chief influence in its selection.[29]

In two brisk paragraphs, Stowe lays a boundary between her artistic wish to interest us in a story of borders and shadows and her commitment to convincing us that slavery is wrong.

The preface outlines why slavery provides a good subject for "romance": it harks "back to the twilight of the feudal ages," providing that literary ideal of a landscape full of "vivid lights, gloomy shadows and grotesque groupings" (*D*, 29). In contrast, she defends the politics of the novel as if it bore no relation to the "work of art" within which they were set. Thus, she states that to decide if "the system of slavery, as set forth in the American slave code" is "*right*," she will try "to do something towards revealing to the people the true character of that system. If the people are to establish such a system, let them do it with their eyes open, with all the dreadful realities before them" (*D*, 29–30). Slavery is to be seen clearly, revealed to "eyes wide open," not pictured in intriguing shades. *Dred* includes appendices of Nat Turner's confessions, legal statutes, and cases, and footnotes such as, "The original document from which this is taken can be seen in the appendix. It appeared in the *Wilmington Journal*, December 18, 1850" (*D*, 627). So much balder is *Dred*'s relationship to the actual world that Stowe must make explicit that although Judge Clayton speaks the words of the real Judge Ruffin, she has taken the "liberty" of inventing his character, "having no personal acquaintance with that gentleman" (*D*, 30). The novel, like the character of Judge Clayton, is split between the rigid reproduction of specific events and the "liberty" of arbitrary invention.

That split is particularly evident in the story of Clayton, the novel's romantic hero but also a believer in the concept of abuses. In *Dred*'s version of *State* v. *Mann*, Clayton prosecutes the case because he sees it as a chance to prove that the slave code protects slaves: "'It is a debt which we owe,' he said, 'to the character of our state, and to the purity of our institutions, to prove the efficiency of the law in behalf of that class of our population whose helplessness places them more particularly under our protection'" (*D*, 382). After he loses his case, Clayton finally sees that the slave law is inherently cruel. But Clayton does not then try to change the law; he moves to Canada with "[his] servants" (*D*, 454), frees them, and settles them in a "township." There Clayton works for the "improvement" of his ex-slaves while taking up a "beautiful residence" (*D*, 672) – the fantasy paternalism of proslavery authors, only without the legal basis that, as Stowe had made Clayton realize, inevitably caused cruelty and violence. But why not imagine a plot where Clayton becomes an abolitionist, let alone a successful one? Stowe will not imagine, in fiction, anything that goes against the current state of the law (such as an emancipated state of Louisiana); nor will she write a fiction that is imagined on the basis of the codes. Instead, there are the codes; and there is a separate, fictional world that borders on fairytale.

Clayton's belief that the slave law is inherently kind is posed against the decision rendered in the case, here delivered not by Judge Ruffin but by Clayton's father, Judge Clayton. As Judge Clayton explains it: "I sit in my seat, not to make laws, nor to alter them, but simply to declare what they are" (*D*, 444). Even though he "felt exceedingly chagrined" (*D*, 444) at the decision he rendered, in keeping with his strict self-control behind the bench Judge Clayton speaks in "tones" which are "passionless" (*D*, 450) as he pronounces, "The end [of slavery] is the profit of the master," not the slave's "personal happiness." Slavery cannot, therefore, exist without "uncontrolled authority over the body" (otherwise no one would submit to it), and consequently slavery requires that the master have complete power over his slave. The "master['s] . . . power is, in no instance, usurped, but is conferred by the laws of man, at least, if not by the law of God" (*D*, 448–49). Judge Clayton stands for the authority of an institution, rather than the moral persuasion of individual persons: Stowe uses most of Ruffin's decision verbatim, and this includes the sentence that recognized "the struggle . . . in the judge's own breast between the feelings of the man and the duty of the magistrate" (*D*, 446).[30] The rigorous formalism of Ruffin's decision, that the law must be carried out, is replicated in Stowe's own writing, in these passages, in that she essentially transcribes Judge Clayton's speech from that delivered by Judge Ruffin and published in *Wheeler's Law of Slavery*.[31]

In its stress on the falsity of Clayton's idea that benevolence and slavery can coexist, Stowe follows Goodell, contending that it is the laws, not the people who implement them or live under them, that are the problem. Yet the difference between Clayton's understanding (that slavery is a paternalistic institution subject only to abuses) and that of his father Judge Clayton (that slavery is a necessarily tyrannical and violent institution) is not entirely convincing. For although Judge Clayton is hardly an abolitionist, he does (like Ruffin) express some regret at the decision he feels compelled to render. His function is to insist on the inherent cruelty of slavery, and Stowe uses that function to forward the claims of abolition. Judge Clayton informs his son that "no reform is possible, unless we are prepared to give up the institution of slavery" (*D*, 455), in words written by Stowe, not taken from the actual case. The matter becomes still more complicated when one looks at the actual case of *State* v. *Mann*. As Saidiya Hartman points out, "Rather than distinguish between implied relations and absolute dominance or separate affections from violence, the court considered them both essential to the maintenance and longevity of the institution of slavery."[32] In Hartman's view, the thing *State* v. *Mann* shows is not just how inherently cruel the form of slave law is (that's what Stowe and Goodell mean it to show), but that it depends on a complementary kindness and sympathy for the slave. This kindness was to be performed, strictly speaking, outside the law, but this extra-legal humanitarianism directly served the needs of the slave state. In the words of Judge Ruffin, it is quite clear that benevolence toward the slaves – that thing which, in Goodell and Stowe's account, had been rigorously distinguished from his implementation of the law, and which might even lead to private belief in abolitionism – is, just as Hartman argues, a necessary correlative to legalized cruelty:

That all powerful motive, the private interest of the owner, the benevolence towards each other, seated in the hearts of those who have been born and bred together, the frowns and deep execrations of the community upon the barbarian, who is guilty of excessive and brutal cruelty to his unprotected slave, all combined, have produced a mildness of treatment, and attention to the comforts of the unfortunate class of slaves, greatly mitigating the rigors of servitude, and ameliorating the condition of the slaves.[33]

Ruffin's position went beyond articulating his personal sorrow over the matter in the face of a legal form he could not influence. He maintained that it was the extra-legal territory of the social (interactions between persons who had lived together, the judgment of the community upon brutal slaveholders, and even mere self-interest) that would do the job of amelioration that the law was being asked, in the case, to do. In this sense, the actual Judge Ruffin's position was not so distinct from that of the character of Clayton (the son, not the Judge): Judge Ruffin believed slavery to be an insitution of legal cruelty perpetuated, made possible even, by extra-legal kindness.

In *Dred*, Stowe gives Judge Clayton seven uninterrupted paragraphs to state his case, and these words are all taken straight from *Wheeler's Law of Slavery*. She marks with ellipses two short places where she elides material deemed unnecessary, but the only significant such elision is of the above-quoted passage about benevolence. That is to say, the only significant portion of the case that Stowe does not put straight into her novel is the part where Judge Clayton explains that benevolence and fellow-feeling for slaves will shore up and complement – not counter – the violence of the institution as law. Her deletion of the passage where Ruffin directly expressed his care for slaves as in symbiosis with the law's violence may indicate a recognition of this aspect of the case as a direct refutation of her point, as might Goodell's elision of the same passage.[34] That Ruffin's words suggested to Stowe an uncomfortable identity of her view that kindness must follow from seeing the inevitable cruelty of slavery might be apparent in her insistence that Clayton is wrong to think that paternalism and slavery go hand in hand. The idea that kindness is proslavery, necessary to and linked to the slave law, is doubly rebuked in the novel by the removal of Clayton's paternalism from the domain of slave law, and the removal from the decision in *State* v. *Mann* of the mention of the role that kindness and concern played in maintaining slavery.

Regardless of Stowe's conscious or unconscious thoughts and feelings on the matter, however, it is evident that what happens in *Dred* is that she both focuses on a case that suggests that committing legalized cruelty and feeling a need to redress that cruelty extra-legally are both effects of the institution's legal form, and, in that focusing, strives to write in such a way as to continue to maintain that slavery is legalized cruelty but, unlike in *Uncle Tom's Cabin*, to insist her fiction was a radical break from, not another natural consequence of, those codes. The project of *Dred*, that is, is to resist its own intimation that the project of reading the codes and cases causes both the enactment of violence and sorrow and outrage over that violence. Indeed, Judge Clayton is capable of enforcing the codes, deeming his actions "regrettable," and suggesting the need for abolition. That might suggest there is no way to differentiate between these responses – as each is, in its way, the ironclad effect of the codes. In this light, we might read Stowe's decision to exile Clayton to Canada as a way to assert by authorial fiat that Clayton's paternalism really *is* different from proslavery paternalism, when the underlying unease would be a sense that this is, as Hartman points out, untrue (and Stowe's decision to make Clayton's father the judge leads to a confusion over their names that might indicate the concern that they were indistinguishable). Still closer to home would be the case of the oddly praised Judge Ruffin: he insists on the necessity of brutal violence in the same breath as he declares his sorrow over it and the need to repeal the laws – this is much the same principle of the abolitionist readings of the codes. The odd decision to kill off the heroine, Nina Gordon, partway through the novel also speaks of a certain exaggerated authorial power over the characters, as though Stowe were newly determined to portray her characters as her own inventions, not as more typical effects of slavery.

In *State* v. *Mann* Judge Ruffin expressed his sorrow at the cruel decision he believed legal formalism demanded of him; in reading it, Goodell maintained both that the form of slavery was the cause of cruelty and that one must resist it. In writing about this case Stowe changed her narrative style.

Instead of picturing the scenes of cruelty that would inevitably occur under the law of slavery, Stowe split her work in two: she drops the facts of *State* v. *Mann* into the book, transcribing passages verbatim from *Wheeler's Law of Slavery*, and she provides unlikely fictional narratives and characters which bear no relation to the reality of specific events and persons. The logic of this move is that the different effects of a single cause, or the multiple steps in a causal chain, cannot properly be distinguished. To be cruel and to be antislavery are both results of the slave code, and being cruel is what leads to being antislavery. Only if this causal chain means that there is no difference between cruelty and antislavery belief, both being determinate effects of the slave code, would Stowe need to uproot them and cease to assert that her fiction writing is the effect of the code, but is rather, on the one hand, its literal reproduction, and, on the other, an alternative, fictional invention. At the beginning of this section, I noted that in one sense, Stowe is committed to the experience of the text as identical to, even identified with, the text. In that regard, her concerns in *Dred* reveal her deepening belief in the identity of multiple effects of a single cause, both with each other and with their common cause.

In Stowe we see one kind of demise of the conception of experience as the projected, possible effect of typical situations. For while she both exemplifies and even seemed to fulfill the ambition of earlier literary nationalism, out of *Uncle Tom's Cabin* and on into the *Key* and *Dred* she begins to think of the effects of her texts as not just likely or normal but necessary and true, and to think of them as something not just to be provoked out of and caused by the text but increasingly written back into it. If on the one hand her suturing of response to her text and to the text of the slave codes makes Stowe seem to approach a New Critical identification of the reader's experience with the text, she herself backs off from that notion in *Dred*, condemning Clayton's rhetoric for its tyrannical "atmosphere" of "force" and "secret power" (*D*, 389, 387). And another way to look back at *Dred* is as an effort to deflect attention from the text itself, to shake off that identification of text with its experience that she had approached in defending *Uncle Tom's Cabin*'s value as evidence.

The suspicion that causes and effects cannot be distinguished, and that multiple effects of a single cause cannot be distinguished from either one another or their shared cause, is not only evident in Stowe; it has been adopted and strengthened in some Stowe criticism. One example of this is Stephen Best's assessment of the movies and plays made out of *Uncle Tom's Cabin* as parts of the novel, insofar as "in the case of Stowe's *Uncle Tom's*

*Cabin*, the plot of the text anticipates the circulation of the text (its logic becomes a chronologic, so to speak)."[35] Another example is Lauren Berlant's argument that the form of sentimentalism is "generate[d]" by *Uncle Tom's Cabin* and inevitably invoked every time the novel is cited, as it is in *The King and I* and in the film *Dimples*.[36] At stake for Berlant in defining not only sentimentality, but *Uncle Tom's Cabin*, as a "form" is the assertion that within a set of generic and rhetorical gestures there is lodged the meaning of a certain ideology: to quote or refer to *Uncle Tom* is to turn the identification with suffering into a ceaselessly repetitive spectacle of commodity entertainment. Similarly, Best suggests a new historical formalism, in which the structure of analogy is seen as having intentionality and effectiveness in the world: "our forms should and do matter."[37] Both Best's and Berlant's accounts of the effects of *Uncle Tom's Cabin* as part of it, and of form as possessing agency and intentionality, are directed toward the negotiation of formal equality with the recognition of historical inequality (a concern also animating recent scholarship applying pragmatist philosophy to American literature). In the case of Berlant, there is no such thing as democracy based on "transcend[ing]" either the past or "corporeal self-knowledge."[38] In Best's case, this is evident in his critique of legal formalism (what Ruffin advocates in evacuating his own views from his task of implementing the codes). Legal formalism both fosters ongoing inequity (as in the case of *Plessy* v. *Ferguson*, where formal equality is the defense of segregation) and is nothing but a front: "There is no . . . concept of equality before the messy struggle to bring one's particular conception of equality to life."[39] On that last point, Best stresses in particular the way that abstract structures of the law are caught up with the materiality of history and the intentions of those framing those laws.

In both Best and Berlant, then, one sees a commitment both to the control of form over its effect, and to the indistinguishability of form from both its animating cause and that which comes after it. That position makes it possible to draw the kind of connections that make literary studies look important, as if it tells us about something other than literature (most often, for Americanists, about democracy and about America). But it also makes it look as if the only way to stop repeating the past is to veer into sheer invention. That dual view – we can only repeat or arbitrarily cross – is what Stowe ran into with *Dred*: she shows the way the laws must work, and then just makes up another universe in which things work on utterly new terms. It is also what Best does when he offers us "two films in one," one a film based on the joke that a man might kiss a black woman instead of a white woman (the joke being at the idea that the women might

be substituted for one another – a joke on the conceit of formal equality), the other an anti-racist film that laughs at the culture that thinks that
race is essential, not "an accident of history."⁴⁰ And it is what Berlant gestures toward in her investigation of cases of "postsentimentality," which
"struggle to encounter the *Uncle Tom* form without reproducing it, declin-
ing to pay the inheritance tax": James Baldwin exemplifies "reading against
the grain," while Robert James Waller suggests how an "inheritance" could
be instead "a disinheritance" that "force[s]" those disinherited "to make living up as they go along."⁴¹ This last moment is one like those we have seen
in Emerson criticism, in which the insistence that we need to kill off the
past actually depends on refiguring or rewriting that past, since the belief
is so central that we never could just leave it behind. Berlant's offer of an
alternative to either repeating the past or projecting a fantastic future is a
constant "present tense" of something called "corporeal self-knowledge that
can neither be alienated into the commodity form nor provide instruction
and entertainment to audiences."⁴² Notwithstanding Berlant's opposition
to anything like transcendence, her concept of a knowledge in and as the
body is transcendental insofar as (by virtue of its perpetual present tense)
it appears immortal.

Best observes that liberal democracy is an abstraction that requires some
figure of corporeality; in place of the body of the king (monarchy's figure
of corporeality), America relies on the body of the slave.⁴³ And he takes
Stowe to be right when she fears that "slavery as a system of exchange has
perhaps progressed so far as to be linked inextricably with its object of
exchange."⁴⁴ He offers, with Berlant and others, the idea that all forms are
saturated with the intentionality of their historical era, such that one can
do historicism by reading texts closely, and one can read texts closely by
reading the history that came before and after the words. I mean, of course,
to recall the discussion from the introduction of the way in which recent
criticism's return to close reading has been accurate in its self-assessment
as a continuation of new historicism, rather than a retreat into an elitist,
aesthetic hall of mirrors.⁴⁵ In such criticism, skepticism regarding the very
possibility of abstraction, seen only as a specious claim to have transcended
history, the body, and identity (or, in another version, a specious claim
that art could be separated from history), has circled back to a vision of
abstractions always caught up with such contingencies. The peculiar effect
is that what was for the New Critics a special feat of art is now a description
of the way things are and have to be. The closeness of these two practices,
seeking to unify the abstract and the contingent through a certain formalist
harmony, is particularly clear in the work of Jehlen and it is also particularly

clear in Best's work. For Best's point throughout is that metaphor is that way in which ostensibly abstract forms are inextricably linked to concrete matter, as the slave's body provides the material form in which can be incarnated the abstractions of both the market and liberalism. As in Jehlen's account of the Guggenheim, Bilbao, while at first the critic's objection is to the attempt to distinguish intention from form, the ultimate belief is that this separation is impossible.

We could, then, think that criticism is faced with choosing between thinking experience matters or that it does not; between thinking meaning, belief, and abstractions are either separate from, part of (indistinguishable from), or in an either necessary or brilliant dynamic exchange with one another. This would mean that looking at something other than the meaning of a text – at its shapes, figures, structures, even experiences – would have to be a commitment to our own experience, and to the related notion of cultural experience. This would also entail thinking of formalism as meaning one of two things (again, this is depending upon our view of the issue, of the choice we make): haywire, ethereal abstractions (either the dream of legal formalism, or even the arbitrary shapes of Gehry's museum) or their very opposite, just another part of subjective experience.[46] Faced with that choice, I would follow the latter route, seeing meaning as distinct from experience and categorizing form as part of experience. But I don't think this choice is the entire situation; aspects of experience are neither entirely subjective nor collapsed with meaning. Of course, there is such a thing as personal and possessive experience, but – as Jay, Terada, and Knapp differently maintain – that is only one aspect of experience. Even Berlant's immortal corporeal knowledge suggests that commitment to experience is more complicated than a commitment to how belief is forged from our personal experience – whose body is that "corporeal self-knowledge," after all? In this respect, what's instructive at all about the aesthetic is that in it we do distinguish within our experience. That's what it means to find a reference to drinking coffee or to personal experience out of place in an architectural critique. And that's why, in contrast, it makes sense for Foster to describe the Guggenheim, Bilbao as mystifying and disorienting: those are references to an experience of the building, not of Foster.

A major concern in the criticism with which I am taking issue is the way that a commitment to the separability of meaning from experience, and a commitment to what one believes as opposed to who one is, seems to launch us into a sunny stratosphere in which we wash our minds and hands alike of the ongoing inequities and sufferings in the world. But I am not arguing for this kind of division – either as a complacent return to the republican citizen or as an inevitable theoretical frame which we must see as always compromised, and in need of still further compromising. This is because thinking experience matters is not the same thing as thinking that all of our experience must matter, nor is it the same thing as thinking that our experience must matter insofar as it is intertwined with or collapsed into our beliefs. And it's only when we believe that thinking experience matters is to think our experience is either part of or a destruction of belief and meaning, that we produce a situation in which we have two choices: thinking all of our subjective experience counts or thinking nothing but the meaning counts. That produces the idea that reading is either to repeat or just to reject the past, defining history as both an empty accident and as an inevitable presence, such that all we can do to escape is jump ship, by adjusting Emerson, flipping a movie's politics, or packing Clayton off to Canada.

My readings have suggested that such ways of thinking about form, meaning and experience precisely do not apply to or appear in a set of American texts that would have seemed most likely to evince them. Hawthorne's emblems are not about the subjective experience of making meaning; Emerson's essays do not offer us resonant embodiments of a heritage of individualism. Even Stowe does not, in *Uncle Tom's Cabin*, suggest the saturation of subjective experience into the text, and when, through the *Key* and on into *Dred*, she starts to be concerned with this possibility, she rips up her own script. I have also suggested that it is not theoretically necessary for reading with interest in form to be inevitably a commitment to what, in Lentricchia and DuBois's phrase, is "embodied there," or to give some special, ethical value to a certain experience of reading. For nineteenth-century American prose authors before the Civil War, specifically engaged in the thought of literary nationalism and Scottish associationism, experience is neither the meaning of the text, nor irrelevant to the text. Subjective experience, what we think of today as experience most immediately, is not relevant; but an order of typical and projected experience – what would be expected of anyone, even if it happened to no one person – is the central medium in which the words and meaning of an author sought to evoke an abstract art of affects, apart from both person and text. These abstractions are, of course, made from texts, authors' intentions, even persons reading – but, I have suggested throughout, this is not to say that they are identical to them or identified with them. That such abstraction might exist neither in opposition to, nor in negotiation with, personal experience indicates that the relationship of literary form to experience in this so-called foundational period of American literature may not be relevant to the current project of adding substantive to formal equality. For the literature is not engaged in the problem of bringing ideals to life, and that political project is more feasible when it is not misconstrued as a literary problem.

The typicality, rather than the objective or subjective quality of such literary experience, means that it can be discussed without becoming a matter of either repetition or willful misreading. In this regard, I intend my own articulations of the shapes, in particular, of projected experience in Neal, Hawthorne, Emerson, Alcott, and Stowe (in her earlier, not later state) to be articulations of forms of experience that are identical neither to the meaning of these author's writing, to the style of their prose, nor to the actual, personal experience – the subjective and the historical – behind or following upon them. All kinds of critical works are strewn with observations about texts that are precisely not accounts of what they mean, nor of how the individual subject felt reading it, but critical performances and explications of this typical experience. In this aspect, finally, I would recall that each text I have examined here, however engaged in practices of fiction, ethical preaching, or pedagogy, has also and at once been engaged in an analytic elaboration of the experience it has been concerned with – that, in other words, in these works the presentation of types, emblems, and standard situations has also been the simultaneous invention and analysis of abstract experience.

# *Notes*

## INTRODUCTION: NEW CRITICAL FORMALISM AND IDENTITY IN AMERICANIST CRITICISM

1 W. H. Gardiner, review of James Fenimore Cooper, *The Spy*, in *North-American Review* 15:36 (July, 1822), 252–53.

2 Van Wyck Brooks, *The Flowering of New England 1815–1865: Emerson, Thoreau, Hawthorne, and the Beginnings of American Literature* (1936; repr. Boston: Houghton Mifflin, 1981); F. O. Matthiessen, *The American Renaissance: Art and Expression in the Age of Emerson and Whitman* (New York: Oxford University Press, 1941).

3 For example, Eric Cheyfitz argued that "the rhetoric of American exceptionalism . . . represents a political entity, the US, as a universal ideal, 'America'" ("The Irresistibleness of Great Literature: Reconstructing Hawthorne's Politics," *American Literary History* 6:3 [Fall 1994]: 539–58).

4 For examples of these approaches, see: Amy Kaplan, *The Anarchy of Empire in the Making of US Culture* (Cambridge, Mass.: Harvard University Press, 2002); Eric Wertheimer, *Imagined Empires: Incas, Aztecs, and the New World of American Literature, 1771–1876* (Cambridge: Cambridge University Press, 1999); Sacvan Bercovitch, *The Rites of Assent: Transformations in the Symbolic Construction of America* (New York: Routledge, 1993); John Carlos Rowe, *At Emerson's Tomb: The Politics of Classic American Literature* (New York: Columbia University Press, 1997); Cornel West, *Democracy Matters: Winning the Fight Against Imperialism* (New York: Penguin, 2004); Denis Donoghue, *The American Classics: A Personal Essay* (New Haven: Yale University Press, 2005).

5 Gardiner, review of *The Spy*, 251.

6 [Charles Briggs], "Uncle Tomitudes," *Putnam's Monthly* 1 (January 1853): 97–102, in *Critical Essays on Harriet Beecher Stowe*, ed. Elizabeth Ammons (Boston: G. K. Hall, 1980).

7 Richard Poirier argued in *A World Elsewhere: The Place of Style in American Literature* (Madison: University of Wisconsin Press, 1985) that American prose works not by representing persons, plots, or stories so much as by projecting through style a world in which the self may come fully into being without the complications of the real. I consider my subject in what follows to be this peculiar, abstracted American prose that, as Poirier maintained, superseded

generic distinctions such as that between novel and romance. However, this was, for Poirier, tied to a larger argument about the specificity of prose, the thrust of which this book counters. On the other hand, insofar as Poirier still focused on the necessary failure of such a stylistic world to sustain itself, my focus on how texts point beyond their style to a projected experience could be seen as an extension and reinvestigation of Poirier's originating arguments.

8 Although the abstraction of experience that I am concerned with might seem more obviously located in Poe or in Melville, I take its foundational presence in texts that seem most interested in experience in the naturalized sense that we would associate with nationalism and identity to be more instructive.

9 Myra Jehlen, *American Incarnation: The Individual, the Nation, the Continent* (Cambridge: Harvard University Press, 1986), 3–4.

10 Jehlen, *American Incarnation*, 3.

11 Dana Nelson, *National Manhood: Capitalist Citizenship and the Imagined Fraternity of White Men* (Durham, N.C.: Duke University Press, 1998), 7. Also see Jared Gardner's *Master Plots: Race and the Founding of an American Literature 1787–1845* (Baltimore: Johns Hopkins University Press, 1998), which analyzed how in both late eighteenth- and early nineteenth-century fictions, the identity of the "American" was thought of as a racial category.

12 Russ Castronovo, *Necro Citizenship: Death, Eroticism, and the Public Sphere in the Nineteenth-Century United States* (Durham, N.C.: Duke University Press, 2001), 17.

13 Lori Merish, *Sentimental Materialism: Gender, Commodity Culture, and Nineteenth-Century American Literature* (Durham, N.C.: Duke University Press, 2000), 20.

14 Richard Brodhead, *Cultures of Letters: Scenes of Reading and Writing in Nineteenth-Century America* (Chicago: University of Chicago Press, 1993); Gillian Brown, *Domestic Individualism: Imagining Self in Nineteenth-Century America* (Berkeley: University of California Press, 1990); Lauren Berlant, *The Anatomy of a National Fantasy: Hawthorne, Utopia, and Everyday Life* (Chicago: University of Chicago Press, 1991).

15 Jay Fliegelman, *Declaring Independence: Jefferson, Natural Language, and the Culture of Performance* (Stanford: Stanford University Press, 1993), 36. Elizabeth Barnes, in *States of Sympathy: Seduction and Democracy in the American Novel* (New York: Columbia University Press, 1997), argues that even in the republican era of the apparently disembodied public sphere, there is a "heteroerotic construction of the body politic" in which the state is conceived of as a family, and vice versa (41). Julie Ellison argues that both sentimental literature and republican literature are intertwined, noting that "rationality [is] a very emotional thing. Rationality has an affect" in *Cato's Tears and the Making of Anglo-American Emotion* (Chicago: University of Chicago Press, 1999), 189.

16 Brown, *Domestic Individualism*, 1. Also see Walter Benn Michaels, *The Gold Standard and the Logic of Naturalism: American Literature at the Turn of the Century* (Berkeley: University of California Press, 1987).

17 Glenn Hendler, *Public Sentiments: Structures of Feeling in Nineteenth-Century American Literature* (Chapel Hill: University of North Carolina Press, 2001). Peter Coviello asserts that "American nation-ness existed, and had meaning, as a kind of relation – for some, an intimacy" in *Intimacy in America: Dreams of Affiliation in Antebellum American Literature* (Minneapolis: University of Minnesota Press, 2005), 5.

18 Stacey Margolis, *The Public Life of Privacy in Nineteenth-Century American Literature* (Durham, N.C.: Duke University Press, 2005), 3.

19 Rei Terada, *Feeling in Theory: Emotion after the "Death of the Subject"* (Cambridge, Mass.: Harvard University Press, 2003), 11.

20 Terada, *Feeling in Theory*, 19, 21.

21 Terada, *Feeling in Theory*, 156.

22 Martin Jay, *Songs of Experience: Modern American and European Variations on a Universal Theme* (Berkeley: University of California Press, 2005), 35, 319.

23 This is one way that Kant's *Critique of Judgment* has been read, particularly insofar as Kant maintains that the aesthetic judgment is a "subjective universal," an experience that is fundamentally "disinterested" and yet cannot be abstracted into the realm of concepts. Immanuel Kant, *Critique of Judgment* (1790), trans. Werner Pluhar (Indianapolis: Hackett, 1987).

24 Jay, *Songs of Experience*, 408.

25 These are the essential ways that reader-response criticism has been concerned with experience: (a) as a study of persons, either as psychological study or as a history of readers' responses, or (b) as an account of the meaning of a text. See Wolfgang Iser, *The Act of Reading: A Theory of Aesthetic Response*, trans. from German (Baltimore: Johns Hopkins University Press, 1978); Stanley Fish, *Is There a Text in this Class? The Authority of Interpretive Communities* (Cambridge, Mass.: Harvard University Press, 1980); David Bleich, *Subjective Criticism* (Baltimore: Johns Hopkins University Press, 1978); Norman Holland, *Five Readers Reading* (New Haven: Yale University Press, 1975).

26 Steven Knapp and Walter Benn Michaels, "Against Theory," *Critical Inquiry* 8 (Summer 1982): 723–42.

27 Walter Benn Michaels, *The Shape of the Signifier: 1967 to the End of History* (Princeton: Princeton University Press, 2004), 11. Subsequent page references in this discussion are given in parenthesis in the text.

28 W. K. Wimsatt and Monroe Beardsley, *The Verbal Icon: Studies in the Meaning of Poetry* (Lexington: University Press of Kentucky, 1954), 27.

29 Wimsatt and Beardsley, *Verbal Icon*, 29. Subsequent page references in this discussion are given in parenthesis in the text.

30 Frank Lenttricchia and Andrew DuBois, eds., *Close Reading: The Reader* (Durham, N.C.: Duke University Press, 2003), ix.

31 Bercovitch, *Rites*, 361. Also see Ellen Rooney, "Form and Contentment," *MLQ* 61:1 (2000): 17–40.

32 Bercovitch, *Rites*, 370.

33 Coviello, *Intimacy in America*, 18.

34 Hendler, *Public Sentiments*, 138.

35 Wimsatt and Beardsley, *Verbal Icon*, 11–12.
36 Jay Grossman, *Reconstituting the American Renaissance: Emerson, Whitman, and the Politics of Resistance* (Durham, N.C.: Duke University Press, 2003), 26.
37 Grossman, *American Renaissance*, 95.
38 Grossman, *American Renaissance*, 97–99.
39 Grossman, *American Renaissance*, 99.
40 Jehlen, *American Incarnation*, 9.
41 Jehlen, *American Incarnation*, 11.
42 Myra Jehlen, *Readings at the Edge of Literature* (Chicago: University of Chicago Press, 2002), 205.
43 Jehlen, *Readings at the Edge of Literature*, 207.
44 Jehlen, *Readings at the Edge of Literature*, 217.
45 Jehlen, *Readings at the Edge of Literature*, 218.
46 Hal Foster, *Design and Crime and Other Diatribes* (London: Verso, 2002), 37, 38. Subsequent page references in this discussion are given in parenthesis in the text.
47 Jehlen, *Readings at the Edge of Literature*, 225.
48 Jehlen, *Readings at the Edge of Literature*, 226.
49 Jehlen, *Readings at the Edge of Literature*, 224.
50 Jehlen, *Readings at the Edge of Literature*, 226–27.
51 Jehlen, *Readings at the Edge of Literature*, 205, 204.
52 Steven Knapp, *Literary Interest: The Limits of Anti-Formalism* (Cambridge: Harvard University Press, 1993), 107.
53 Knapp, *Literary Interest*, 2–3.
54 Knapp, *Literary Interest*, 47. Compare Donald Davidson, "What Metaphors Mean," *Inquiries into Truth and Interpretation* (Oxford: Clarendon Press, 1984), 245–64.
55 Knapp, *Literary Interest*, 61.
56 Knapp, *Literary Interest*, 65.
57 Knapp, *Literary Interest*, 66.
58 Wimsatt, quoted in Knapp, *Literary Interest*, 66.
59 Knapp, *Literary Interest*, 67.
60 Knapp, *Literary Interest*, 83–84.
61 Matthiessen, *American Renaissance*, 235.
62 Knapp, *Literary Interest*, 139.
63 Stendhal, *The Life of Henry Brulard*, new edn, trans. John Sturrock (New York: New York Review Books Classics, 2001), 172.

1 TYPES OF INTEREST: SCOTTISH THEORY, LITERARY NATIONALISM, AND JOHN NEAL

1 Henry Home, Lord Kames, *Elements of Criticism* (1761), ed. James R. Boyd (New York: A. S. Barnes, 1855), 82. Hereafter cited parenthetically and abbreviated to *E*.

2 See Walter Jackson Bate, *From Classic to Romantic: Premises of Taste in Eighteenth Century England* (New York: Harper & Row, 1946); András Horn, "Kames and the Anthropological Approach to Criticism," *Philological Quarterly* 44 (1965): 211–33; Arthur E. McGuinness, *Henry Home, Lord Kames* (New York: Twayne, 1970); Helen Whitcomb Randall, *The Critical Theory of Lord Kames* (Northampton: Smith College, 1944); Ian Simpson Ross, *Lord Kames and the Scotland of his Day* (Oxford: Clarendon Press, 1972), and "Scots Law and Scots Criticism: The Case of Lord Kames," *Philological Quarterly* 45 (1966): 614–23; Dabney Townsend, "Archibald Alison: Aesthetic Experience and Emotion," *British Journal of Aesthetics* 28:2 (Spring 1988): 132–44; Mary Warnock, *Imagination* (Berkeley: University of California Press, 1976); and René Wellek, *A History of Modern Criticism, 1750–1950*, vol. 1, *The Later Eighteenth Century* (New Haven: Yale University Press, 1955).

3 Adela Pinch, *Strange Fits of Passion: Epistemologies of Emotion, Hume to Austen* (Stanford: Stanford University Press, 1996), 1.

4 See William Charvat, *The Origins of American Critical Thought, 1810–1835* (Philadelphia: University of Pennsylvania Press, 1936); Terence Martin, *The Instructed Vision: Scottish Common Sense Philosophy and the Origins of American Fiction* (Bloomington: Indiana University Press, 1961); Gilman M. Ostrander, "Lord Kames and American Revolutionary Culture," in *Essays in Honor of Russel B. Nye*, ed. Joseph J. Waldmeir and David C. Meade (East Lansing: Michigan State University Press, 1978); James D. Wallace, *Early Cooper and His Audience* (New York: Columbia University Press, 1986); Franklin E. Court, "Scottish Literary Teaching in North America," in *The Scottish Invention of English Literature*, ed. Robert Crawford (Cambridge: Cambridge University Press, 1998), 134–63; John Paul Pritchard, *Criticism in America: An Account of the Development of Critical Techniques from the Early Period of the Republic to the Middle Years of the Twentieth Century* (Norman, Okla.: University of Oklahoma Press, 1956).

5 Martin, *Instructed Vision*, 85–86.

6 Martin, *Instructed Vision*, 141.

7 Michael Davitt Bell, *The Development of American Romance: The Sacrifice of Relation* (Chicago: University of Chicago Press, 1980), 18.

8 Bell, *Development of American Romance*, 19. This logic also informs Lori Merish's account of the Scottish Enlightenment's influence in the United States. In her analysis, the Scots provide an essential dynamic in which the subject identifies with the cultural commodity, displacing his internal experience onto the books and artworks he owns and thereby turning the reality of power relations between persons and between persons and objects under capitalism into a fantasy of emotional attachments and duties (*Sentimental Materialism*, ch. 1).

9 Bate, *From Classic to Romantic*, 95. Also see Horn, 'Kames.'

10 Randall notes that Kames's account of the train of thought "differs hardly at all" from that of Hume, and also that his distinction of perception and idea is

directly adopted from Hume (*Critical Theory of Lord Kames*, 32, 40; see also Ross, *Lord Kames*, on Kames's debt to Hume).

11 Warnock explains that the imagination knits a whole from scattershot impressions (*Imagination*, 23–24); her point implies that it is in the subject that the external world attains coherence (see also Horn, "Kames," 213–14). Randall adopts the Kamesian idea that wholeness is made in the subject, not in the object, in her argument that Kames's *Elements* is complete only when it is brought together in its reader's mind (see *Critical Theory of Lord Kames*, 24, 39, and 60–61). Randall notes that Kames is one source for Coleridge's concept of the creative imagination (47; see also Ross, *Lord Kames*, 289–90), which again suggests that wholeness is a product of the mind rather than a characteristic of the world. But I wish to stress that in Kames the imagination doesn't truly create anything except a certain coherence in a segment of its own experience – it doesn't produce a lasting form.

12 On the similarity of perceptions and ideas in Locke, Berkeley, and Hume, see Warnock, *Imagination*, 14, and Pinch, *Strange Fits*.

13 See Charvat, *Origins of American Critical Thought*, and Townsend, "Archibald Alison."

14 Archibald Alison, *Essays on the Nature and Principles of Taste*, 5th edn (Edinburgh, 1817), 5. Hereafter cited parenthetically and abbreviated to *T*.

15 Charvat has described how early American critics, influenced by writers including Kames and Alison, skirted questions of literary form: "Questions of art and technique were too often neglected" (*Origins of American Critical Thought*, 6). Fliegelman's *Declaring Independence* shows that American rhetoricians emphasized the transparency of language because reading or listening to someone is a proxy experience of whatever the speaker describes, not an experience of his speech. Distaste for the binding, we might say, of experience to language is part of what Michael Warner details in *Letters of the Republic: Publication and the Public Sphere in Eighteenth-Century America* (Cambridge, Mass.: Harvard University Press, 1990), although his book and Fliegelman's paint different pictures of republican culture. Distrust of language imbued with value is also central to Larzer Ziff's *Writing in the New Nation: Prose, Print and Politics in the Early United States* (New Haven: Yale University Press, 1991), which details "the powerful drift from immanence to representation in both literature and society, from a common belief that reality resided in a region beneath appearance and beyond manipulation to the belief that it could be constructed and so made identical to appearances" (xi). Christopher Looby's *Voicing America: Language, Literary Form, and the Origins of the United States* (Chicago: University of Chicago Press, 1996) also touches on this, in that he understands the nation to be premised upon a conviction of oral immediacy; in his analysis, writing is in itself a threat to the nation's legitimacy. I think that the insistence on linguistic transparency – the idea, in Charvat's phrase, that "description is a means, not an end" (*Origins of American Critical Thought*, 92) – lies behind the mass of contradictory writing in the period as to what constitutes

good oratory. See Laurence Buell, *New England Literary Culture from Revolution to Renaissance* (Cambridge and New York: Cambridge University Press, 2000), on the plethora and inconsistency of rhetorical theories.

16 Townsend argues that in Alison's account arbitrary responses become conventional, and are then reified as innate; also see Ross, *Lord Kames*, on Kames's failure to explicate the difference between a general convention and an essential connection.

17 Townsend, "Archibald Alison," 139.

18 Edward Everett, review of *A Tour on the Prairies* by Washington Irving, *North-American Review* 88, July, 1835: 12–13.

19 Everett, review of *A Tour*, 12.

20 Everett, review of *A Tour*, 3.

21 Washington Irving, *The Sketch-Book*, in *History, Tales, and Sketches*, ed. James W. Tuttleton (New York: Literary Classics of the United States, 1983), 753.

22 Henry Wadsworth Longfellow, "Graduation Address" [1825], in *The Native Muse: Theories of American Literature*, ed. Richard Ruland vol. 1 (New York: E. P. Dutton, 1972), 238.

23 John Neal, *Rachel Dyer* (1828; reprint, Amherst, N.Y.: Prometheus Books, 1996), xvi. Hereafter abbreviated to *R* and cited parenthetically.

24 William Ellery Channing, "Remarks on National Literature," in *Selected Writings*, ed. David Robertson (New York: Paulist Press, 1985), 168.

25 Everett, review of *A Tour*, 6.

26 James Fenimore Cooper, *The Spy: A Tale of the Neutral Ground* (New York: Wiley and Halsted, 1821), vii. Michael Gilmore credits Cooper with transforming the novel into a genre of public history instead of private sentiment, although he avers that Cooper never quite finished that transformation or maintained it consistently throughout his work. Gilmore, "The Literature of the Revolutionary and Early National Periods," in *The Cambridge History of American Literature*, vol. 1, ed. Sacvan Bercovitch (Cambridge: Cambridge University Press, 1994). In a different vernacular, Sergio Perosa also sees Cooper attempting to make the particular into the universal (*American Theories of the Novel, 1793–1903* [New York: New York University Press, 1983], 32).

27 Gardiner, review of *The Spy*, 278.

28 Edward Tyrell Channing, review of Charles Brockden Brown, *North-American Review* (June 1819): 68.

29 Alexis de Tocqueville, *Democracy in America*, transl. George Lawrence, ed. J. P. Mayer (New York: Harper & Row, 1969); James Fenimore Cooper, *Notions of the Americans: Picked up by a Traveling Bachelor*, ed. Gary Williams (Albany: State University of New York Press, 1991).

30 Everett, review of *A Tour*, 12. *n oss*

31 Gardiner, review of *The Spy*, 255.

32 Cooper, *The Spy* (1821), vii.

33 Everett, review of *A Tour*, 12.

34 Cooper, *The Pioneers* (1823), ed. Donald A. Ringe (New York: Penguin, 1988), 6.

35 Gardiner, review of *The Spy*, 251.

36 Longfellow, "Graduation Address," 238.

37 Cooper, *The Spy*, vii.

38 Gardiner, review of *The Spy*, 256.

39 See Court, "Scottish Literary Teaching," in Crawford, 152–54.

40 E. Channing, review of Charles Brockden Brown, 65. Subsequent pages references to this review are given in parenthesis in the text.

41 Alan Axelrod stresses Brown's abstractness, but finds that at the moment of yellow fever, Brown manages to connect: "the horse remains sharply present to the senses, not as an emblem, but as a highly wrought synecdoche of 'torpor and decay'" (*Charles Brockden Brown: An American Tale* [Austin: University of Texas Press, 1983], 117). On the tensions between empiricism and imagination in Brown, also see Norman Grabo, *The Coincidental Art of Charles Brockden Brown* (Chapel Hill: University of North Carolina Press, 1981), and Arthur Kimball, *Rational Fictions: A Study of Charles Brockden Brown* (McMinnville, Ore.: Linfield Research Institute, 1986).

42 E. Channing, review of Charles Brockden Brown, 65–66.

43 William Cullen Bryant, review of Catherine Maria Sedgewick, *Redwood*, in *North-American Review* [1825], in *Native Muse*, ed. Ruland, 216–17.

44 Quoted in F. L. Pattee's introduction to John Neal, *American Writers: A Series of Papers contributed to Blackwood's Magazine, 1824–1825* (Durham, N.C.: Duke University Press, 1937), 21. Hereafter abbreviated to *A* and cited parenthetically.

45 See David S. Reynolds's mention of Neal in *Beneath the American Renaissance: The Subversive Imagination in the Age of Emerson and Melville* (New York: Alfred A. Knopf, 1988), 203–4; Peter D. King, "John Neal as a Benthamite," *New England Quarterly* 39:1 (March 1966): 47–65; John D. Seelye's introduction to Neal, *Rachel Dyer* (Gainesville: Scholars' Facsimiles and Reprints, 1964), v–vi; Benjamin Lease, *That Wild Fellow John Neal and the American Literary Revolution* (Chicago: University of Chicago Press, 1972); Donald A. Sears, *John Neal* (Boston: Twayne, 1978).

46 On Neal's experiments with dialect, diction, and syntax, see Harold C. Martin, "The Colloquial Tradition in the Novel: John Neal," *New England Quarterly* 32:4 (Dec. 1959): 455–75.

47 Channing, review of Neal, *North-American Review* [1818], in *Native Muse*, ed. Ruland.

48 See Bell, *Hawthorne and the Historical Romance of New England* (Princeton: Princeton University Press, 1971).

49 Neal, *Randolph* ("Published For Whom It May Concern," 1823), 181, 180.

50 *Randolph*, 219.

51 Teresa A. Goddu, *Gothic America: Narrative, History, and Nation* (New York: Columbia University Press, 1997), 58, 72.

52 Nelson, *National Manhood*, 88.

53 Goddu, *Gothic America*, 70.

54 *Randolph*, 238.

## 2 SENSING HAWTHORNE: THE FIGURE
## OF HAWTHORNE'S AFFECT

1 Nathaniel Hawthorne, *The Scarlet Letter* (1850), in *Collected Novels*, selected and with notes by Millicent Bell (New York: Literary Classics of the United States, 1983), 146. Hereafter abbreviated to *S* and cited parenthetically. "Young Goodman Brown," in *Tales and Sketches*, selected by Roy Harvey Pearce (New York: Literary Classics of the United States, 1982), 288.

2 See John Stubbs, *The Pursuit of Form: A Study of Hawthorne and the Romance* (Urbana: University of Illinois Press, 1970), 50; Gordon Hutner's *Secrets and Sympathy: Forms of Disclosure in Hawthorne's Novels* (Athens, Ga.: University of Georgia Press, 1988) argues that by obscuring meaning, Hawthorne teaches readers to intuit meaning through sympathy; Richard Millington focuses on the moral meanings of Hawthorne's work in *Practicing Romance: Narrative Form and Cultural Engagement in Hawthorne's Fiction* (Princeton: Princeton University Press, 1992). Kenneth Dauber's observation that Hawthorne's "purpose is to engage us, and we must not mistake his hospitality for anything intellectually more substantial" is closer to my own suggestion of a certain vacuity in Hawthorne's intimacy (*Rediscovering Hawthorne* [Princeton: Princeton University Press, 1977], 18.

3 The same issue also included a story by Neal, observes Joel Pfister in *The Production of Personal Life: Class, Gender, and the Psychological in Hawthorne's Fiction* (Stanford: Stanford University Press, 1991).

4 Nathaniel Hawthorne, "The Minister's Black Veil," in *Tales and Sketches*, 371. Hereafter abbreviated to "M" and cited parenthetically.

5 See Rosemary Freeman, *English Emblem Books* (London: Chatto & Windus, 1948), and Mario Praz, *Studies in Seventeenth-Century Imagery*, 2nd edn (Rome: Edizioni di Storia e Letteratura, 1964).

6 Jeffrey Steele, *The Representation of the Self in the American Renaissance* (Chapel Hill: University of North Carolina Press, 1987), 159.

7 Berlant, *Anatomy of a National Fantasy*, 20–21.

8 These readings share a sense of the importance of the social to Hawthorne, which has been explored recently by Stacey Margolis in terms of Hawthorne's concern with party affiliations which, she argues, are more prominent than national ones in Hawthorne (*The Public Life of Privacy*, 19–23). The idea that in Hawthorne the self is put in dialogue with a larger community, which becomes responsible for the making of meaning, is explored by Donald Pease as a way in which American Renaissance writing contributes to the sustenance of the republican ideal of the public sphere in *Visionary Compacts: American Renaissance Writings in Cultural Context* (Madison: University of Wisconsin Press, 1987), 49.

9 Sharon Cameron, *The Corporeal Self: Allegories of the Body in Melville and Hawthorne* (New York: Columbia University Press, 1991), 119.

10 [Henry Wadsworth Longfellow], from a review in the *North-American Review* 45 (July 1837), 59–73, in J. Donald Crowley, *Hawthorne: The Critical*

*Heritage* (New York: Barnes and Noble, 1970), 58; [Anne W. Abbott], "*The Scarlet Letter,*" *North-American Review* 71:148 (July 1850), 135–48, in *Nathaniel Hawthorne: The Contemporary Reviews*, ed. John L. Idol Jr. and Buford Jones (Cambridge: Cambridge University Press, 1994), 131.

11 Abbott, "*The Scarlet Letter,*" 131.

12 [Evert A. Duyckinck], "*The Scarlet Letter,*" *Literary World* 6 (30 March 1850), in Crowley, *Critical Heritage*, 193.

13 Melville, "Hawthorne and His Mosses," *Literary* World, 7 (August 17 and 24, 1850), in *Contemporary Reviews*, ed. Idol and Jones, 108.

14 Ibid.

15 Philip Rahv, "The Dark Lady of Salem," in *Image and Idea: Fourteen Essays on Literary Themes* (New York: New Directions, 1949), 23.

16 Frederick C. Crews, *Sins of the Fathers: Hawthorne's Psychological Themes* (Oxford: Oxford University Press, 1966), 270, 240, 243; Crews's emphasis.

17 Lionel Trilling, "Hawthorne in Our Time," in *Beyond Culture: Essays on Literature and Learning* (New York: Viking Press, 1965), 186.

18 Trilling, "Hawthorne," 185, 192.

19 Trilling, "Hawthorne," 192.

20 Ibid.

21 Trilling, "Hawthorne," 206, 207.

22 In this regard, Michael Gilmore's account of "Surface and Depth" as a central theme of American literature is a continuing recourse to figuration to explain or point towards an experience that does not rest in the depths of the text or the mind (*Surface and Depth: The Quest for Legibility in American Culture* [New York: Oxford University Press, 2003]).

23 Henry James, *Nathaniel Hawthorne* [1879], ed. with a foreword by Dan McCall (Ithaca: Cornell University Press, 1966), 2–3.

24 Nathaniel Hawthorne, *The House of the Seven Gables*, in *Collected Novels*, 451. Hereafter abbreviated to *H* and cited parenthetically.

25 Nathaniel Hawthorne, *The American Notebooks*, ed. Claude M. Simpson (Columbus: Ohio State University Press, 1972). Hereafter abbreviated to *AN* and cited parenthetically.

26 Thus, while previous critics have discussed this passage as exploring the relationship between metaphoric and literal representation, I point to the way it proposes the making of the literalized emblems as an iterative gesture. For Hutner (*Secrets and Sympathy*, 26–27) the issue is dismemberment, and for Cameron it is how allegory's relationship of the "literal and figural" projects the question of "how the body is related to itself" (*The Corporeal Self*, 87).

27 Angus Fletcher, *Allegory: The Theory of a Symbolic Mode* (Ithaca: Cornell University Press, 1964), 66.

28 Dorrit Cohn, *The Distinction of Fiction* (Baltimore: Johns Hopkins University Press, 1999), 12.

29 There is always the possibility that the moment of original experience is a stage in Hawthorne's life we are not seeing, but my point is that in conceiving

of experience he does not distinguish the actual experience and the abstract connection which brings forth the emblem.

30 James, *Hawthorne*, 33.

31 I am thinking here particularly of Bill Brown's account of things in Henry James in *A Sense of Things: The Object Matter of American Literature* (Chicago: University of Chicago Press, 2003).

32 Stubbs, *Pursuit of Form*, 6. Stubbs uses Frye's definition of romance as occurring in "a world in which the ordinary laws of nature are slightly suspended . . . between the realm of gods in myth and the realm of human beings in realism" (xiii).

33 Lora Romero, *Home Fronts: Domesticity and Its Critics in the Antebellum United States* (Durham, N.C.: Duke University Press, 1997), 102.

34 Lydia Maria Child, *Hobomok and Other Writings on Indians* [1824], ed. with introduction by Carolyn L. Karcher (New Brunswick: Rutgers University Press, 2001), 116.

35 Child, *Hobomok*, 3–4.

36 Pearl is right to see the two of them together as a threat, since for Hester and Dimmesdale as characters to reunite would destroy Pearl's need for being, or to incorporate her back into the form of human relationships. Merish points out that such incorporation into human relationships is precisely Pearl's fate at the end of the novel, when Pearl "would grow up amid human joys and sorrows" (*S*, 279, quoted in Merish, *Sentimental Materialism*, 174). But while Merish argues that this shows that "exchanges of sympathetic identification are localized within the patriarchal domestic economy of sex and gender" (174), the Pearl who becomes "a woman" lacks the fascination of the Pearl who is a space moving across a threshold.

37 Sacvan Bercovitch, *The Office of the Scarlet Letter* (Baltimore: Johns Hopkins University Press, 1991), 18.

38 See Cheyfitz, "Irresistibleness of Great Literature," on the equivocality of Bercovitch's judgment of liberal ideology; it seems critical but is fundamentally celebratory.

39 Richard Harter Fogle notes that Hawthorne approaches "organic unity or synthesis," but ultimately unravels his metaphors: he "conceives synthesis but presents it in parts" in *Hawthorne's Imagery: The "Proper Light and Shadow" in the Major Romances* (Norman: University of Oklahoma Press, 1969), 29, 8.

40 Edgar A. Dryden, *Monumental Melville: The Formation of a Literary Career* (Stanford: Stanford University Press, 2004), 55.

41 Of course, there is a major difference in that Knapp's position indicates the inevitability of making a choice and committing to a belief, while Bercovitch's suggests a constant hanging back from such commitments in the restricted plurality of multiply legitimate, contrasting beliefs.

42 "Young Goodman Brown," in *Tales and Sketches*, 288.

43 Charles Feidelson, *Symbolism and American Literature* (Chicago: University of Chicago Press, 1953), 52. Also see Fogle, *Hawthorne's Imagery*, and Harry Levin, *The Power of Blackness: Hawthorne, Poe, Melville* (New York: Knopf, 1958), 75.

44 Jonathan Arac, "Reading the Letter," *Diacritics* 9:2 (Summer, 1979): 42–52; 49.

45 Evan Carton, *The Rhetoric of American Romance* (Baltimore: Johns Hopkins University Press, 1985), 12. Also see Dryden's discussion of the prefaces in *The Form of American Romance* (Baltimore: Johns Hopkins University Press, 1988).

46 Carton, *Rhetoric of American Romance*, 213.

47 See Fletcher, *Allegory*, 7.

48 On obscuring the bodies of women, see Brown, *Domestic Individualism*, 95; on obscuring the changeability of American life by turning away from mimetic representation to the idealistic vacuum of romance, see Michaels, *Gold Standard*, 100–1.

## 3 "LIFE IS AN ECSTACY": RALPH WALDO EMERSON AND A. BRONSON ALCOTT

1 Ralph Waldo Emerson, "Illusions," in *Essays and Poems*, ed. Joel Porte, Harold Bloom, and Paul Kane (New York: Literary Classics of the United States, 1996), 942. Hereafter abbreviated to "I" and cited parenthetically.

2 "The Poet," in *Essays and Poems*, 468. Hereafter abbreviated to "P" and cited parenthetically.

3 For the history of Transcendentalism's relation to Locke, the best source is B. L. Packer, "The Assault on Locke," in "The Transcendentalists," in *The Cambridge History of American Literature*, vol. ii, ed. Sacvan Bercovitch (Cambridge: Cambridge University Press, 1994).

4 Christopher Newfield, *The Emerson Effect: Individualism and Submission in America* (Chicago: University of Chicago Press, 1996), 25.

5 Poirier, *A World Elsewhere*, 248.

6 In addition to Newfield, the criticism on Emerson's individualism includes: Charles E. Mitchell, *Individualism and Its Discontents: Appropriations of Emerson, 1880–1950* (Amherst: University of Massachusetts Press, 1997); George Kateb, *Emerson and Self-Reliance* (Thousand Oaks, Calif.: Sage Publications, 1995); Bercovitch, *Rites of Assent*.

7 "Thoughts on Modern Literature," 1:2 (October, 1840): 147. Emerson's distinction between the subjective and the personal is one of the affinities of American with Kantian Transcendentalism. Yet it remains a fairly superficial affinity: neither a rigorous agreement nor a genetic derivation. See Stanley M. Vogel, *German Literary Influences on the American Transcendentalists* (New Haven: Archon Books, 1970); René Wellek, *Confrontations: Studies in the Intellectual and Literary Relations between Germany, England, and the United States During the Nineteenth Century* (Princeton: Princeton University Press, 1965), 211; and Bruce Kuklick, *The Rise of American Philosophy: Cambridge, Massachusetts 1860–1930* (New Haven: Yale University Press, 1977). For arguments that Emerson is responding directly to Kant, see David Van Leer, *Emerson's Epistemology* (Cambridge: Cambridge University Press, 1986); and Stanley Cavell, "Finding as Founding," in *This New Yet Unapproachable America: Lectures After Emerson After Wittgenstein* (Albuquerque: Living Batch Press, 1989) and *In Quest of the*

*Ordinary: Lines of Skepticism and Romanticism* (Chicago: University of Chicago Press, 1988).

8 Rowe, *At Emerson's Tomb*, 248.

9 Grossman, *Reconstituting the American Renaissance*, 204.

10 Jonathan Levin, *The Poetics of Transition: Emerson, Pragmatism, and American Literary Modernism* (Durham, N.C.: Duke University Press, 1999), 25.

11 Gregg D. Crane, *Race, Citizenship and Law in American Literature* (Cambridge: Cambridge University Press, 2002), 87.

12 Notably in Poirier, *A World Elsewhere* and Sharon Cameron, "The Way of Life by Abandonment: Emerson's Impersonal," *Critical Inquiry* 25 (Autumn 1998): 1–31. Her argument is that because Emerson does not ground his knowledge in "God or Law," he must then base it in an epiphany occurring "to someone *in particular*, who, by virtue of that particularity, is in a position to describe it" (26). Yet Emerson presents no such personal epiphany and only imagines the impersonal, which he tries to ground in its representation. Cameron argues Emerson offers "the representation of an encounter whose truth is somehow tied to its stylistic or rhetorical singularity" (22). That is, the essays' rhetoric is insufficient to the task of presenting the the the impersonal.

13 "Fate," in *Essays and Poems*, 793.

14 In contrast, Emerson's essay title "Experience" is more properly concerned with an attempt to recuperate subjective experience. The essay's very difficulty with this approach to experience, the attempt to recapture the feeling of possession, bespeaks the extent of Emerson's investment in the contrary notion of a universal experience.

15 "Circles," in *Essays and Poems*, 403. Hereafter abbreviated to "C" and cited parenthetically.

16 Crane, *Race, Citizenship and Law*, 91.

17 Levin, *Poetics of Transition*, 39.

18 B. L. Packer, *Emerson's Fall: A New Interpretation of the Major Essays* (New York: Continuum, 1982), 193–94. Or, as Poirier observed, Emerson "invested less of his energy in stylistic ingenuities than his positions required" (*World Elsewhere*, 90).

19 "An Address delivered before the Senior Class in Divinity College, Cambridge, Sunday Evening, July 15, 1838," in *Essays and Poems*, 80.

20 Moreover, this means that Emerson must be distinguished from pragmatist aesthetics, not identified with it as Levin has argued. Emerson isn't interested in "find[ing] meaningful drama in" ordinary activities such as "playing with a pet or planning and cooking a meal" or "infus[ing] life with deeper (but never definitive or absolute) meanings" (*Poetics of Transition*, 5) – not, that is, in the sense that Levin means, of seeing ordinary experience as full of the ideal and even aesthetic in a way that would heal the breach of art and life.

21 For Cameron, his writing is voiced from an impersonal speaking position, such that Emerson as author does not own up, so to speak, to the fact that he wrote the essays ("The Way of Life by Abandonment," 31). Poirier's account of Emerson in *The Renewal of Literature: Emersonian Reflections* (New York:

Random House, 1987) – somewhat differently from that in *World Elsewhere* – also suggests that the words do not quite belong to a person or have an identifiable point; in his terms, genius supersedes human powers, and this must be communicated in words which are never allowed to settle into static, humanly graspable, terms. Newfield objects to the poet's absence of individual activity: "The poet watches his intellectual processes as though they were not part of his consciousness, but distinct from and prior to it, part of some other power" (*The Emerson Effect*, 49). Jehlen argues in *American Incarnation* that the individual speaker in Emerson disappears into the general voice of nature: "the forms of both nature and language carry their meanings organically, so that one might say they speak us rather than we them . . . the necessary speaker can be seen as one who personal power to speak is realized in the reproduction of the language of nature" (106).

22 Oscar W. Firkins, *Ralph Waldo Emerson* (Boston: Houghton Mifflin, 1915), 256.
23 Stanley Cavell, *Philosophical Passages: Wittgenstein, Emerson, Austin, Derrida* (Cambridge, Mass.: Basil Blackwell, 1995), *Conditions Handsome and Unhandsome: The Conditions of Emersonian Perfectionism* (Chicago: University of Chicago Press, 1990), and "Finding as Founding."
24 "Quotation and Originality," in *Essays and Poems*, 1030.
25 Packer, *Emerson's Fall*, 6.
26 Pamela Schirmeister, *Less Legible Meanings: Between Poetry and Philosophy in the Work of Emerson* (Stanford: Stanford University Press, 1999), 16; Levin, *Poetics of Transition*, 15.
27 Schirmeister, *Less Legible Meanings*, 16.
28 Cavell, "Finding as Founding," in *This New Yet Unapproachable America*, 118.
29 West, *Democracy Matters*, 70.
30 Grossman, *Reconstituting the American Renaissance*, 137, 147.
31 Kateb, *Emerson and Self-Reliance*, Chapter 3.
32 Mitchell, *Individualism*, 11.
33 Ibid.
34 Crane, *Race, Citizenship and Law*, 103.
35 Newfield, *The Emerson Effect*, 4; emphasis in original.
36 Newfield, *The Emerson Effect*, 215; my emphasis.
37 Newfield, *The Emerson Effect*, 38.
38 Newfield, *The Emerson Effect*, 218.
39 "The American Scholar," in *Essays and Poems*, 53, 68. Hereafter abbreviated to "AS" and cited parenthetically.
40 As Jehlen observes, "If pictures are rare in Emerson's writing, stories are rarer still" (*American Incarnation*, 124).
41 Maurice Gonnaud's description of the world as the "biography" of a "Universal Spirit," which belongs to all men, then, doesn't acknowledge the need of the spirit for objects, or the sense in which its manifestation in form is the crucial theatre of its coming into existence (*An Uneasy Solitude: Individual and Society in the Work of Ralph Waldo Emerson*, trans. Lawrence Rosenwald [Princeton: Princeton University Press, 1987], 189).

42 Michaels, *Shape of the Signifier*, 95.

43 Jehlen, *American Incarnation*, 102.

44 "Emerson's meaning is incarnate in the body of his essay, as the meaning of America is in the body of the continent" (Jehlen, *American Incarnation*, 92).

45 A. Bronson Alcott, "Days from a Diary," *The Dial* 2.4 (April, 1842), 435.

46 *Emerson in His Journals*, ed. Joel Porte (Cambridge: Belknap Press of Harvard University, 1982), 196.

47 Alcott, "Days from a Diary," 431, 432, 433.

48 Elizabeth Palmer Peabody, from "Explanatory Preface," *Record of a School: Exemplifying the General Principles of Spiritual Culture*, 2nd edn (Boston: Russell, Shattuck; New York: Leavitt, Lord, 1836), in Joel Myerson, ed., *Transcendentalism: A Reader* (New York: Oxford University Press), 111.

49 On the school's history in general see Packer's account in the *Cambridge History*, 385–91; Frederick C. Dahlstrand, *Amos Bronson Alcott: An Intellectual Biography* (East Brunswick, N.J.: Associated University Presses, 1982); and Megan Marshall, *The Peabody Sisters: Three Women Who Ignited American Romanticism* (Boston: Houghton Mifflin, 2005), 294–98, 307–26. *Amos Bronson Alcott and Elizabeth Peabody, Conversations with Children on the Gospels*, 2 vols. (Boston: James Munroe and Company, 1836–37) Hereafter abbreviated to *C* and cited parenthetically.

50 In *Record of a School* Peabody took pains to defend Alcott from the charge that his methods of "self-analysis" led the students into "egotism" (111, 101).

51 Packer, *Cambridge History*, 388.

52 "Days from a Diary," 414.

53 Gillian Brown comments that Fruitlands was run on the principle that labor could be spiritualized through "the denial of desires," and that "Alcott's pursuit of the pure life did not follow the principles of abstinence as far as Lane's" (108). My point would be that Alcott's commitment to sexual activity at Fruitlands would, to him, not have been inconsistent with the denial of individual desire, but the cornerstone of a way of evoking how spirit could inform – be conceived in – every piece of matter. Also see Richard Francis's *Transcendental Utopias: Individual and Community at Brook Farm, Fruitlands, and Walden* (Ithaca: Cornell University Press, 1997), 180 ff, for a discussion of sexuality and the family in Lane, Alcott, and other Transcendentalists.

54 For Eve Kosofsky Sedgewick, Alcott teaches by pointing at things and ideas alike, waiting for students to recognize what they already know (*Touching Feeling: Affect, Pedagogy, Performativity* [Durham, N.C.: Duke University Press, 2003]). But Alcott's pedagogy is not merely deictic, for it involves a precise process of exploring emblematic images and responses, of producing conversations about them that begin to educe some spirit that is apart from the content as well as the form of the class. I would also suggest that it's important that the goal is to bring an experience into being, not to practice an extreme form of knowing, or rather not to practice a kind of knowing that can be said to even compete with or compare to the conveying of beliefs from one person to another.

## 4 LAWS OF EXPERIENCE: TRUTH AND FEELING IN HARRIET BEECHER STOWE

1 [Briggs], "Uncle Tomitudes," 41, 35.

2 Harriet Beecher Stowe, *Uncle Tom's Cabin* [1852], ed. Jean Fagan Yellin (New York: Oxford University Press, 1998), 447. Hereafter abbreviated to *UTC* and cited parenthetically.

3 Stowe, *A Key to Uncle Tom's Cabin; Presenting the Original Facts and Documents upon which the Story is Founded. Together with Corroborative Statements Verifying the Work* ([1853]; repr. Bedford, Mass.: Applewood Books, 1998), 2. Hereafter abbreviated to *K* and cited parenthetically.

4 Mary H. Eastman, *Aunt Phillis's Cabin; or, Southern Life as It is* ([1852]; repr. New York: Negro Universities Press, 1968).

5 Susan Warner, *The Wide, Wide World* (1850), with an afterword by Jane Tompkins (New York: The Feminist Press at the City University of New York, 1987), 12. Jane Tompkins points out the "claustrophobic" atmosphere of the novel, as well as the way it "draws the reader into its own circuit of attention" so that "the reader has to pay attention to what Ellen pays attention to" in *Sensational Designs: The Cultural Work of American Fiction, 1790–1860* (New York: Oxford University Press, 1985), 177. Margolis discusses in *The Public Life of Privacy* how in this novel there is no self-knowledge or regulation, except in and through others.

6 Warner, *Wide, Wide World*, 284.

7 Warner, *Wide, Wide World*, 241, 220.

8 See Janet Todd, *Sensibility: An Introduction* (New York: Methuen, 1986); David Marshall, *The Surprising Effects of Sympathy: Marivaux, Diderot, Rousseau, and Mary Shelley* (Chicago: University of Chicago Press, 1988).

9 See, for example, Philip Fisher, *Hard Facts: Setting and Form in the American Novel* (New York: Oxford University Press, 1987); Saidiya V. Hartman, *Scenes of Subjection: Terror, Slavery, and Self-Making in Nineteenth-Century America* (New York: Oxford University Press, 1997); Karen Sánchez-Eppler, *Touching Liberty: Abolition, Feminism, and the Politics of the Body* (Berkeley: University of California Press, 1993); Marianne Noble, "The Ecstasies of Sentimental Wounding in *Uncle Tom's Cabin*," in *The Masochistic Pleasures of Sentimental Literature* (Princeton: Princeton University Press, 2000).

10 See both Hendler, *Public Sentiments* and Margolis, *The Public Life of Privacy*.

11 This would contribute to June Howard's re-emphasis on the connection between sympathy and sentimentalism in "What Is Sentimentality?" *American Literary History* 11:1 (Spring, 1999): 63–81. Also see Gregg Camfield, *Sentimental Twain: Samuel Clemens in the Maze of Moral Philosophy* (Philadelphia: University of Philadelphia Press, 1994), chap. 2 for an account of the ongoing pertinence of sympathy, rather than sentimentalism, to Stowe.

12 Lauren Berlant, "The Female Woman: Fanny Fern and the Form of Sentiment," in *The Culture of Sentiment: Race, Gender, and Sentimentality in*

*Nineteenth-Century America*, ed. Shirley Samuels (New York: Oxford University Press, 1992), 278.

13 See E. Bruce Kirkham, *The Building of Uncle Tom's Cabin* (Knoxville: University of Tennessee Press, 1977); Thomas F. Gossett, *Uncle Tom's Cabin and American Culture* (Dallas: Southern Methodist University Press, 1985), 291; Eric Sundquist, introduction to *New Essays on Uncle Tom's Cabin*, ed. Sundquist (Cambridge: Cambridge University Press, 1986); Alice Crozier, *The Novels of Harriet Beecher Stowe* (New York: Oxford University Press, 1969); and Lisa Whitney, "In the Shadow of Uncle Tom's Cabin: Stowe's Vision of Slavery from the Great Dismal Swamp," *New England Quarterly* 66:4 (December 1993): 552–69.

14 Cindy Weinstein, *Family, Kinship, and Sympathy in Nineteenth-Century American Literature* (Cambridge: Cambridge University Press, 2004).

15 Ann Douglas, *The Feminization of American Culture* (New York: Alfred A. Knopf, 1977); Tompkins, *Sensational Designs*, xvii.

16 Lorenzo D. Turner's *Anti-Slavery Sentiment in American Literature Prior to 1865* (Washington, D.C.: Association for the Study of Negro Life and History, 1929) provides a broad picture of the conventions spanning antislavery literature, and of Stowe's adaptation as well as invention of those conventions. An early school of criticism paid a fair amount of attention to Stowe as a realist, in the specific sense that she pays attention to everyday details of material life and speech, and is avowedly committed to writing from her own experience. See Crozier, *The Novels of Harriet Beecher Stowe*; Gossett, *"Uncle Tom's Cabin"*; Charles H. Foster, *The Rungless Ladder: Harriet Beecher Stowe and New England Puritanism* (Durham, N.C.: Duke University Press, 1954); Kirkham, *The Building of Uncle Tom's Cabin*; and Camfield, *Sentimental Twain*.

17 George Lippard, *The Quaker City; or, the Monks of Monk Hall. A Romance of Philadelphia Life, Mystery, and Crime* [1845], ed. and intro. David S. Reynolds (Amherst: University of Massachusetts Press, 1995), 119.

18 Berlant, "Poor Eliza," *American Literature*, No More Separate Spheres! 70:3 (September, 1998): 635–68, 636.

19 Crane, *Race, Citizenship and Law*, 58.

20 Kenneth Warren, "The Persistence of Uncle Tom and the Problem of Critical Distinction," in *Black and White Strangers: Race and American Literary Realism* (Chicago: University of Chicago Press, 1993). For an argument about Stowe's policing of the boundary of the abstraction demanded by the social and the embodiment it must exclude, see Jonathan Elmer, *Reading at the Social Limit: Affect, Mass Culture and Edgar Allan Poe* (Stanford: Stanford University Press, 1995), chap. 2.

21 Sánchez-Eppler, *Touching Liberty*, 47, 31, 48.

22 Sundquist, *New Essays on Uncle Tom's Cabin*, 1. Also see Foster, *Rungless Ladder*; Tompkins, *Sensational Designs*; Berlant, "Poor Eliza"; Edmund Wilson, *Patriotic Gore: Studies in The Literature of the American Civil War* (New York: W. W. Norton, 1962); and Stephen M. Best, *The Fugitive's Properties: Law and the Poetics of Possession* (Chicago: University of Chicago Press, 2004).

23 For a recent such dismissal of Stowe, see Donoghue, *The American Classics*.

24 The effect is similar to that in the Greuze paintings Michael Fried describes in *Absorption and Theatricality: Painting and Beholder in the Age of Diderot* (Chicago: University of Chicago Press, 1980), where emotional response is objectified and incorporated into paintings by the presence of a figure watching and responding to a central scene.

25 My account of abolitionism and the legal issues it involves derives from Don E. Fehrenbacher, *Slavery, Law, and Politics: The Dred Scott Case in Historical Perspective* (New York: Oxford University Press, 1981); Robert William Fogel, *Without Consent or Contract: The Rise and Fall of American Slavery* (New York: W. W. Norton, 1989); Louis S. Gerteis, *Morality and Utility in American Antislavery Reform* (Chapel Hill: University of North Carolina Press, 1987); Daniel J. McInerney, *The Fortunate Heirs of Freedom: Abolitionism and Republican Thought* (Lincoln: University of Nebraska Press, 1994); Perry Miller, *The Life of the Mind in America: From the Revolution to the Civil War* (New York: Harcourt, Brace, and World, 1965); Gerald Sorin, *The New York Abolitionists: A Case Study of Political Radicalism* (Westport, Conn.: Greenwood, 1971); and James Brewer Stewart, *Holy Warriors: The Abolitionists and American Slavery* (New York: Hill and Wang, 1976).

26 William Goodell, *The American Slave Code in Theory and Practice: Its Distinctive Features Shown by its Statutes, Judicial Decisions, and Illustrative Facts* (London, 1853). Hereafter abbreviated to *ASC* and cited parenthetically. The prefatory letter by William Jay states, "It is more easy to make than to refute a charge of exaggeration against a work of fiction like Mrs. Stowe's; but your book is as impregnable against such a charge as is Euclid's Geometry, since, like that, it consists of propositions and demonstrations" (iii–iv). He adds that Goodell "giv[es] a solemn sanction to the atrocities portrayed by Mrs. Stowe" (v), a statement that upholds the truth of Stowe's fiction but also suggests its insufficiency as proof.

27 Lydia Maria Child, *An Appeal in Favor of that Class of Americans Called Africans* (Boston: Allen and Ticknor, 1833); William Wells Brown, *Narrative of William W. Brown, an American Slave: Written by Himself* (London: C. Gilpin, 1849).

28 See Crane, *Race, Citizenship and Law*; Whitney, "In the Shadow of Uncle Tom's Cabin"; and Susan M. Ryan, "Charity Begins at Home: Stowe's Antislavery Novels and the Forms of Benevolent Citizenship," *American Literature* 72:4 (December, 2000): 751–82.

29 Harriet Beecher Stowe, *Dred: A Tale of the Great Dismal Swamp* [1856], ed. Judie Newman (Edinburgh: Edinburgh University Press, 1999), 29. Hereafter abbreviated to *D* and cited parenthetically.

30 The *State* v. *Mann*, Dec. T. 1829. 2 Devereaux's North Carolina Rep. 263, in Jacob D. Wheeler, ed., *A Practical Treatise on the Law of Slavery. Being a Compilation of all the Decisions made on that Subject, in the Several Courts of the United States and State Courts. With Copious Notes and References to the Statutes and other Authorities, Systematically Arranged* (Allan Pollock, Jr., 1837; reprint, New York: Negro Universities Press, 1968), 244.

31 This commitment to the law is a position that Stowe allows to prevail without any criticism. In fact, when Judge Clayton tells his wife of his moral misgivings about the decision he is about to render, neither Stowe nor Mrs. Clayton make any suggestion that he should act differently. In *Uncle Tom's Cabin*, Senator Bird returns home after voting for the Fugitive Slave Law only to find himself confronted first by his wife's arguments and then by Eliza; he ends up helping Eliza in her escape. In *Dred*, Clayton urges that the man who has murdered a slave should be convicted as a murderer – and Stowe has his good-intentioned plan fail, with the force of the law prevailing. The plots, then, are very different: in *Uncle Tom's Cabin*, morally inspired argument undergirds abolitionist transgressions of the law, while in *Dred* morally inspired argument brings out a benevolent but proslavery misinterpretation of the laws. However, it is crucial that in *Dred* the problem with Clayton's moral fervor is that he mistakenly thinks it is grounded in the law; were he right about the law such moral power would be legitimate. In *Dred*, Stowe suggests that slavery must be righted not just through moral or rhetorical pleading, nor even through reform, but through direct abolition of the laws. My point is that this is exactly the position which Stowe has maintained in *Uncle Tom's Cabin* and in the *Key*: the same view as in Goodell, that the laws' essence is to produce cruel actions.

32 Hartman, *Scenes of Subjection*, 91.

33 Wheeler, *A Practical Treatise on the Law of Slavery*, 247.

34 Goodell elides this passage too, but because Stowe includes some material that Goodell had not, hers is unlikely to be an unconscious repetition of his editing.

35 Best, *Fugitive's Properties*, 150.

36 Berlant, "Poor Eliza," 645.

37 Best, *Fugitive's Properties*, 25.

38 Berlant, "Poor Eliza," 665.

39 Best, *Fugitive's Properties*, 272.

40 Best, *Fugitive's Properties*, 266–67.

41 Berlant, "Poor Eliza," 655, 659, 662.

42 Berlant, "Poor Eliza," 665.

43 Best, *Fugitive's Properties*, 8.

44 Best, *Fugitive's Properties*, 2.

45 As in, for example, Pierre Bourdieu's critique of taste as the cultivation of distinctions and comparisons without end in *Distinction: A Social Critique of the Judgment of Taste*, trans. Richard Nice (1985; reprint, Cambridge: Harvard University Press, 2002).

46 Hal Foster objects of the Guggenheim, Bilbao: "Why this curve, swirl, or blob here, and not that one? Formal articulation requires a resistant material, structure or context; without such constraint architecture quickly becomes arbitrary or self-indulgent" (*Design and Crime*, 40).

# Bibliography

[Abbott, Anne W.]. "*The Scarlet Letter.*" *North-American Review* 71:148 (July 1850): 135–48. In *Nathaniel Hawthorne: The Contemporary Reviews*, ed. Crowley.

Alcott, Amos Bronson. "Days from a Diary." *The Dial* 2:4 (April 1842): 409–37.

Alcott, Amos Bronson, and Elizabeth Peabody. *Conversations with Children on the Gospels.* 2 vols. Boston: James Munroe and Company, 1836–37.

Alison, Archibald. *Essays on the Nature and Principles of Taste.* 5th edn. Edinburgh, 1817.

Ammons, Elizabeth, ed. *Critical Essays on Harriet Beecher Stowe.* Boston: G. K. Hall, 1980.

Arac, Jonathan. "Reading the Letter." *Diacritics* 9:2 (Summer 1979): 42–52.

Axelrod, Alan. *Charles Brockden Brown: An American Tale.* Austin: University of Texas Press, 1983.

Barnes, Elizabeth. *States of Sympathy: Seduction and Democracy in the American Novel.* New York: Columbia University Press, 1997.

Bate, Walter Jackson. *From Classic to Romantic: Premises of Taste in Eighteenth Century England.* New York: Harper & Row, 1946.

Bell, Michael Davitt. *The Development of American Romance: The Sacrifice of Relation.* Chicago: University of Chicago Press, 1980.

　*Hawthorne and the Historical Romance of New England.* Princeton: Princeton University Press, 1971.

Bercovitch, Sacvan. *The Office of the Scarlet Letter.* Baltimore: Johns Hopkins University Press, 1991.

　*The Rites of Assent: Transformations in the Symbolic Construction of America.* New York: Routledge, 1993.

Berlant, Lauren. *The Anatomy of a National Fantasy: Hawthorne, Utopia, and Everyday Life.* Chicago: University of Chicago Press, 1991.

　"The Female Woman: Fanny Fern and the Form of Sentiment." In *The Culture of Sentiment*, ed. Samuels.

　"Poor Eliza!" *American Literature.* No More Separate Spheres! 70:3 (September 1998): 635–68.

Best, Stephen M. *The Fugitive's Properties: Law and the Poetics of Possession.* Chicago: University of Chicago Press, 2004.

Blassingame, John W., ed. *Slave Testimony: Two Centuries of Letters, Speeches, Interviews, and Autobiographies*. Baton Rouge: Louisiana State University Press, 1977.

Bleich, David. *Subjective Criticism*. Baltimore: Johns Hopkins University Press, 1978.

Bourdieu, Pierre. *Distinction: A Social Critique of the Judgment of Taste*. trans. Richard Nice, 1985. Repr., Cambridge: Harvard University Press, 2002.

[Briggs, Charles]. "Uncle Tomitudes." *Putnam's Monthly* 1 (January 1853): 97–102. In *Critical Essays on Harriet Beecher Stowe*, ed. Ammons.

Brodhead, Richard. *Cultures of Letters: Scenes of Reading and Writing in Nineteenth-Century America*. Chicago: University of Chicago Press, 1993.

Brooks, Van Wyck. *The Flowering of New England 1815–1865: Emerson, Thoreau, Hawthorne, and the Beginnings of American Literature*. 1936. Repr., Boston: Houghton Mifflin, 1981.

Brown, Bill. *A Sense of Things: The Object Matter of American Literature*. Chicago: University of Chicago Press, 2003.

Brown, Gillian. *Domestic Individualism: Imagining Self in Nineteenth-Century America*. Berkeley: University of California Press, 1990.

Brown, William Wells. *Narrative of William W. Brown, an American Slave. Written by Himself*. London: C. Gilpin, 1849.

Buell, Laurence. *Literary Transcendentalism: Style and Vision in the American Renaissance*. Ithaca: Cornell University Press, 1973.

   *New England Literary Culture from Revolution to Renaissance*. Cambridge: Cambridge University Press, 2000.

Bryant, William Cullen. Review of Catherine Maria Sedgewick, *Redwood*. *The North-American Review* (1825). In *Native Muse*, ed. Ruland, 212–221.

Cameron, Sharon. *The Corporeal Self: Allegories of the Body in Melville and Hawthorne*. New York: Columbia University Press, 1981, 1991.

   "The Way of Life by Abandonment: Emerson's Impersonal." *Critical Inquiry* 25 (Autumn 1998): 1–31.

Camfield, Gregg. *Sentimental Twain: Samuel Clemens in the Maze of Moral Philosophy*. Philadelphia: University of Philadelphia Press, 1994.

Carton, Evan. *The Rhetoric of American Romance*. Baltimore: Johns Hopkins University Press, 1985.

Castronovo, Russ. *Necro Citizenship: Death, Eroticism, and the Public Sphere in the Nineteenth-Century United States*. Durham, N.C.: Duke University Press, 2001.

Cavell, Stanley. *Conditions Handsome and Unhandsome: The Conditions of Emersonian Perfectionism*. Chicago: University of Chicago Press, 1990.

   "Finding as Founding." In *This New Yet Unapproachable America: Lectures After Emerson After Wittgenstein*. Albequerque: Living Batch Press, 1989.

   *In Quest of the Ordinary: Lines of Skepticism and Romanticism*. Chicago: University of Chicago Press, 1988.

   *Philosophical Passages: Wittgenstein, Austin, Derrida*. Cambridge, Mass.: Basil Blackwell, 1995.

Channing, Edward Tyrell. "Brown's Life and Writings." *North-American Review* 9:24 (June 1819): 58–77.

Review of John Neal. *North-American Review* (1816). In *Native Muse*, ed. Ruland, 85–91.

Channing, William Ellery. "Remarks on National Literature." In *Selected Writings*, ed. David Roberston. New York: Paulist Press, 1985.

Charvat, William. *The Origins of American Critical Thought, 1810–1835*. Philadelphia: University of Pennsylvania Press, 1936.

Cheyfitz, Eric. "The Irresistibleness of Great Literature: Reconstructing Hawthorne's Politics." *American Literary History* 6:3 (Fall 1994): 539–58.

Child, Lydia Maria. *An Appeal in Favor of that Class of Americans Called Africans.* Boston: Allen and Ticknor, 1833.

*Hobomok and Other Writings on Indians* [1824], ed. with introduction by Carolyn L. Karcher. New Brunswick: Rutgers University Press, 2001.

Cohn, Dorrit. *The Distinction of Fiction.* Baltimore: Johns Hopkins University Press, 1999.

Cooper, James Fenimore. *Notions of the Americans: Picked up by a Traveling Bachelor*, ed. Gary Williams. Albany: State University of New York Press, 1991.

*The Pioneers* [1823], ed. Donald A. Ringe. New York: Penguin, 1988.

*The Spy: A Tale of the Neutral Ground.* New York: Wiley and Halsted, 1821.

*The Spy: A Tale of the Neutral Ground*, introduction and notes by Wayne Franklin. New York: Penguin, 1997.

Court, Franklin E. "Scottish Literary Teaching in North America." In *The Scottish Invention of English Literature*, ed. Robert Crawford. Cambridge: Cambridge University Press, 1998, 134–63.

Coviello, Peter. *Intimacy in America: Dreams of Affiliation in Antebellum American Literature.* Minneapolis: University of Minnesota Press, 2005.

Crane, Gregg D. *Race, Citizenship and Law in American Literature.* Cambridge: Cambridge University Press, 2002.

Crews, Frederick C. *The Sins of the Fathers: Hawthorne's Psychological Themes.* New York: Oxford University Press, 1966.

Crowley, J. Donald. *Hawthorne: The Critical Heritage.* New York: Barnes and Noble, 1970.

Crozier, Alice. *The Novels of Harriet Beecher Stowe.* New York: Oxford University Press, 1969.

Dahlstrand, Frederick C. *Amos Bronson Alcott: An Intellectual Biography.* East Brunswick, N.J.: Associated University Presses, 1982.

Dauber, Kenneth. *Rediscovering Hawthorne.* Princeton: Princeton University Press, 1977.

Davidson, Donald. *Inquiries into Truth and Interpretation.* Oxford: Clarendon Press, 1984.

Donoghue, Denis. *The American Classics: A Personal Essay.* New Haven: Yale University Press, 2005.

Douglas, Ann. *The Feminization of American Culture.* New York: Alfred A. Knopf, 1977.

Dryden, Edgar A. *The Form of American Romance.* Baltimore: Johns Hopkins University Press, 1988.

  *Monumental Melville: The Formation of a Literary Career.* Stanford: Stanford University Press, 2004.

[Duyckinck, Evert A.]. "*The Scarlet Letter.*" *Literary World* 6 (30 March 1850). In *Critical Heritage*, ed. Crowley, 191.

Eastman, Mary H. *Aunt Phillis's Cabin; or, Southern Life as It is* [1852]. Repr., New York: Negro Universities Press, 1968.

Ellison, Julie. *Cato's Tears and the Making of Anglo-American Emotion.* Chicago: University of Chicago Press, 1999.

Elmer, Jonathan. *Reading at the Social Limit: Affect, Mass Culture and Edgar Allan Poe.* Stanford: Stanford University Press, 1995.

Emerson, Ralph Waldo. *Emerson in His Journals,* sel. and ed. Joel Porte. Cambridge, Mass.: Belknap Press, Harvard University, 1982.

  *Essays and Poems,* ed. Joel Porte, Harold Bloom, and Paul Kane. New York: Literary Classics of the United States, 1996.

  "Thoughts on Modern Literature." *The Dial* 1:2 (October, 1840): 137–58.

Everett, Edward. Review of Washington Irving, *A Tour on the Prairies. North-American Review* 88 (July 1835): 1–28.

Fehrenbacher, Don E. *Slavery, Law, and Politics: The Dred Scott Case in Historical Perspective.* New York: Oxford University Press, 1981.

Feidelson, Charles. *Symbolism and American Literature.* Chicago: University of Chicago Press, 1953.

Firkins, Oscar W. *Ralph Waldo Emerson.* Boston: Houghton Mifflin, 1915.

Fish, Stanley. *Is There a Text in this Class? The Authority of Interpretive Communities.* Cambridge, Mass.: Harvard University Press, 1980.

Fisher, Philip. *Hard Facts: Setting and Form in the American Novel.* New York: Oxford University Press, 1987.

Fletcher, Angus. *Allegory: The Theory of a Symbolic Mode.* Ithaca: Cornell University Press, 1964.

Fliegelman, Jay. *Declaring Independence: Jefferson, Natural Language, and the Culture of Performance.* Stanford: Stanford University Press, 1993.

Fogle, Richard Harter. *Hawthorne's Imagery: The "Proper Light and Shadow" in the Major Romances.* Norman: University of Oklahoma Press, 1969.

Fogel, Robert William. *Without Consent or Contract: The Rise and Fall of American Slavery.* New York: W.W. Norton, 1989.

Foster, Charles H. *The Rungless Ladder: Harriet Beecher Stowe and New England Puritanism.* Durham, N.C.: Duke University Press, 1954.

Foster, Hal. *Design and Crime and Other Diatribes.* London: Verso, 2002.

Francis, Richard. *Transcendental Utopias: Individual and Community at Brook Farm, Fruitlands, and Walden.* Ithaca: Cornell University Press, 1997.

Freeman, Rosemary. *English Emblem Books.* London: Chatto & Windus, 1948.

Fried, Michael. *Absorption and Theatricality: Painting and Beholder in the Age of Diderot.* Chicago: University of Chicago Press, 1980.

Gardiner, W. H. Review of James Fenimore Cooper, *The Spy. North-American Review* 15:36 (July, 1822): 250–83.

Gardner, Jared. *Master Plots: Race and the Founding of an American Literature 1787–1845.* Baltimore: Johns Hopkins University Press, 1998.

Gerteis, Louis S. *Morality and Utility in American Antislavery Reform.* Chapel Hill: University of North Carolina Press, 1987.

Gilmore, Michael T. "The Literature of the Revolutionary and Early National Periods." In *The Cambridge History of American Literature*, vol. I, ed. Sacvan Bercovitch. Cambridge: Cambridge University Press, 1994.

   *Surface and Depth: The Quest for Legibility in American Culture.* New York: Oxford University Press, 2003.

Goddu, Teresa. *Gothic America: Narrative, History, and Nation.* New York: Columbia University Press, 1997.

Gonnaud, Maurice. *An Uneasy Solitude: Individual and Society in the Work of Ralph Waldo Emerson*, trans. Lawrence Rosenwald. Princeton: Princeton University Press, 1987.

Goodell, William. *The American Slave Code in Theory and Practice: Its Distinctive Features shown by its Statutes, Judicial Decisions, and Illustrative Facts.* 4th edn. New York: American and Foreign Anti-Slavery Society, 1853.

Gossett, Thomas F. *"Uncle Tom's Cabin" and American Culture.* Dallas: Southern Methodist University Press, 1985.

Grabo, Norman. *The Coincidental Art of Charles Brockden Brown.* Chapel Hill: University of North Carolina Press, 1981.

Grossman, Jay. *Reconstituting the American Renaissance: Emerson, Whitman, and the Politics of Resistance.* Durham, N.C.: Duke University Press, 2003.

Hartman, Saidiya V. *Scenes of Subjection: Terror, Slavery, and Self-Making in Nineteenth-Cnetury America.* New York: Oxford University Press, 1997.

Hawthorne, Nathaniel. *The American Notebooks*, ed. Claude M. Simpson. *The Centenary Edition of the Works of Nathaniel Hawthorne*, vol. VIII. Columbus: Ohio State University Press, 1972.

   *Collected Novels*, selected with notes by Millicent Bell. New York: Literary Classics of the United States, 1983.

   *Tales and Sketches*, selected by Roy Harvey Pearce. New York: Literary Classics of the United States, 1982.

Hendler, Glenn. *Public Sentiments: Structures of Feeling in Nineteenth-Century American Literature.* Chapel Hill: University of North Carolina Press, 2001.

Holland, Norman. *Five Readers Reading.* New Haven: Yale University Press, 1975.

Holmes, George F. Review of "Uncle Tom's Cabin." *Southern Literary Messenger* 18 (October, 1852): 630–38. In *Critical Essays on Harriet Beecher Stowe*, ed. Ammons.

Horn, András. "Kames and the Anthropological Approach to Criticism." *Philological Quarterly* 44 (1965): 211–33.

Howard, June. "What Is Sentimentality?" *American Literary History* 11:1 (Spring, 1999): 63–81.

Hutner, Gordon. *Secrets and Sympathy: Forms of Disclosure in Hawthorne's Novels.* Athens, Ga.: University of Georgia Press, 1988.

Idol, John L. Jr. and Buford Jones, eds. *Nathaniel Hawthorne: The Contemporary Reviews.* Cambridge: Cambridge University Press, 1994.

Irving, Washington. *History, Tales, and Sketches,* ed. James W. Tuttleton. New York: Literary Classics of the United States, 1983.

Iser, Wolfgang. *The Act of Reading: A Theory of Aesthetic Response.* Baltimore: Johns Hopkins University Press, 1978.

James, Henry. *Nathaniel Hawthorne* [1879], ed. Dan McCall. Ithaca: Cornell University Press, 1966.

Jay, Martin. *Songs of Experience: Modern American and European Variations on a Universal Theme.* Berkeley: University of California Press, 2005.

Jehlen, Myra. *American Incarnation: The Individual, the Nation, the Continent.* Cambridge: Harvard University Press, 1986.

*Readings at the Edge of Literature.* Chicago: University of Chicago Press, 2002.

Kames, Henry Home, Lord. *Elements of Criticism* [1761], ed. James R. Boyd. New York: A. S. Barnes, 1855.

Kant, Immanuel. *Critique of Judgment* [1790], trans. Werner Pluhar. Indianapolis: Hackett, 1987.

Kaplan, Amy. *The Anarchy of Empire in the Making of US Culture.* Cambridge: Harvard University Press, 2002.

Kateb, George. *Emerson and Self-Reliance.* Thousand Oaks, Calif.: Sage Publications, 1995.

Kimball, Arthur. *Rational Fictions: A Study of Charles Brockden Brown.* McMinnville, Ore.: Linfield Research Institute, 1986.

King, Peter D. "John Neal as a Benthamite." *New England Quarterly* 39:1 (March 1966): 47–65.

Kirkham, E. Bruce. *The Building of Uncle Tom's Cabin.* Knoxville: University of Tennessee Press, 1977.

Knapp, Steven. *Literary Interest: The Limits of Anti-Formalism.* Cambridge: Harvard University Press, 1993.

Knapp, Steven and Walter Benn Michaels. "Against Theory." *Critical Inquiry* 8 (Summer 1982): 723–42.

Kuklick, Bruce. *The Rise of American Philosophy: Cambridge, Massachusetts 1860–1930.* New Haven: Yale University Press, 1977.

Lease, Benjamin. *That Wild Fellow John Neal and the American Literary Revolution.* Chicago: University of Chicago Press, 1972.

Lenttricchia, Frank and Andrew DuBois, eds. *Close Reading: The Reader.* Durham, N.C.: Duke University Press, 2003.

Levin, Harry. *The Power of Blackness: Hawthorne, Poe, Melville.* New York: Knopf, 1958.

Levin, Jonathan. *The Poetics of Transition: Emerson, Pragmatism, and American Literary Modernism.* Durham, N.C.: Duke University Press, 1999.

Lippard, George. *The Quaker City: Or, The Monks of Monk Hall. A Romance of Philadelphia Life, Mystery, and Crime* [1845], ed. David S. Reynolds. Amherst: University of Massachusetts Press, 1995.

Longfellow, Henry Wadsworth. "Graduation Address" [1825]. In *Native Muse*, ed. Ruland, 237–39.

Looby, Christopher. *Voicing America: Language, Literary Form, and the Origins of the United States*. Chicago: University of Chicago Press, 1996.

Margolis, Stacey. *The Public Life of Privacy in Nineteenth-Century American Literature*. Durham, N.C.: Duke University Press, 2005.

Marshall, David. *The Surprising Effects of Sympathy: Marivaux, Diderot, Rousseau, and Mary Shelley*. Chicago: University of Chicago Press, 1988.

Marshall, Megan *The Peabody Sisters: Three Women Who Ignited American Romanticism*. Boston: Houghton Mifflin, 2005.

Martin, Harold C. "The Colloquial Tradition in the Novel: John Neal." *New England Quarterly* 32:4 (December 1959): 455–75.

Martin, Terence. *The Instructed Vision: Scottish Common Sense Philosophy and the Origins of American Fiction*. Bloomington: Indiana University Press, 1961.

Matthiessen, F. O. *The American Renaissance: Art and Expression in the Age of Emerson and Whitman*. New York: Oxford University Press, 1941.

McGuinness, Arthur E. *Henry Home, Lord Kames*. New York: Twayne, 1970.

McInerney, Daniel J. *The Fortunate Heirs of Freedom: Abolitionism and Republican Thought*. Lincoln: University of Nebraska Press, 1994.

Melville, Herman. "Hawthorne and His Mosses." *Literary World* 7 (August 17 and 24, 1850). In *Contemporary Reviews*, ed. Idol and Jones.

Merish, Lori. *Sentimental Materialism: Gender, Commodity Culture, and Nineteenth-Century American Literature*. Durham, N.C.: Duke University Press, 2000.

Michaels, Walter Benn. *The Gold Standard and the Logic of Naturalism: American Literature at the Turn of the Century*. Berkeley: University of California Press, 1987.

*The Shape of the Signifier: 1967 to the End of History*. Princeton: Princeton University Press, 2004.

Miller, Perry. *The Life of the Mind in America: From the Revolution to the Civil War*. New York: Harcourt, Brace, and World, 1965.

Millington, Richard. *Practicing Romance: Narrative Form and Cultural Engagement in Hawthorne's Fiction*. Princeton: Princeton University Press, 1992.

Mitchell, Charles E. *Individualism and Its Discontents: Appropriations of Emerson, 1880–1950*. Amherst: University of Massachusetts Press, 1997.

Myerson, Joel, ed. *Transcendentalism: A Reader*. New York: Oxford University Press, 2000.

Neal, John. *American Writers: A Series of Papers Contributed to Blackwood's Magazine, 1824–1825*, ed. F. L. Pattee. Durham, N.C.: Duke University Press, 1937.

*Rachel Dyer* [1828]. Repr. Amherst, New York: Prometheus Books, 1996.

*Rachel Dyer*, ed. John D. Seelye. Gainesville: Scholars' Facsimiles and Reprints, 1964.

*Randolph*. "Published For Whom It May Concern," 1823.

Nelson, Dana. *National Manhood: Capitalist Citizenship and the Imagined Fraternity of White Men*. Durham, N.C.: Duke University Press, 1998.

Newfield, Christopher. *The Emerson Effect: Individualism and Submission in America*. Chicago: University of Chicago Press, 1996.

Noble, Marianne. *The Masochistic Pleasures of Sentimental Literature*. Princeton: Princeton University Press, 2000.

Ostrander, Gilman M. "Lord Kames and American Revolutionary Culture." In *Essays in Honor of Russell B. Nye*, ed. Joseph J. Waldmeir and David C. Meade. East Lansing: Michigan State University Press, 1978.

Packer, B. L. *Emerson's Fall: A New Interpretation of the Major Essays*. New York: Continuum, 1982.

——— "The Transcendentalists." In *The Cambridge History of American Literature*, vol. II, ed. Sacvan Bercovitch. Cambridge: Cambridge University Press, 1994.

Peabody, Elizabeth Palmer. "Explanatory Preface." In *Record of a School: Exemplifying the General Principles of Spiritual Culture*. 2nd edn. Boston: Russell, Shattuck; New York: Leavitt, Lord, 1836. In *Transcendentalism*, ed. Myerson.

Pease, Donald. *Visionary Compacts: American Renaissance Writings in Cultural Context*. Madison: University of Wisconsin Press, 1987.

Perosa, Sergio. *American Theories of the Novel, 1793–1903*. New York: New York University Press, 1983.

Pfister, Joel. *The Production of Personal Life: Class, Gender, and the Psychological in Hawthorne's Fiction*. Stanford: Stanford University Press, 1991.

Pinch, Adela. *Strange Fits of Passion: Epistemologies of Emotion, Hume to Austen*. Stanford: Stanford University Press, 1996.

Poirier, Richard. *The Renewal of Literature: Emersonian Reflections*. New York: Random House, 1987.

——— *A World Elsewhere: The Place of Style in American Literature*. Madison: University of Wisconsin Press, 1985.

Praz, Mario. *Studies in Seventeenth-Century Imagery*. 2nd edn. Rome: Edizioni di Storia e Letteratura, 1964.

Pritchard, John Paul. *Criticism in America: An Account of the Development of Critical Techniques from the Early Period of the Republic to the Middle Years of the Twentieth Century*. Norman, Okla.: University of Oklahoma Press, 1956.

Rahv, Philip. *Image and Idea: Fourteen Essays on Literary Themes*. New York: New Directions, 1949.

Randall, Helen Whitcomb. *The Critical Theory of Lord Kames*. Northampton: Smith College, 1944.

Reynolds, David S. *Beneath the American Renaissance: The Subversive Imagination in the Age of Emerson and Melville*. New York: Alfred A. Knopf, 1988.

Rice, Grantland S. *The Transformation of Authorship in America*. Chicago: University of Chicago Press, 1997.

Romero, Lora. *Home Fronts: Domesticity and its Critics in the Antebellum United States*. Durham, N.C.: Duke University Press, 1997.

Rooney, Ellen. "Form and Contentment." *MLQ* 61:1 (2000): 17–40.

Rose, Anne. *Transcendentalism as a Social Movement, 1830–1850*. New Haven: Yale University Press, 1981.

Ross, Ian Simpson. *Lord Kames and the Scotland of his Day*. Oxford: Clarendon Press, 1972.

"Scots Law and Scots Criticism: The Case of Lord Kames." *Philological Quarterly* 45 (1966): 614–23.

Rowe, John Carlos. *At Emerson's Tomb: The Politics of Classic American Literature*. New York: Columbia University Press, 1997.

Ruland, Richard. *The Native Muse: Theories of American Literature*, vol. 1. New York: E. P. Dutton, 1972.

Ryan, Susan M. "Charity Begins at Home: Stowe's Antislavery Novels and the Forms of Benevolent Citizenship." *American Literature* 72:4 (December 2000): 751–82.

Samuels, Shirley, ed. *The Culture of Sentiment: Race, Gender, and Sentimentality in Nineteenth Century America*. New York: Oxford University Press, 1992.

Sánchez-Eppler, Karen. *Touching Liberty: Abolition, Feminism, and the Politics of the Body*. Berkeley: University of California Press, 1993.

Schirmeister, Pamela. *Less Legible Meanings: Between Poetry and Philosophy in the Work of Emerson*. Stanford: Stanford University Press, 1999.

Sears, Donald A. *John Neal*. Boston: Twayne, 1978.

Sedgewick, Eve Kosofsky. *Touching Feeling: Affect, Pedagogy, Performativity*. Durham, N.C.: Duke University Press, 2003.

Sorin, Gerald. *The New York Abolitionists: A Case Study of Political Radicalism*. Westport, Conn.: Greenwood, 1971.

Steele, Jeffrey. *The Representation of the Self in the American Renaissance*. Chapel Hill: University of North Carolina Press, 1987.

Stendhal. *The Life of Henry Brulard*. New edn, trans. John Sturrock. New York: New York Review Books Classics, 2001.

Stern, Julia. *The Plight of Feeling: Sympathy and Dissent in the Early American Novel*. Chicago: University of Chicago Press, 1997.

Stewart, James Brewer. *Holy Warriors: The Abolitionists and American Slavery*. New York: Hill and Wang, 1976.

Stowe, Harriet Beecher. *Dred: A Tale of the Great Dismal Swamp* [1856], ed. Judie Newman. Edinburgh: Edinburgh University Press, 1999.

*A Key to Uncle Tom's Cabin; Presenting the Original Facts and Documents upon which the Story is Founded. Together with Corroborative Statements Verifying the Work* [1853]. Repr. Bedford, Mass.: Applewood Books, 1998.

*Uncle Tom's Cabin* [1852], ed. Jean Fagan Yellin. New York: Oxford University Press, 1998.

Stubbs, John. *The Pursuit of Form: A Study of Hawthorne and the Romance*. Urbana: University of Illinois Press, 1970.

Sundquist, Eric, ed. *New Essays on Uncle Tom's Cabin*. Cambridge: Cambridge University Press, 1986.

Terada, Rei. *Feeling in Theory: Emotion after the "Death of the Subject."* Cambridge, Mass.: Harvard University Press, 2003.

Tocqueville, Alexis de. *Democracy in America*, trans. George Lawrence, ed. J. P. Mayer. New York: Harper & Row, 1969.

Todd, Janet. *Sensibility: An Introduction.* New York: Methuen, 1986.

Tompkins, Jane. *Sensational Designs: The Cultural Work of American Fiction 1790–1860.* New York: Oxford University Press, 1985.

Townsend, Dabney. "Archibald Alison: Aesthetic Experience and Emotion." *British Journal of Aesthetics* 28:2 (Spring 1988): 132–44.

Trilling, Lionel. *Beyond Culture: Essays on Literature and Learning.* New York: Viking Press, 1965.

Turner, Lorenzo D. *Anti-Slavery Sentiment in American Literature Prior to 1865.* Washington, D.C.: Association for the Study of Negro Life and History, 1929.

Van Leer, David. *Emerson's Epistemology.* Cambridge: Cambridge University Press, 1986.

Vogel, Stanley M. *German Literary Influences on the American Transcendentalists.* New Haven: Archon Books, 1970.

Waggoner, Hyatt. *The Presence of Hawthorne.* Baton Rouge: Louisiana State University Press, 1979.

Wallace, James D. *Early Cooper and His Audience.* New York: Columbia University Press, 1986.

Warner, Michael. *Letters of the Republic: Publication and the Public Sphere in Eighteenth-Century America.* Cambridge, Mass.: Harvard University Press, 1990.

Warner, Susan. *The Wide, Wide World* [1850], with an afterword by Jane Tompkins. New York: The Feminist Press at the City University of New York, 1987.

Warnock, Mary. *Imagination.* Berkeley: University of California Press, 1976.

Warren, Kenneth. *Black and White Strangers: Race and American Literary Realism.* Chicago: University of Chicago Press, 1993.

Weinstein, Cindy. *Family, Kinship, and Sympathy in Nineteenth-Century American Literature.* Cambridge: Cambridge University Press, 2004.

Wellek, René. *Confrontations: Studies in the Intellectual and Literary Relations between Germany, England, and the United States during the Nineteenth Century.* Princeton: Princeton University Press, 1965.

*A History of Modern Criticism, 1750–1950,* vol. 1. *The Later Eighteenth Century.* New Haven: Yale University Press, 1955.

Wertheimer, Eric. *Imagined Empires: Incas, Aztecs, and the New World of American Literature, 1771–1876.* Cambridge: Cambridge University Press, 1999.

West, Cornel. *Democracy Matters: Winning the Fight Against Imperialism.* New York: Penguin, 2004.

Wheeler, Jacob D. *A Practical Treatise on the Law of Slavery. Being a Compilation of all the Decisions made on that Subject, in the Several Courts of the United States and State Courts. With Copious Notes and References to the Statutes and other Authorities, Systematically Arranged* [1837]. Repr. New York: Negro Universities Press, 1968.

Whitney, Lisa. "In the Shadow of Uncle Tom's Cabin: Stowe's Vision of Slavery from the Great Dismal Swamp." *New England Quarterly* 66:4 (December 1993): 552–69.

Wiegman, Robyn. *American Anatomies: Theorizing Race and Gender.* Durham, N.C.: Duke University Press, 1995.

Wilson, Edmund. *Patriotic Gore: Studies in the Literature of the American Civil War.* New York: W. W. Norton, 1962.

Wimsatt, W. K. and Monroe Beardsley. *The Verbal Icon: Studies in the Meaning of Poetry.* Lexington: University Press of Kentucky, 1954.

Ziff, Larzer. *Writing in the New Nation: Prose, Print and Politics in the Early United States.* New Haven: Yale University Press, 1991.

# Index

Abbott, Anne, 78, 79

abolitionism, 139, 147, 149–51, 153–55, 157

abstraction, 160; in Alcott, 129–31, 133, 134; in allegory, 83; and American prose authors, 162; in Best, 161; in criticism, 161; in Emerson, 110, 113–15, 119, 120, 123; and experience, 4, 28; and form; in Hawthorne, 74, 81–88, 94, 96, 98–99, 105, 107, 108; Jay on, 6; Kames on, 35, 38; in Neal, 56, 71; neoclassical, 3; in nineteenth-century American literature, 28, 29; in Poe and Melville, 165; and reason, 4; in Scottish Common Sense philosophy, 31; in Stowe, 138, 147; and subjective experience, 4, 8; in Transcendentalism, 137; and typicality, 3

actuality: in Hawthorne, 91, 99; Knapp on, 24; and literary nationalism, 55; in Neal, 67; in Scottish Common Sense philosophy, 31; in Stowe, 143–45; see also reality

aesthetics: Alison on, 39, 40, 42; in Bate and Wellek, 37; in Emerson, 110; and judgment, 15–16; Kames on, 32, 42; Kant on, 12, 13, 166; in Scottish Common Sense philosophy, 30; in Wimsatt and Beardsley, 12–16; see also surface aesthetic, in Hawthorne

affective criticism, 18

affective fallacy, 12–16

affect(s): about object vs. subject, 14, 15; and American prose authors, 162; in Hawthorne, 74–78, 80, 84, 87, 90, 96, 97, 99, 105, 107; and meaning, 15; in Stowe, 148; see also emotion

agency: in Hawthorne, 92, 105; Knapp on, 27; in Lippard, 146; in Stowe, 146, 153, 159

Alciati, Andrea, 81

Alcott, A. Bronson, 3, 125–35, 137; *Conversations with Children on the Gospels*, 126–35; "Days from a Diary," 126; and Emerson, 125–26, 132, 135–37; and Hawthorne, 134

Alcott, Louisa May, *Work*, 17

Alison, Archibald: and American literature, 44; and associationist artworks, 67; and

Channing, 50–52; and Emerson, 113, 119; on emotion, 39–40, 42, 52, 148; *Essays On Taste*, 39–44; on experience, 31–33, 39–42, 44, 113, 148; and form, 169; and Hawthorne, 84; and Neal, 60; reader in, 40, 41, 43, 50, 52, 148

allegory: in Alcott, 130; in Carton, 98; in Emerson, 116; in Hawthorne, 83–85, 87, 88, 92, 98–99, 102, 103

Americanist criticism, 4, 5, 7, 8, 26

American Renaissance, 172

analogy: in Emerson, 113–15; and Stowe, 159

analysis, in Stowe, 143, 146

appearance, in Neal, 56–58

Arac, Jonathan, 98

art/artwork: Alison on, 40–41, 148; associationist, 32, 44, 67–68; in Bate and Wellek, 37; Kames on, 148; and meaning, 23; Michaels on, 11; in Stowe, 153; and subjectivity, 16

associationism, 43; affective element of, 37; art in, 32, 44, 67–68; and Channing, 49; and empiricism, 30; experience in, 44, 148, 162; and Hawthorne, 84, 100; insufficiency of, 43; reader in, 32, 148; and Stowe, 148

associations: Alison on, 41, 43, 52; Channing on, 49–52; in Emerson, 119; Gardiner on, 47, 48; Kames on, 47; and literary nationalism, 48, 54, 55; in Neal, 57, 59, 66–68, 73

*Aunt Phillis's Cabin*, 139

Austen, Jane, 28

authenticity: in literary nationalism, 54; in Stowe, 138, 139

author: Alison on, 40; disembodied, 99; in Hawthorne, 84, 90, 94, 97, 99, 102–4, 106; psychology of, 17; reader's experience as work of, 148; in Stowe, 143

authorial voice: in Hawthorne, 95, 96; in Neal, 56, 68–70; see also narrator/narrative voice; voice(s)

awareness, in Emerson, 111, 115

Axelrod, Alan, 171

194